AMERICA

ON THE ICE

American scientist on the South Polar Plateau.

AMERICA

ON THE ICE

Antarctic Policy Issues

Frank G. Klotz

1990

National Defense University Press

NDU PRESS Fort Lesley J. Mc Nair

Washington, DC

National Defense University Press Publications

To increase general knowledge and inform discussion, NDU Press publishes books on subjects relating to US national security.

Each year, in this effort, the National Defense University, through the Institute for National Strategic Studies, hosts about two dozen Senior Fellows who engage in original research on national security issues. NDU Press publishes the best of this research.

In addition, the Press publishes other especially timely or distinguished writing on national security, as well as new editions of out-of-print defense classics, and books based on University-sponsored conferences concerning national security affairs.

The photograph on page 15, and on which the cover art is based, is protected by copyright; permission to reprint it must be obtained from Nationaal Scheepvaartmuseum, Antwerp. Other portions of this book may be quoted or reprinted without permission, provided that a standard source credit line is included. NDU Press would appreciate a courtesy copy of reprints or reviews.

William A. Palmer, Jr., Cheltenham, Md., proofread the page proofs of this book, under contract DAHC32-90-A-0035. Connie Moy, Editorial Experts, Inc., Alexandria, Va., indexed this book, under contract DAHC32-90-0032.

NDU Press publications are sold by the US Government Printing Office. For ordering information, call (202) 783-3238 or write to the Superintendent of Documents, US Government Printing Office, Washington, DC 20402.

Library of Congress Cataloging-in-Publication Data
Klotz, Frank G., 1950-
     America on the ice : Antarctic policy issues / Frank G. Klotz.
        p.   cm.
     Includes bibliographical references (p.   ) and index.
     1. Antarctic regions—International status.   2. United States—Foreign relations—
     1945- I. Title
JX4084.A5K56   1990
341.2'9'09989—dc 20   90-13300
                                                                           CIP
First printing, November 1990.

To my wife, Nancy,
and our favorite "adventurers,"
Justin and David

Contents

Illustrations

Maps

Photographs

Tables

Foreword

Working together under the highly successful Antarctic Treaty of 1959, the United States and other nations have quietly and peacefully pursued exploration and scientific research in Antarctica. The treaty, however, could be subject to major revision in 1991 and possibly even elimination. It is therefore important to review US national interests in anticipation of a new treaty arrangement that may necessitate modifying US policy toward Antarctica.

Frank Klotz examines Antarctica before the 1959 treaty, and then scrutinizes the operation of the treaty itself. In doing so, he notes that three significant challenges to continued cooperation in the Antarctic have arisen despite 30 years of international cooperation. First, as the world has become more aware of dwindling natural resources, the modest discoveries in the Antarctic are attracting more attention. Second, certain nations, not signatories to the treaty, have questioned the right of the treaty members to control resource development. Third, disputes over territorial sovereignty remain to be resolved.

As competition for resources increases, the issue of "who owns the Antarctic" could lead to contention. This thoughtful study provides a sound framework for crafting a US strategy on these emerging Antarctic issues.

J. A. BALDWIN
Vice Admiral, US Navy
President, National Defense University

Preface

Most works on the Antarctic describe the region with a series of forbidding extremes. The continent is said to be the coldest, driest, highest, windiest, and most remote place on earth. At least one other extreme merits inclusion on this list: Antarctica also is the most neglected continent in both the practice and study of American national security policy.

The reasons for this neglect are not hard to fathom.

Precisely because of all Antarctica's extremes, only a handful of Americans have ever expressed an interest in the region. During the late eighteenth and early nineteenth centuries, sailors from New England explored the waters of the Southern Ocean in search of seals for trade. Later, commercial exploitation of the region's living resources gave way to heroic feats by famous explorers. The adventures of Roald Amundsen, Robert Falcon Scott, and Admiral Richard Byrd opened up the Antarctic in both a literal and figurative sense, as the popular imagination became seized with the haunting images of the last earthly frontier.

Yet, for all its majestic beauty, the Antarctic never possessed sufficient wealth or strategic significance to command broad and sustained attention from the American body politic. Even as more Americans became aware of the region, Antarctica remained the province of the few. Indeed today, it is populated only by a small circle of scientists, and the civilian and military officials who support their research.

Not surprisingly then, US decisionmakers have generally paid only scant attention to Antarctica. Consequently, policy toward the region traditionally has suffered from a lack of strong direction from the top and a corresponding air of ambivalence. For example, in the first half of this century, the State Department carefully laid the foundation for a territorial claim there. However in the end, the United States never mustered the wherewithal to assert such a claim, even though seven other nations did.

Despite the relatively low priority assigned to Antarctica within US Government circles, the United States nevertheless has been one of the most active nations in the region, as well as one of the most influential players in the international politics of the continent. The United States in fact took the lead in negotiating an agreement to end international competition for Antarctic territory and to promote cooperation "on the ice."

The resulting Antarctic Treaty of 1959 and its associated procedures and measures—commonly referred to as the Antarctic Treaty system—have successfully governed the activities of nations in the region for nearly 30 years. The treaty reduces the potential for armed conflict in Antarctica by suspending all claims to territory and by "demilitarizing" the continent and its adjacent waters. The treaty also provides for virtually unrestricted access to the region for scientific and other peaceful pursuits. At the same time, the treaty establishes a process for its signatories to consult regularly on problems affecting the region. This consultative process has yielded an impressive body of national law and international agreements regulating Antarctic affairs. The United States continues to be one of the staunchest supporters of this system, because the system has protected virtually every American interest in the region.

Though the treaty system has worked remarkably well to date, its continued operation should not be taken for granted. The treaty has no expiration date. However, starting in 1991, any consultative party to the treaty (a term defined later) can call for a formal review that ultimately could result in significant revision or even the demise of the treaty. At the moment, no nation appears intent on invoking this provision of the treaty. Nevertheless, the existing treaty system is under pressure from several quarters. This pressure has three interrelated components.

First, interest in the *potential* living and mineral resources of the Antarctic is growing in response to perceived shortages elsewhere in the world and tantalizing discoveries (for example, traces of hydrocarbon gas) in the region. The treaty, however, does not address resource development. To fill this gap, the treaty members already have put into place systems to regulate sealing and fishing in the Southern Ocean. They are now coming to grips with the more difficult task of setting up mechanisms for regulating possible oil and mineral activities in Antarctica.

Meanwhile, several developing countries have challenged the right of the Antarctic Treaty nations to make rules governing resource development in the region. The treaty opponents have asserted that any resources discovered in Antarctica ought to be equitably distributed among all nations, not just the privileged few who are parties to the treaty. Accordingly, critics have called for the creation of a new system to manage Antarctic affairs—one that involves the entire world community in any decisions affecting Antarctic resources.

Finally, while the treaty system reacts to these pressures, the unresolved question of territorial sovereignty lurks just beneath the surface. As one scholar aptly put it, the Antarctic Treaty never answered the question of "who owns the Antarctic?"* However, as interest in resource development has grown, ownership issues have become more pressing. Failure to resolve these issues in a manner satisfactory to all parties with territorial claims conceivably could lead one or more countries to conclude that their national interests would be better served by ignoring the treaty altogether and attempting to exercise direct control over Antarctic territory.

Because of these pressures, the Antarctic Treaty—which has been the cornerstone of American policy in the region for a generation—could be in danger of significant revision, or even collapse. Without the treaty, the scramble for control over the continent that marked the pre-treaty era could resume, with a corresponding increase in the potential for armed conflict.

Given the ever-present risk of renewed competition and conflict in the region, Antarctica can no longer remain the exclusive province of a handful of specialists. Rather, officials from several different sectors of the policy community—*including those concerned primarily with national security issues*—must become engaged in questions concerning the nature, level, and costs of American activities in the region. Decisions affecting

---

*Evan Luard, "Who Owns the Antarctic?", *Foreign Affairs*, Vol. 62, No. 5, Summer 1984, pp. 1175-93.

the number and location of Antarctic stations, for example, or the scope of the American military involvement in supporting scientific activities on the ice cannot be framed solely in terms of the specific requirements for conducting research. They also must address the larger and far more important issue of the ability of the United States to project its influence into the region, either to buttress the status quo or have a large voice in framing alternatives.

In defining specific policies for the Antarctic over the next decade, American officials ought to be guided by a coherent and integrated strategy that relates fundamental objectives in the region to the resources available to support them and constraints imposed by the international and domestic policy context. This study seeks to provide basic data and the framework necessary to devise such a strategy. It does so by providing the general reader with background information on the international political status of Antarctica; operation of the Antarctic Treaty system; current American activities on the ice; and recent developments that may ultimately force a change in the treaty system and, with it, a change in basic American policy toward the region. The final section suggests basic criteria to guide American officials in defining the precise elements of US policy in the Antarctic in the years ahead, including the role the American military can and should play in implementing that policy.

The importance of developing a coherent, forward-looking strategy to guarantee that American interests are met in the Antarctic should not be underestimated—even if the region rarely, if ever, appears on the front page of leading newspapers. Prior to 1982, only a handful of people in the defense policy community knew the location, much less the tangled history, of a set of islands very close to the Antarctic both in geography and history: the Falklands (or *Malvinas*). Yet, in the spring of that year, two American allies (Great Britain and Argentina) waged a costly war over this remote territory, clearly demonstrating the wide-ranging consequences of territorial disputes that get out of hand.

For now and for the foreseeable future, the Antarctic is calm, governed by a treaty often hailed as a model for international cooperation. However, disputes over sovereignty—every bit as contentious as the dispute over the Falklands—could erupt under the right (or wrong) set of circumstances, plunging two or more countries into the very conflict the Antarctic Treaty system thus far has averted.

The individual policy and programmatic choices made today concerning the size and scope of American activities on the ice will directly bear on US influence in Antarctic diplomacy. That influence, in turn, will help decide whether the Antarctic remains peaceful.

Acknowledgments

Many individuals contributed to this book during the three years it took to research, write, and publish it.

The author is especially grateful to those specialists in Antarctic affairs who kindly agreed to discuss various aspects of US policy toward the region: Raymond Arnaudo, David Bresnahan, Harlan Cohen, Sherman Garnett, Guy Gutheridge, Michael Harris, Anton Inderbitzen, Lee Kimball, Richard Malow, George Martin, and Jack Talmadge.

Special thanks also go to Howie DeWolf, Bob Hughes, Nancy Klotz, Alex Larzelere, Tom Mahr, Tom McDaniel, Barry Pavel, and Bill Taylor who "volunteered" to review the manuscript during different stages of its development.

Winifred Reuning of the National Science Foundation made available many of the photograhs used in the text.

Throughout the writing of this book, Dr. Fred Kiley provided the wise counsel and nurturing support for which he is justly known. Ed Seneff not only edited the manuscript with sharp-eyed skill, he also supplied the wit and good humor every writer needs at critical junctures in the publication process.

Responsibility for any sins of commission or omission rests squarely on the shoulders of the author.

Chronology

Discovery and Early Exploration

Early exploration of Antarctica motivated primarily by commercial interests, though imperial ambition and scientific curiosity also play roles.

1772-75	Captain James Cook (UK) circumnavigates Antarctic continent. Discovers new sub-Antarctic islands, but does not actually lay eyes on continent.
1820	Nathaniel Palmer (US) and Edward Bransfield (UK) sail separately into Antarctic waters in search of seals. Subsequently make rival claims to first sighting of Antarctic continent.
1821	Fabian von Bellingshausen (Russia) discovers Peter I and Alexander I islands.
1820s and 1830s	American and British sealers make repeated voyages to region until diminishing seal population renders seal trade not economically attractive.
1835-41	Ross (UK), Wilkes (US), and D'Urville (France) mount separate expeditions into Antarctic region.
1870s and 1880s	Revived seal trade and growing interest in Southern Ocean whaling lead to resumption of expeditions to Antarctic waters.

"Heroic Age"

Series of daring expeditions achieve several "firsts" in region. Meanwhile, nations begin to lay claim to Antarctic territory.

1894-95	H.J. Bull's (Norway) expedition first to land on continent (at Cape Adare).
1898-99	Adrien de Gerlache's (Belgium) expedition first to "winter over" in region; his ship—*Belgica*—becomes lodged in ice.

1898-1900	C.J. Borchgrevink's (Norway/UK) expedition first to "winter over" on continent itself.
1903	William Bruce (UK) establishes first permanent research station at Laurie Island, off Antarctic peninsula.
1908	London issues first of 2 Letters of Patent confirming its claim to several South Atlantic islands and a sector of Antarctic territory encompassing Antarctic peninsula.
1911	Roald Amundsen's (Norway) expedition first to reach South Pole.
1912	Four weeks later, Robert Falcon Scott (UK) also reaches Pole; he and his companions perish while returning to their base camp.
1923	By an Order in Council, Great Britain formally claims sector of territory encompassing Ross Ice Shelf, placing it under administration of New Zealand.
1924	French president formally annexes Adelie Land in East Antarctica and several Southern Ocean islands (including Kerguelen and Crozet).
1928	Sir Hubert Wilkins (UK) makes first airplane flight in region (across Antarctic peninsula).
1929	Richard Byrd (US) first explorer to fly over South Pole.
1928-39	Richard Byrd and Lincoln Ellsworth mount several major expeditions to region, reinforcing basis for American claim to Antarctic territory—though Washington never actually makes one.
1933	Great Britain asserts sovereignty over 2 large sectors of Antarctic territory on behalf of Australia.
1939	Norway claims region of continent known as Queen Maud land, which Riiser-Larsen expedition had explored 10 years earlier.
1940	Chile decrees its authority over sector of Antarctic territory that includes most of Antarctic peninsula and adjacent islands.

| 1940 | Argentina makes first of several pronouncements claiming title to Antarctic territory in peninsula region. |
| 1941-45 | UK establishes 3 bases in peninsula region as part of *Operation Tabarin*, ostensibly to interdict German naval forces in South Atlantic. |

"Postwar" Era

After Second World War, territorial rivalries in region intensify. Meanwhile, 2 "superpowers" establish major presence on continent.

1946-47	During *Operation Highjump*, US military stages expedition to Antarctic to provide training in polar operations. Dozen ships and 4,700 personnel involved.
1947-48	Following year, US Navy sends smaller expedition—*Operation Windmill*—to region.
	UK, Argentina, and Chile sail naval vessels into Antarctic waters, but agree following year not to dispatch warships south of 60° south latitude.
1950	Soviet Union formally asserts historic interests in Antarctica, and declares intention to play active role in decisions affecting region.
1952	Armed clash occurs between British and Argentine personnel at Hope Bay. Though no one is hurt, incident illustrates potential for conflict arising from conflicting claims.
1956-57	US Navy begins constructing permanent research stations in Antarctica during first *Operation Deep Freeze*.
1957-58	As part of *International Geophysical Year* (IGY), 12 nations conduct scientific programs at 60 different stations in Antarctic. Under so-called "gentlemen's agreement," scientists have unrestricted access to all parts of region for research, regardless of existing territorial claims.
1958	US Government invites the 12 nations that had IGY programs in region to Conference on Antarctica.

Antarctic Treaty System

Antarctic Treaty puts territorial claims on hold, "demilitarizes" region, and enshrines principle of free access to entire continent for peaceful purposes. Also establishes system for cooperative management of scientific, environmental, and resource issues.

1959	Antarctic Treaty signed by all 12 participants at Washington Conference on Antarctica.
1961	After sufficient number of ratifications in hand, Antarctic Treaty formally enters into force.
1961	First Antarctic Treaty Consultative Meeting (ATCM) convenes in Canberra, Australia. Subsequent consultative meetings held roughly every 2 years thereafter.
1964	Third ATCM approves set of environmental provisions known as "Agreed Measures for the Conservation of Antarctic Fauna and Flora."
1966	First commercial tourist venture to Antarctica takes place.
1972	Convention for Conservation of Antarctic Seals signed in London. (Actually enters into force in 1978.)
1979	New Zealand DC-10 crashes into Mount Erebus, killing all 257 tourists and crew on board.
1980	Convention on Conservation of Antarctic Marine Living Resources signed in Canberra. (Actually enters into force in 1982.)
1982	UK and Argentina go to war in territorial dispute involving nearby Falkland (*Malvinas*) and South Georgia Islands.
1983	United Nations debates "Question of Antarctica" for first time in UN history.
1988	Negotiations for Convention on Regulation of Antarctic Mineral Resource Activities completed in Wellington, New Zealand. (This convention *not* yet entered into force.)
1989	Argentine supply ship *Bahia Paraiso* runs aground off Antarctic peninsula, spilling oil that seriously threatens local animal life.

AMERICA

ON THE ICE

1

Antarctica Before the Treaty

FROM THE OUTSET, THE INTERNATIONAL LEGAL AND political status of the Antarctic region has been ambiguous and, therefore, subject to dispute. Prior to its discovery early in the nineteenth century, the continent was uninhabited and belonged to no one. Moreover, no universally accepted principles or treaties governed activities in the Antarctic or decided jurisdiction over its territory and resources. Antarctica was what international lawyers refer to as *terra nullius*—literally, nobody's land.[1]

In the years following its discovery, several countries attempted to impose their own laws and authority over large tracts of Antarctic territory. For several decades, sailors and explorers from different nations visited the region and, in some cases, claimed territory on behalf of their native countries. By the early twentieth century, governments began to formally declare that they exercised sovereignty over certain areas. The ensuing scramble for a piece of Antarctic territory resembled in many respects the carving up of Africa after the 1884-85 Conference of Berlin, with all the attendant potential for armed conflict among rival claimants.

6,000-year-old "dirty ice" in the Antarctic.

After the Second World War, the Cold War competition for power and influence between East and West interjected yet another element of danger into the already confused Antarctic political situation. By the fifties, no statesman could confidently predict the future of the region: A continuation of the unstable status quo, a division of the continent into separate territories or spheres of influence, or some altogether new approach to resolving international disputes over contested territory.

Rival Territorial Claims

Great Britain was the first country to officially enter the sovereignty sweepstakes. The British government based its case for control over Antarctic territory on the principle of discovery and possession by its explorers.[2] Captain James Cook circumnavigated Antarctica during his voyage of 1772-75. In 1820, an English sailor, Edward Bransfield, may have been the first person to lay eyes on the continent—though the United States and the Soviet Union dispute this claim; they attribute the first sighting to sailors from their own countries.[3] British seamen continued to visit the Antarctic region throughout the nineteenth century. During the so-called "heroic age" of Antarctic exploration (early in the twentieth century), British subjects—most notably Robert Falcon Scott and Ernest Shackleton—mounted major expeditions to the continent with encouragement from the British government.

Commercial interests, however, ultimately prompted the British government to make its first formal claims to Antarctic territory. In response to growing interest in whaling in the Southern Ocean, London issued Letters of Patent in 1908 and 1917 confirming its claim to several South Atlantic islands and a sector of Antarctic territory encompassing the Antarctic peninsula. (See Map 1 for territorial claims in the Antarctic.) These territories were assigned to

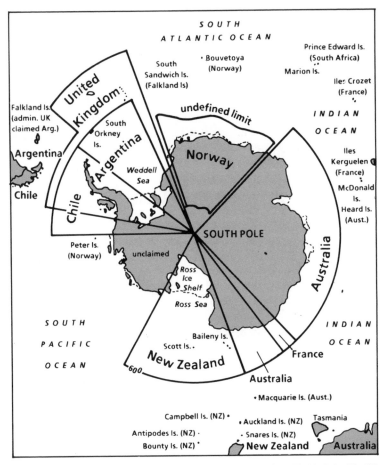

Map 1. Territorial claims in the Antarctic

the governor of the Falkland Islands for administration. The British followed up their claim by issuing whaling regulations and licenses, and collecting fees from foreign companies operating within the claim, thus lending some internationally recognized legitimacy to the asserted right to exercise jurisdiction within that area.[4]

By 1920, the British government had privately adopted a policy of gradually acquiring control over the entire Antarctic continent. The British were motivated by a mixture of imperial sentiment, the allure of fishing and mineral resources in the region, and concern that an enemy could use the Antarctic for bases to attack British interests in the Southern Hemisphere.[5] The government's strategy for achieving this objective was not to claim the whole continent outright, but rather to assert additional claims on behalf of its dominions. By an Order in Council in 1923, Great Britain formally claimed a sector encompassing the Ross Ice Shelf (from which Scott and Shackleton had staged expeditions into the continent's interior) and placed it under the administration of New Zealand.[6] In 1933, a similar order asserted sovereignty over two large sectors on behalf of Australia. The Australian legislature subsequently confirmed this move by passing the Australian Antarctic Acceptance Act that same year.[7] Thus, by the early thirties, Great Britain and its two former colonies had laid claim to roughly two-thirds of the continent.

However, before the British could stake out the entire Antarctic region, other countries entered the territorial competition.

France had long claimed rights to Adelie Land in East Antarctica on the basis of its discovery by Captain Dumont d'Urville in 1840. In 1924, the French president officially annexed Adelie Land and several Southern Ocean islands (including Kerguelen and Crozet).[8] Two factors apparently led to the French action: A mounting concern with British designs on the continent; and a desire to protect fishing rights off their sub-Antarctic islands.[9] In 1938, the French government formally extended its claim from Adelie Land to the

South Pole, thus following the "sector principle" employed by the British.[10] As indicated on Map 1, the French sector lies in the midst of the large Australian claim.

In 1939, Norway claimed a region of the continent known as Queen Maud Land, which a Norwegian expedition had explored the previous decade. Earlier, the Norwegian government had annexed the sub-Antarctic islands of Bouvetoya (1928) and Peter I (1931) to support whaling interests in the Southern Ocean. The claim to Queen Maud Land likewise was designed to preclude rivals from encroaching on areas frequented by Norwegian whalers. Additionally, the Norwegian government wanted to forestall a claim by the German Third Reich, which had ordered an expedition to Queen Maud Land.

Unlike the British and French, the Norwegians did not contend that their Antarctic territory extended from the coastal areas to the Pole, although Roald Amundsen's success in beating Scott to the Pole in December 1911 probably gave Norway as much right to claim it as any other nation at that time. Instead, the Norwegians purposely rejected the sector principle in asserting their Antarctic rights, presumably because they did not wish to lend any credence to Soviet efforts to apply the same approach in regions closer to Norwegian vital interests—the Arctic, to be specific. Consequently, the Norwegians left both the northern and southern boundaries of their Antarctic claim undefined.[11]

The early exploration of Antarctica was largely an outgrowth of European commercial and imperial interests. Not surprisingly, the first countries to officially claim title to the continent were European powers, or their former colonies. However, with the onset of the Second World War in Europe, interest in the Antarctic broadened and two non-European nations joined the ranks of the claimant states.

The first to do so was Chile. In 1940, the Chilean government formally decreed that it exercised authority over a sector of Antarctic territory that included most of the Antarctic peninsula and its adjacent islands.[12] Significantly, the Chilean claim overlapped part of the sector already staked out by Great Britain. Thus, it might appear that Chile had entered the game of carving up the continent a bit too late. The Chilean government, however, stated that its 1940 decree did not create a title, but only clarified the boundaries of a title that had existed even before the rival British claim.[13]

The Chilean government advanced several unique arguments in support of its position. It contended that Chile's right to a slice of Antarctic territory actually originated with the papal bulls of Pope Alexander VI (1493) and the Treaty of Tordesillas (1494), which together divided the unexplored world—including any lands that might be found to the far south—between Spain and Portugal. Thus, according to the argument, when Chile won its independence from Spain in 1810, it also inherited this and other Spanish rights in the New World, including an historic right to Antarctica—even though it had not been discovered yet. In addition to this questionable legal logic, the Chileans also employed the notions of geographic contiguity (Antarctica was the geographic and geological extension of South America) and geographical proximity (Chile was the closest country to the Antarctic peninsula) to add more weight to its case. Finally, the government cited Chilean fishing and whaling activities in the region and administrative decrees dating from 1902 as evidence of Chilean intent to exercise sovereignty in the claimed region.[14]

In announcing their claim, Chilean officials also made clear their reasons for doing so. Like the British and the Norwegians, the Chileans wanted to protect their interests in whaling and in the presumed mineral resources of the region. At the same time, the Chilean government emphasized the strategic importance of its claimed territory, describing it as the "veritable guardian" of the Drake Passage connecting the Atlantic and Pacific oceans south of Tierra del Fuego.[15]

Argentina was the second non-European nation to formally claim title to Antarctic territory. The Argentine government articulated its position in a series of unilateral pronouncements and diplomatic demarches between 1940 and 1947. The Argentines advanced a case similar in many respects to the one employed by Chile—ancient historic rights, continuity, contiguity, the sector principle, Argentine activities on the continent (such as the continuous occupation of a weather station in the South Orkney Islands since 1904), and the performance of various administrative acts.[16]

A unique feature of the Argentine position was its relationship to the long-standing dispute with the British regarding sovereignty over the Falkland (or *Malvinas*) Islands. The Argentines considered their claim to these islands to be incontrovertible. As noted above, the British Letters of Patent of 1908 and 1917 assigned the Antarctic territories claimed by Great Britain to the so-called Falkland Islands Dependencies. Thus, an administrative measure on the part of the British established a link between the fates of both the Falklands and the Antarctic. For Argentina, the uncompromising assertion of a claim to Antarctica became an important facet of its passionately pursued objective of gaining control of the Malvinas.[17]

The actual Argentine claim encompassed part of the Antarctic peninsula, as well as the South Orkney, South Shetland, and other adjacent islands. Significantly, it overlapped both the British and Chilean claims. Since the Argentine government totally rejected the British position, the "only problem that remains to be settled," according to the Argentine foreign minister in 1940, "is that of the Chilean-Argentine Antarctic frontier."[18]

Thus, by the end of the Second World War, territorial claims in the Antarctic had become a contentious political issue. Seven different nations had formally asserted title to Antarctic territory—Great Britain, New Zealand, Australia, France, Norway, Chile, and Argentina. Three of the claims—those of Chile, Argentina, and Great Britain—overlapped. The dispute between the latter two countries was inextricably linked to conflicting claims outside the immediate Antarctic region. Finally, a substantial portion of the continent had yet to be claimed, though (as will be seen below) other nations were poised to assert their own rights to Antarctic territory. In other words, the so-called "last continent" was becoming the object of the same kinds of disputes over territory and sovereignty that had long preoccupied the international affairs of the major powers. As in other territorial disputes, the claimant nations attempted to employ the traditional tools of diplomacy, international law, and (ultimately) military force to support their respective positions.

The diplomatic efforts of rival claimants took several forms. For example, each claimant asserted its rights in formal state documents and in diplomatic correspondence addressed to rival claimants, as well as other members of the international community. The claimant states justified their respective positions in several different ways. As one might expect, each government seized on supposed principles of international law that best suited its particular historical circumstances.

In reality, international law provided no definitive answers to the issue of territorial claims in the Antarctic. Legal norms for laying claim to uninhabited territory were based on only a few adjudicated cases. Consequently, precedent in this area of international law was not strong. The precedent that did exist suggested that discovery or possession established an "inchoate title," which ultimately had to be perfected by "effective occupation." The definition of "effective occupation," however, was elusive, particularly when applied to relatively inaccessible areas with forbidding climates. Moreover, not every claimant agreed that effective occupation by itself established a superior claim to title.[19]

Presumably, rival claimants could have subjected their cases to formal adjudication or arbitration. In fact, on several occasions between 1947 and 1955, the British government separately proposed to the Argentines and Chileans that they submit their differences to the International Court of Justice or some other form of international arbitration.[20] Both Latin American governments consistently refused, suggesting that an international conference should decide the issue.[21] In May 1955, the British government unilaterally applied to the International Court of Justice to hear its side of the story. Nothing came of the application, and the Antarctic Treaty ultimately rendered it moot.[22]

In the absence of any definitive legal standards for validating Antarctic territorial claims, the international community for the most part refused to endorse positions taken by claimants in the region. Common political interest did lead to some mutual recognition of claims. Great Britain, New Zealand, and Australia, of course, accepted the legitimacy of the three large claims the London government had asserted on their behalves. In 1938, the three Commonwealth countries and France mutually recognized each other's position in the Antarctic.[23] The circle of mutual recognition expanded to include Norway the following year.[24] Despite having made overlapping claims, Argentina and Chile demonstrated Latin American solidarity by explicitly recognizing each other's "unquestionable" right to Antarctic territory and agreeing in principle to negotiate a precise demarcation of sovereignty in the region.[25] However, the recognition of claims stopped with these two clusters of claimant nations. No other country recognized any of the seven outstanding claims to Antarctic territory.

In cases in which legal or diplomatic approaches failed to resolve territorial disputes, the use or threatened use of military force often resulted. The Antarctic was no exception. During the Second World War, the British established three bases in the Antarctic peninsula region as part of *Operation Tabarin*. The bases were supposed to enhance British capabilities to interdict German naval forces in the South Atlantic and to deny them safe haven in Antarctic harbors. An equally important justification for constructing the bases was to establish a military presence in the Antarctic at the very time Chile and Argentina were publicly asserting claims that overlapped the British sector. Significantly, *Operation Tabarin* was a joint venture of the Admiralty and the Colonial Office.[26]

During 1947-48, Britain, Argentina, and Chile sailed several warships into the region. At the same time, the Argentines and Chileans established bases on or near the Antarctic peninsula manned by naval personnel. Obviously concerned about the mounting potential for conflict, all three governments jointly agreed in January 1949 not to dispatch warships south of 60° south latitude—an agreement they regularly renewed in subsequent years.[27]

Nevertheless, armed clashes still occurred. In 1952, a British party landed at Hope Bay to rebuild a base destroyed by fire several years earlier. Personnel from an Argentine base at Hope Bay fired machine gun bursts over the heads of the British party and forced them at gunpoint to return to their ship. The British later returned to Hope Bay and, under Marine protection, completed the reconstruction.[28] In 1953, the British government instructed the Acting Governor General of the Falklands to dismantle an Argentine and a Chilean base on Deception Island. In the process, two Argentine citizens were arrested and "deported" for violating the Falkland Islands Aliens Ordinance.[29]

In the final analysis, these incidents were relatively minor—no lives were lost. Moreover, the actions probably resulted more (in the words of the Argentine foreign minister) from "an excess of zeal" on the part of officials on the scene than from any deliberate policy of the central governments.[30] Clearly the stakes in the region were not high enough at the time to warrant more drastic military measures. Still, the incidents dramatically affirmed that the use of force was an option in backing up a territorial claim, and once unleashed it could prove difficult to control. As a US National Security Council report noted in 1948, "While it seems unlikely that war could break out over disputed claims in Antarctica, it cannot be denied that wars in the past have grown out of disputes of even more trivial nature."[31]

Cold War Dimension

The clashes that occurred in the early fifties only involved three claimants and were restricted to disputes around the Antarctic peninsula. However, the emerging global competition between the United States and the Soviet Union threatened to embroil the entire Antarctic continent in a much more serious conflict over territory. In the late forties and early fifties, both superpowers devoted increasing attention to the continent far from their respective borders.

The United States had played a major role in the discovery and later exploration of the Antarctic. An American, Nathaniel Palmer, claimed to have sighted the continent in 1820 during a sealing expedition to the Southern Ocean. From 1838 to 1842, Charles Wilkes explored and mapped the East Antarctic Coast during an expedition sponsored by the US Navy. The seal trade continued to attract American ships to the area during the remainder of the nineteenth century. An American, Dr. Frederick Cook, was a member of the *Belgica* expedition that "wintered over" in Antarctica during 1898-99. Starting in 1928, expeditions led by Richard Byrd and Lincoln Ellsworth used airplanes to map large areas of unexplored territory in the region. By the Second World War, the United States could easily claim that American explorers had traversed

Belgica, **shown here in a June 1898 photograph by moonlight, served as transportation and home for the first expedition to "winter over" in the Antarctic. An American, Dr. Frederick Cook, was a member of *Belgica*'s party.**

more of the continent than had explorers from any other nation.[32]

Despite extensive exploration of the Antarctic by American citizens, the US Government did not engage in the land grab that started with the British Letter of Patents in 1908. Instead, the United States adopted a twofold policy of (1) pointedly refusing to recognize claims of other nations to Antarctic territory and (2) reserving all "rights" that resulted from the actions of American citizens in the region. This latter point carried a thinly veiled warning that the United States might at some point announce its own territorial claim based on explorations made by Americans.

The US Government based its non-recognition policy on the premise that existing claims did not meet the test of international law regarding the acquisition of *terra nullius* (nobody's land). For example, in 1924, Secretary of State Charles Evans Hughes informed the Norwegian government that discovery and formal taking of possession did not constitute a sufficient basis for sovereignty over previously uninhabited lands.[33] (European and Commonwealth countries, as noted above, relied heavily on these two doctrines in asserting their rights in the region.) The US State Department sounded the same theme 10 years later, telling the British—who were upset about some of Byrd's actions in the New Zealand sector—that "it could not admit that sovereignty accrues from mere discovery unaccompanied by occupancy and use."[34] The French government received a similarly worded note in 1939 regarding its claims to Adelie Land.[35] Likewise, the State Department refuted the sector principle as a basis for extending claims from coastal areas to poles in the Antarctic as well as the Arctic.[36]

While Hughes and subsequent spokesmen categorically rejected discovery as a sufficient basis for an Antarctic claim, the US Government was less clear about specific legal requirements for perfecting title. Secretary Hughes had stated in 1924 that some form of settlement was required, though he did not say what form. In 1947, an internal State Department policy statement admitted that "normal rules of international law regarding acquisition of territory by discovery and effective occupation cannot reasonably be applied to the Antarctic Continent." However, the State Department was apparently at a loss to come up with an acceptable principle.[37] By 1951, it could only conclude that in the future "title to such regions may be acquired by some form of control short of actual settlement."[38]

Even though it had no definitive view on a sufficient basis for Antarctic claims, the US Government still took several measures to bolster such a claim in the event it ever decided to assert one. For example, a postmaster

First mail from home in 12 months arrives aboard USS *BEAR* at West Base in the Antarctic on 10 January 1941 during the 1939-41 US Antarctic Expedition.

accompanied Byrd's expedition in 1933 and canceled mail at his Antarctic base, much to the chagrin of the British. The State Department secretly informed Ellsworth that he should drop notes during his 1939 expedition to assert claims on behalf of the United States.[39] The US government sponsored Byrd's third expedition to the Antarctic, under the aegis of the US Antarctic Service with "the specific purpose of establishing and strengthening US claims within the sector previously explored by Admiral Byrd and Lincoln Ellsworth."[40] President Roosevelt privately instructed Byrd that

> members of the Service may take any appropriate
> steps such as dropping written claims from airplanes,
> depositing such writings in cairns, et cetera, which

might assist in supporting a sovereignty claim by the
United States.[41]

Similar actions were quietly taken during official expeditions after the Second World War. By the late forties, US officials were confident the United States could assert a claim as strong if not stronger than those advanced by the seven claimant countries.[42]

Thus for much of this period, US policy toward the Antarctic was designed primarily to preserve future options by insisting on certain undefined rights in the region. Even though American citizens had assumed a major role in Antarctic exploration—a role that had excited public interest—US officials saw little reason to adopt a more activist policy toward the continent. Immediately after the Second World War, the US Government clearly regarded the immediate economic and strategic value of the Antarctic region to be small, though it did support continued exploration of the continent on "scientific and technical grounds." While some interest was shown at the working level within the State Department for negotiating an international administration for the region, Secretary of State James Byrnes ruled out any major US initiatives. He told reporters that with all the other diplomatic activities of the moment, "it would not be essential immediately to call a conference on Antarctic questions which are *not very important*" (emphasis added).[43]

This policy of benign neglect did not last long. By late 1947, Antarctic affairs assumed increasing importance in US foreign policy considerations. Ironically, the impetus for this shift in focus had more to do with the Soviet Union than with events on the ice.

Specifically, Antarctica created special problems for America's emerging strategy of containing Soviet power and influence across the globe. In March 1947, the American President had publicly announced the "Truman Doctrine" of providing US assistance to countries resisting

Before World War II, US naval aviators explored vast stretches of Antarctic territory during survey flights. A pilot flies back to West Base from a survey flight over the Bay of Whales during the third US Antarctic Expedition. West Cape, footed by broken pressure ice, passes beneath; beyond lies East Cape and the camp.

direct or indirect aggression. That summer, Washington launched the Marshall Plan for the economic recovery of Europe. And, in September 1947, the United States and several Latin American states signed the Rio Treaty that provided for the collective self-defense of the hemisphere.

The squabbling over rival claims in the Antarctic interjected a troublesome and potentially disruptive element into this coalition-building process. It placed the United States in the middle of an increasingly acrimonious conflict between a major European ally (Great Britain) on one side and two important South American allies (Argentina and Chile) on the other. All three countries looked to their superpower ally for support on this issue. The Latin American countries, in fact, took the position that the Rio Treaty might obligate the United States to help them defend their Antarctic interests against "armed threats" by the British.[44] The US Government refused to accept this interpretation of the pact and studiously attempted to pursue an even-handed approach to all three countries.[45] Nevertheless, American officials concluded that dissension within western ranks was an embarrassment which the Soviet Union could potentially exploit to its advantage.[46]

In an effort to avert a clash among its allies, the US Government took the lead in framing a diplomatic solution to the Antarctic claims dispute. The basic American strategy was to "internationalize" the Antarctic by merging separate national interests and vesting them in a special regime. Specific proposals for international administration of the region varied over time. The State Department initially recommended placing the Antarctic under a United Nations trusteeship administered by the seven claimant nations and the United States.

The British, however, were cool to the trusteeship concept since it might give the Soviet Union a pretext for meddling in Antarctic matters. The State Department consequently modified its proposal by suggesting a condominium arrangement administered by the same eight states.

The United States then presented its ideas to the Latin Americans. Peron's government in Argentina took a militant position, refusing to discuss any scheme that relinquished its presumed sovereignty in the area. The Chileans presented a counterproposal: Instead of merging individual interests, they suggested that claims in the region simply be frozen for five to ten years as a means of reducing tension.[47] The United States, apparently pleased to have any movement on the issue, correspondingly agreed to the Chilean proposal for a *modus vivendi* as a basis for pushing ahead on a diplomatic solution. However, negotiations to implement the concept bogged down; by the mid-fifties, little if any progress had been made.[48]

The US proposal to internationalize Antarctica also sprang from a concern related to the broader objectives of the containment strategy: The United States and its allies wanted to keep the Soviet Union out of Antarctica and Antarctic affairs. The underlying reason for excluding the Soviets was geostrategic in nature. American military officials concluded that the Antarctic had little military significance in peacetime—aside from serving as a training ground for cold weather operations that, for political reasons, could not easily be conducted in the Arctic.

However, the Antarctic's strategic importance could change considerably in wartime. If, for example, the United States and its allies were denied use of the Panama Canal in a major conflict, the only feasible sea route between the east and west coasts of North and South America would be the Drake Passage—which is bordered by Tierra del Fuego on the north and the Antarctic peninsula on the south. (See Map 2.) By basing air or naval forces on either side of Drake Passage, an adversary could interdict the sea line of communications linking the Atlantic and Pacific oceans. For this reason, the Defense Department argued that it was

> imperative that sovereignty or active participation in control of the Antarctic, under trusteeship arrangement or otherwise, should be denied groups of nations which include our most probable enemies.[49]

The State Department came to the same conclusion.[50]

Despite its concern about the Antarctic falling into the wrong hands during a war, the Defense Department did not argue for a permanent military presence in the region.[51] No good reason could be shown to spend scarce resources to base forces in such an inhospitable climate. In 1946-47, the military had staged a very large expedition to

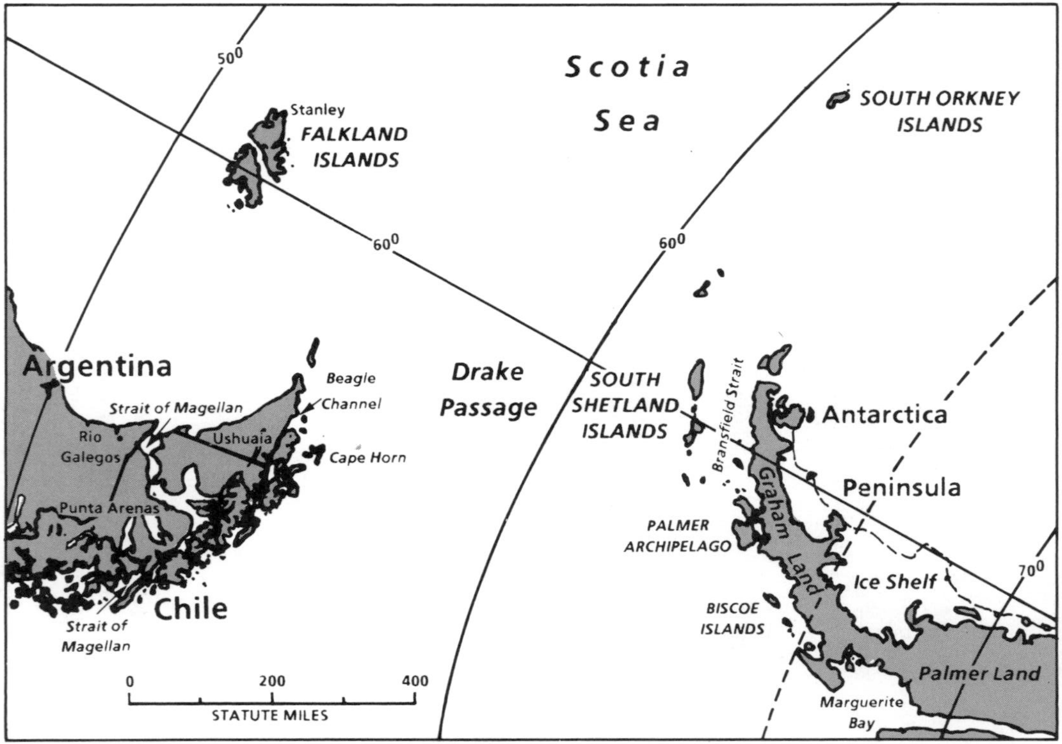

Map 2. Drake Passage

Source: CIA. *Polar Regions Atlas*, 1978

Rear Admiral Richard E. Byrd at Little America in February 1947, during *Operation Highjump*. The pipe and tobacco, as well as the isolated hut in which he is seated, were left over from Admiral Byrd's 1933-35 Antarctic Expedition.

the Antarctic—*Operation Highjump*—to provide training in polar operations and strengthen the basis for a possible American territorial claim. The expedition involved a dozen naval ships (including an aircraft carrier and a submarine) and some 4,700 personnel. The following year, the Navy dispatched a smaller expedition to the region—*Operation Windmill*.[52] In addition to their stated objectives, these movements of men and supplies also demonstrated that the United States had the capability to project military forces to the Antarctic should the need arise. To preserve the option of doing so, the military objected to an early State Department proposal to demilitarize the Antarctic as part of a negotiated settlement of the claims dispute.[53]

For its part, the Soviet Union had no intention of being frozen out of Antarctic affairs by an American-engineered solution to the claims dispute. In 1949, the president of the Soviet All-Union Geographic Society claimed that the Russian sailors Thaddeus Bellingshausen and Mikhail Lazarev had in fact been the first to discover parts of the Antarctic continent during their 1819-21 voyage. Consequently, the Soviet Union felt it had as much right to assert a claim to Antarctic territory as France. These comments received wide play in the official Soviet press, and the US and British governments braced themselves for the next shoe to drop.[54]

It fell the following year, when the Soviet government formally expressed its views on Antarctica in a demarche to the United States and six of the seven claimant nations. (The Soviet Union did not have diplomatic relations with Chile at the time.) The Soviet note made reference to the State Department's ongoing discussions with claimant nations regarding the continent's future. In the Soviet opinion, the circle of participants was too small. Citing historical, whaling, and scientific interests in the region, the Soviet government insisted on its right to take part in any negotiations on a new regime for the Antarctic. Moreover, it threatened to withhold recognition of any decision made without its involvement.[55]

Though the United States chose not to respond to the note, the Soviets clearly had laid down a marker. The western hope of excluding the Soviets from the continent had proven to be rather naive. The rivalry between East and West for power and influence now extended to Antarctica as well.

The twin goals of settling claims disputes and excluding the Soviet Union from the Antarctic rekindled pressures within the US national security bureaucracy to formally assert an American territorial claim. Officials concluded that such a move would provide the United States added clout in negotiating a new international regime for the region, as well as the legitimacy needed to participate fully in that regime. They also felt that a US claim might forestall the Soviets from asserting rights to the unclaimed sector.[56] Despite growing interest in a claim at the working level, the US Government remained cool to the notion of joining the ranks of claimant countries.

Several considerations argued against asserting a claim. For one thing, officials never were quite clear where the United States should actually stake a claim. Proposed areas included the large unclaimed sector and the Antarctic peninsula. The latter area was more desirable from a strategic and climatological point of view. Moreover, American officials concluded that US rights in the peninsula could be defended from a legal standpoint. However, as the Central Intelligence Agency argued, a US claim to the peninsula might only serve to antagonize American allies and complicate, rather than ameliorate, ongoing disputes.[57]

President Eisenhower finally put the issue to rest in 1954, when he opted against announcing a formal claim. The President decided instead to continue the policy of asserting undefined "rights" in the region and negotiating a settlement to the claims dispute. He also expressed "hearty agreement" with the desire to exclude the Soviet Union from negotiations on the future of Antarctica.[58]

Eisenhower, however, did break new ground by approving two significant shifts in the American approach toward the Antarctic. *First*, he decided that the United States should maintain a presence in the region through a program of periodic expeditions and permanent bases. (No official expedition had been made to the region since *Operation Windmill* in 1948.) *Second*, this program would be "for scientific purposes only" and would support the upcoming global scientific program known as the International Geophysical Year.[59] While the United States continued to define Antarctic issues in terms of its larger global containment policy, a new element had thus crept into official American thinking about the region. The folkways of science, rather than the traditional tools of great power diplomacy, were emerging as the preferred approach to reducing the potential for conflict over the last continent.

International Geophysical Year

With the International Geophysical Year (IGY), scientific research replaced exploration as the central human activity in the Antarctic.[60] The IGY was a worldwide program of research in several different scientific disciplines that took place between July 1957 and December 1958. The original idea for such an effort came from a group of American and British scientists who wanted to take advantage of improved scientific instruments and equipment (such as the rocket) to expand the existing body of data on geophysical phenomena. The timing of the IGY coincided with an expected period of maximum sunspot activity. The International Council of Scientific Unions (ICSU) endorsed the concept in 1952, and established a *Comité Spécial de l'Année Géophysique Internationale* (CSAGI) to coordinate the research agenda of various national IGY committees. Sixty-seven countries ultimately participated in the IGY. For 18 months, several thousand scientists collected data from monitoring stations located throughout the world, including Antarctica.[61]

Efforts to coordinate IGY research in the Antarctic began at a Paris conference in June 1955. Principles and procedures adopted at this meeting had an important bearing on Antarctic affairs for years to come. Specifically, the conferees decided that their dealings with one another would be exclusively scientific in nature and that they would not concern themselves with political questions. They also agreed that research requirements might dictate placing some scientific stations in relatively close proximity. In making this concession to the needs of science, the conferees obviously sought to avoid the kind of clashes that had occurred at Hope Bay only three years earlier. (The Argentine and Chilean delegates—the only professional diplomats at the conference—were quick to point out, however, that the consensus on station siting was a temporary measure and would not modify existing relations in the region.)[62] Finally, the conferees established procedures for sharing weather information on the continent that envisioned Soviet scientists working at American stations, and vice versa.[63] The Paris conference produced what is usually referred to as a ''gentlemen's agreement'' not to allow territorial disputes and Cold War rivalries to stand in the way of science. Instead, scientists would have free access to all areas of the Antarctic to carry out IGY research.[64]

The scale of IGY research activities in the Antarctic was unprecedentedly large. Twelve nations ultimately conducted programs in the region—the seven claimant nations plus the United States, the Soviet Union, Belgium, Japan, and South Africa—at 60 different stations.[65] The scientific investigation ranged across a number of fields and demonstrated the importance of the Antarctic as a research ''laboratory'' virtually unsullied by pollution and other contamination from the inhabited world. The IGY also taught scientists and logisticians how to survive the rigors of Antarctica for prolonged periods, paving the way for permanent stations on the continent.

The American IGY program in the Antarctic was particularly impressive in this regard. In keeping with President Eisenhower's 1954 decision to expand the US presence, the US Government renewed expeditions to the continent and established several stations there. During the

Rear Admiral Richard E. Byrd (left) meets with Rear Admiral George Dufek, USN, and Admiral Jerry Wright, USN, aboard USS *ARNEB* (AKA 56) as she prepares to depart for *Operation Deep Freeze I* in November 1955.

1954-55 austral (southern) summer, the US Navy icebreaker USS *ATKA* surveyed the Antarctic coast for possible station sites and carried out scientific observations. The following summer, the US Navy—responsible for Antarctic logistics during the American IGY program—conducted its first *Operation Deep Freeze*. That season saw construction of Little America Station on the Ross Ice Shelf and an air facility on Ross Island in McMurdo Sound. During the 1956-57 *Operation Deep Freeze II*, five additional stations, including the Amundsen-Scott station at the South Pole, were completed.[66] While the polar site was important for studying glacial and auroral* phenomena, it also was rich in political symbolism. Since the various claimed sectors all converged at the Pole, the Amundsen-Scott station in effect gave the United States a foot in each territorial claim. Furthermore, in building a station with material delivered totally by air, the United States had demonstrated an ability to project and support an American presence virtually anywhere on the continent.[67]

By the end of the IGY, the United States—though not a claimant country—had reaffirmed its right to have a major say in the future of Antarctica.

The IGY also was the occasion for the first Soviet expeditions and bases on the Antarctic continent. The Soviet government had unequivocally signaled its interest in Antarctic affairs in 1950. But it had done little beyond whaling to establish a presence in the region. Initially, some scientists doubted whether the Soviets would take part in the Antarctic portion of IGY research programs. In the end, the Soviets mounted a very significant research effort on the ice, constructing six stations in East Antarctica. The overland transport of supplies to build their inland bases ranks as one of the most substantial achievements of the IGY.[68]

Even though the IGY was avowedly non-political, Soviet involvement in Antarctica created some consternation among nations previously active in the region. Some Australian officials, for example, reportedly expressed reservations about the Soviet decision to locate IGY stations within the Australian sector. After the launch of *Sputnik* in October 1957, a few pundits even went so far as to suggest

---

*The aurora is a radiant emission in the upper atmosphere that sporadically occurs toward both polar regions. These emissions take the form of luminous bands or streamers. They usually are white or green, but sometimes can be multi-hued. The aurora most likely is the result of charged particles from the sun—guided toward the poles along magnetic lines of force—colliding with molecules in the upper atmosphere.

that the Soviets might use the Antarctic as a base for missiles aimed at Southern Hemisphere targets or as a base for submarines. Thus, the Soviet announcement that it would continue its Antarctic operations beyond the termination date of the IGY led in part to a one-year extension of the research program—under the rubric of the International Geophysical Cooperation program—as a means of perpetuating the "gentlemen's agreement" a bit longer.[69] The prospect of continued Soviet presence on the ice also increased pressure within the United States to maintain stations on the continent after the IGY, particularly at the South Pole.[70]

Regardless of any action the United States or its allies might take, the IGY already had led to the emergence of the Soviet Union as a major player in Antarctic affairs. The policy of excluding the Soviets from the region had been overtaken by events; the most the US Government could hope to do was to ensure that Soviet presence on the ice did not jeopardize American and allied interests there.

While the IGY demonstrated the capacity for international cooperation within the Antarctic, it did not eliminate disputes over sovereignty. The seven claimant countries had not abandoned their interests in the region. Despite the "gentlemen's agreement" to place politics on hold for the program's duration, claimants carefully located their stations within their respective sectors.[71] Paradoxically, the IGY also gave the claimants—as well as the United States and the Soviet Union—greater legal ammunition for asserting title to Antarctic territory. Before the IGY, the principle of effective occupation could only be applied at best in the peninsula region. However, during the course of the IGY, participants had proven their capabilities for operating on the continent for sustained periods. As a result, they were in a far better position to press claims under existing concepts of international law.[72]

During preparations for the IGY, another factor threatened to exacerbate the already complicated issue of Antarctica's legal status. In 1956, the Indian government formally requested the United Nations General Assembly to consider measures to ensure that Antarctica was used "entirely for peaceful purposes and for the general welfare." This proposal encountered stiff resistance from countries already active in the region, and the Indians subsequently withdrew their recommendation. However, two years later, the Indian government again attempted to place the "question of Antarctica" on the UN General Assembly agenda, noting that the subject was "of great importance to the international community as a whole and not merely for certain countries."[73] As before, the Indians backed down in the face of opposition. Nevertheless, the Indian initiatives demonstrated that interest in the region was expanding. Future control over Antarctic affairs was obviously an issue of interest beyond the relatively small circle of nations with pre-existing claims and programs in the area.

Against this backdrop—a winding down of the IGY and the "gentlemen's agreement," Soviet intentions to remain on the ice, lingering territorial disputes, and the prospect of wider international interest in the Antarctic— the US Government decided to resume its earlier efforts to negotiate a new regime for the Antarctic. The objective, as before, was to protect American interests. The model was the IGY experience.

Conference on Antarctica

On 2 May 1958, the US Government invited the 11 other countries with IGY programs in the Antarctic to a conference on Antarctica. As stated in the letter of invitation, the purpose of the conference was to draft a treaty that would perpetuate the principles of cooperation worked out for the IGY. Thus, like the informal "gentlemen's agreement," the treaty would guarantee freedom of scientific investigation and promote international scientific cooperation.[74]

The United States also sought to ensure that the Antarctic was used for peaceful purposes only and to prevent Antarctica from becoming, in President Eisenhower's words, "an object of political conflict."[75] To this end, the US invitation proposed a solution to the territorial question along the lines of the *modus vivendi* first proposed by the Chileans in 1948. Participating nations would not be required to renounce any "historic rights" or "claims of sovereignty." Instead, any existing rights or claims "would remain unaffected while the treaty is in force" and no new rights or claims would be asserted "during the duration of the treaty." In short, "the legal status quo in Antarctica would be frozen for the duration of the treaty, permitting cooperation in scientific and administrative matters."[76]

In a not-so-subtle attempt to apply pressure to attend the conference, the US note recalled the extensive record of American involvement in the Antarctic since the early part of the nineteenth century and reiterated the long-held US position of reserving all rights in the region, "including the right to assert a territorial claim or claims." In other words, if the claimants or potential claimants did not want to work toward a diplomatic solution to Antarctica's tangled legal status, then the United States was fully prepared to pursue a more confrontational course. Indeed, some American officials actually preferred to forgo an international approach in favor of staking a US claim once and for all.[77]

The US Government also went to some lengths in its invitation to rationalize the decision to include in the Antarctic conference only those nations active in IGY research. The US note stressed that even if participation in the negotiations were restricted in this manner, any agreement reached by the 12 would hold benefits for other

nations as well. Moreover, the treaty would entail cooperation with UN technical agencies—an oblique effort, no
doubt, to satisfy concerns raised by the Indian initiatives.[78]

All nations with Antarctic IGY programs ultimately
accepted the US call for a conference. The Commonwealth
nations already had discussed among themselves the need
for a diplomatic solution to the continuing dispute over
claims after the IGY and were receptive to the American
initiative. The Argentines and Chileans resisted the notion
of an international conference that might prejudice what
they considered their immutable rights of sovereignty. But
they ultimately accepted the US invitation, with
reservations.[79]

Informal preparatory talks for the conference began in
June 1958 in Washington. Representatives from the 12
countries met once or twice a week at the National Academy of Sciences. Discussions proceeded at a snail's pace,
slowed in part by Soviet insistence that the preparatory
meetings deal strictly with procedural details. In the meantime, US representative Paul Daniels continued to circulate
substantive proposals.[80]

After 60-or-so sessions, the participants agreed to
convene a formal conference in October 1959 in Washington. Because many issues already had been decided in
the preparatory meetings, negotiations went quickly.[81] On
1 December 1959, all 12 participants signed the Antarctic
Treaty. The treaty entered into force on 23 June 1961,
after ratification by all signatory governments.

Participants in the Washington Conference expressed
great satisfaction in concluding the first treaty ever to
govern Antarctic affairs. Given the animosity surrounding
the territorial disputes and the deep suspicions inherent in
the Cold War, it was remarkable that 12 nations with very
different cultures and political-economic systems agreed
on a regime to regulate national activities across an entire
continent. The closing comment of the British delegate

best captured both the political reality and the promise of
the Antarctic Treaty:

> No Treaty of course ever gives complete satisfaction
> to all its signatories.... Others have made conces-
> sions in the interest of mutual agreement just as we
> have ourselves.... The International Geophysical
> Year showed what could be achieved by interna-
> tional cooperation in scientific research in the Ant-
> arctic. It is our belief that the present Treaty will
> serve as a firm framework within which co-operation
> will continue in the scientific field and be extended
> to others.[82]

Before discussing specific provisions of the Antarctic
Treaty, a final point regarding its negotiation is worth
emphasizing: The new Antarctic regime was drafted by a
very small group of nations. The entire negotiation process
involved only those countries originally invited by the
United States—despite an apparent effort by the Soviet
Union to open the conference to all interested parties.
Moreover, the preparatory and formal sessions were held
in private. While very good political and practical reasons
certainly could be given for these restrictions, this legacy
of secretiveness eventually would come back to haunt the
original signatories.

2

The Antarctic
Treaty System

S INCE 1961, THE ANTARCTIC TREATY SYSTEM HAS
governed the activities of nations in the Antarctic
region. Though some disagreements have surfaced over
the precise definition of this "system," most officials and
scholars agree that it refers to the provisions of the treaty
itself, as well as the procedures and principles member
governments have adopted in implementing it.[1] This system of agreements forms the context in which policies of
nations active in the region have operated for nearly three
decades.

Understanding the Antarctic Treaty system is essential
in evaluating current and future American strategy toward
the region. Accordingly, this chapter describes the key features of the Antarctic Treaty, and then examines the continuing process of consultation among treaty members.
(See Appendix A for the text of the Antarctic Treaty.)

The Antarctic Treaty

One way to approach the Antarctic Treaty is to view
it as several different agreements in one. The treaty is in

NSF Photo

National flags of the Antarctic Treaty's 12 original signatories are displayed in front of the Amundsen-Scott station at the South Pole in this 1975 photo.

effect an arms control measure, a claims settlement (of sorts), a science compact, and a framework for a limited system of administration in Antarctic affairs. This chapter employs this "agreement-within-an-agreement" approach in examining key aspects of the treaty below. Before doing so, two basic dimensions of the Antarctic Treaty—its duration and its geographic scope—should be considered.

DURATION   As stated in its preamble, one objective of the treaty is to preserve the Antarctic for peaceful purposes "forever." Accordingly, the treaty has no expiration date and could conceivably remain in force indefinitely. However, the treaty specifies procedures for amendment and for a review conference, both of which could lead to withdrawal by one or more signatories and ultimately result in de facto termination of the treaty.

An *amendment* can be offered at anytime by a consultative party* to the treaty. Before the amendment can take effect, all consultative parties must approve it and their respective governments must formally ratify it. Any other signatory nation that fails to ratify the amendment within two years "shall be deemed to have withdrawn" from the treaty.[2] Thus, as convoluted as it may appear, a government bent on withdrawing from the treaty could propose an amendment sure to win the approval of the consultative parties, and then subsequently refuse to ratify the amendment.[3] As it turns out, no amendments have been offered since the treaty entered into force in 1961.[4]

A *review conference* can be convened anytime after the thirtieth anniversary of the treaty's entry into force. Consequently, the first time a review conference could be held is 1991. Contrary to some accounts, a review conference is not mandatory; rather, a consultative party must formally request one. Amendment of the treaty under this procedure requires only majority approval. Any nation that fails to ratify the changes made in a review conference within two years may give notice of its intent to withdraw from the treaty. The withdrawal notification would take effect after an additional two years.[5]

The amendment and review conference provisions provide the only means within the treaty by which a signatory can legitimately withdraw. Thus, until an amendment is approved or a review conference is convened, the measures first agreed in 1959 will remain in force and continue to bind the signatories.

---

*One of the original 12 signatory states, or a subsequent signatory granted consultative status in accordance with procedures described later in this chapter. See Table 1 for the current list of consultative parties.

Table 1
Parties to the Antarctic Treaty (as of 1 June 1990)

Country	Status*	Accession Date	CP Status Date
1. United Kingdom	OS/CP	31 May 60	OS
2. South Africa	OS/CP	21 Jun 60	OS
3. Belgium	OS/CP	26 Jul 60	OS
4. Japan	OS/CP	4 Aug 60	OS
5. United States	OS/CP	18 Aug 60	OS
6. Norway	OS/CP	24 Aug 60	OS
7. France	OS/CP	16 Sep 60	OS
8. New Zealand	OS/CP	1 Nov 60	OS
9. Soviet Union	OS/CP	2 Nov 60	OS
10. Poland .	AS/CP	8 Jun 61	29 Jul 77
11. Argentina	OS/CP	23 Jun 61	OS
12. Australia	OS/CP	23 Jun 61	OS
13. Chile	OS/CP	23 Jun 61	OS
14. Czechoslovakia	AS	14 Jun 62	
15. Denmark	AS	20 May 65	
16. The Netherlands	AS**	30 Mar 67	
17. Romania	AS	15 Sep 71	
18. German Democratic Republic	AS/CP	19 Nov 74	5 Oct 87
19. Brazil	AS/CP	16 May 75	12 Sep 83

(Continued on next page)

Table 1—Cont'd
Parties to the Antarctic Treaty (as of 1 June 1990)

Country	Status*	Accession Date	CP Status Date
20. Bulgaria	AS	11 Sep 78	
21. Federal Republic of Germany	AS/CP	5 Feb 79	3 Mar 81
22. Uruguay	AS/CP	11 Jan 80	7 Oct 85
23. Papua New Guinea	AS	16 Mar 81	
24. Italy	AS/CP	18 Mar 81	5 Oct 87
25. Peru	AS	10 Apr 81	9 Oct 89
26. Spain	AS/CP	31 Mar 82	22 Sep 88
27. People's Republic of China	AS/CP	8 Jun 83	7 Oct 85
28. India	AS/CP	19 Aug 83	12 Sep 83
29. Hungary	AS	27 Jan 84	
30. Sweden	AS/CP	24 Apr 84	22 Sep 88
31. Finland	AS	15 May 84	9 Oct 89
32. Cuba	AS	16 Aug 84	
33. Republic of Korea	AS	28 Nov 86	9 Oct 89
34. Greece	AS	8 Jan 87	
35. Democratic People's Republic of Korea	AS	21 Jan 87	
36. Austria	AS	25 Aug 87	
37. Ecuador	AS**	15 Sep 87	
38. Canada	AS	4 May 88	
39. Colombia	AS	31 Jan 89	

*OS = original signatory; CP = consultative party; AS = acceding state. Under the treaty, an original signatory is automatically a consultative party.
**Ecuador and the Netherlands have formally notified the treaty's depositary government (the United States) of their desire to become consultative parties.

Sources: John Heap, ed., *Handbook of the Antarctic Treaty System*, 6th ed. (Cambridge, England: Polar Publications, April 1989), and Office of Oceans Affairs, US Department of State.

SCOPE   The geographic scope of the treaty is the area south of 60° south latitude. (See Map 3.) It encompasses the entire Antarctic continent—including the peninsula— and the South Orkney and South Shetland Islands. The treaty's provisions also apply to "all ice shelves," which the US Government has defined as "thick portions of ice attached to the land and extending seaward." However, the treaty explicitly states that nothing in its provisions will prejudice any nation's rights under international law with regard to the "high seas" within that area.[6]

The treaty thus leaves room for other international legal customs and agreements to govern certain activities within the area south of 60° south latitude. Unfortunately, the treaty failed to resolve the ambiguity surrounding the concept of "high seas" as it applies to the Antarctic. Claimant and non-claimant nations would of course disagree on the existence of maritime zones within the treaty area and, therefore, on the boundaries of the high seas.[7] The chief American negotiator at the 1959 Conference on Antarctica—Herman Phleger—testified that the issue was so controversial that the conferees deliberately left the definition of high seas "indefinite."[8] The question has grown even more complicated over time, particularly in light of more recent discussions surrounding the United Nations Law of the Sea Conference.

The choice of the geographic scope of the treaty was to some extent an arbitrary decision. The definition of what constitutes "the Antarctic" varies according to the context in which the term is used. Many scientists, for example, consider the so-called Antarctic Convergence (also referred to as the Polar Frontal Zone) as the natural boundary for the region. (See Map 4.)

The Antarctic Convergence, which is roughly 20 to 30 miles wide, marks the point at which the colder, less saline waters surrounding the Antarctic continent collide with the warmer, saltier waters of the more northern climes. Its distance from the Antarctic continent varies,

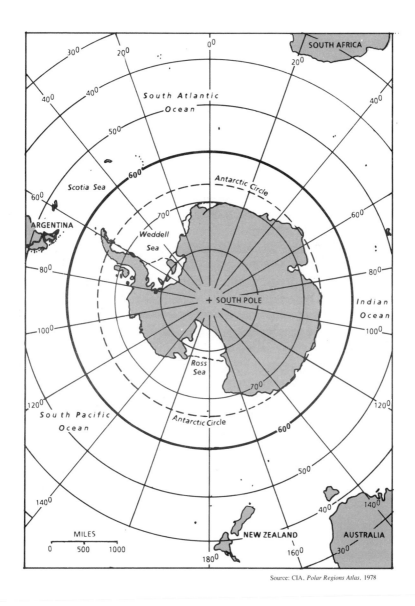

Source: CIA, *Polar Regions Atlas*, 1978

Map 3. Geographic scope of the Antarctic Treaty is the area south of 60° south latitude.

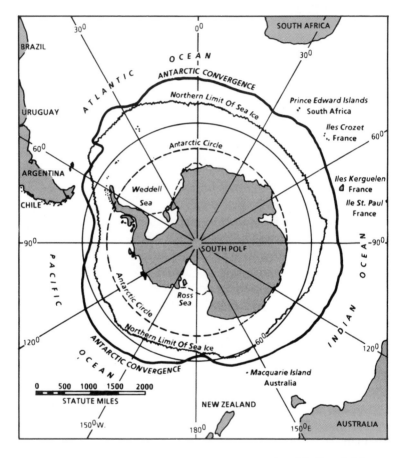

Map 4. The Antarctic Convergence

but averages about 1,000 miles. Because of differences in temperature and salinity on either side, the Antarctic Convergence forms a kind of biological barrier that blocks most aquatic life from passing through it. (Large, migratory animals—such as whales—are obvious exceptions.) Thus, the waters south of the Antarctic Convergence constitute in effect a single and separate ecosystem—a fact germane to the conduct of scientific research and protection of the Antarctic environment.[9]

The Soviet delegate to the Washington preparatory meetings had recommended using the Antarctic Convergence to define the geographic scope of the treaty. While this approach may have made scientific sense, it was not acceptable for practical as well as political reasons. For one thing, the precise location of the Antarctic Convergence fluctuates according to season and prevailing currents. Moreover, a number of islands and island groups claimed by several signatories, but not directly tied to any claims on the continent, lie within the Antarctic Convergence. The claimant nations clearly had no interest in intertwining the issue of sovereignty over these islands with the more contentious issue of sovereignty over the continent.[10]

In the end, the geographic scope of the treaty coincided with the northernmost boundaries of most of the sectoral claims. (The northern and southern limits of the Norwegian sector are not defined.) The continuing claims dispute had after all motivated much of the diplomatic activity that ultimately led to the 1959 Conference on Antarctica. The negotiators obviously wanted to include the main areas of contention under the purview of the treaty. Otherwise, the meeting had little meaning. At the same time, no compelling political reason existed to exacerbate an already vexing issue by expanding the scope of the treaty above 60° south latitude.

AN ARMS CONTROL AGREEMENT   Article I of the Antarctic Treaty states that ''Antarctica shall be used for peaceful purposes only." To this end, "any measures of a military nature" are prohibited, such as military bases and fortifications, manuevers, and weapons testing. Additionally, Article V of the treaty prohibits any nuclear explosions in Antarctica, as well as the disposal of radioactive waste in the region. The treaty also states that should all its contracting parties also become parties to other international agreements on nuclear energy, explosions, or wastes, then those agreements also become binding in the Antarctic. To date, this particular provision has had no bearing on the region.[11]

The Antarctic Treaty is thus said to have "demilitarized" the region—though this characterization begs the question of whether the Antarctic was ever militarized in the first place. As such, the treaty addressed two long-standing concerns of the United States and its allies. *First*, it sharply reduced the prospects of conflict in the Antarctic arising from territorial disputes, such as the incidents at Hope Bay and Deception Island. By limiting military weapons and bases in the region, the treaty also limited the risk of armed clashes resulting from deliberate design or miscalculation. *Second*, this provision assuaged the fear (perhaps somewhat exaggerated) that the Soviet Union (or one of its allies) would use the Antarctic as a base to disrupt commercial and naval traffic through Drake Passage or launch missiles at Southern Hemisphere targets.

The treaty did not, however, altogether rule out the possibility of military deployments to the area south of 60° south latitude. As noted above, Article VI provides that nothing in the treaty will prejudice a signatory's rights with respect to the high seas. A generally recognized right in this regard is for naval vessels and military aircraft to transit the high seas and the airspace above them. Thus, it is entirely conceivable that a signatory could send military forces to the Antarctic region and still be in compliance with the treaty as long as those forces remained on the high seas.[12]

The treaty makes another important exception to its general prohibition against military "measures" in the

American military personnel routinely support scientific activities in Antarctica. For example, US Navy pilots fly the ski-equipped LC-130 aircraft (background) that transport scientists to remote research sites.

treaty area. Prior to the treaty, military personnel from various nations had been intimately involved in the early exploration of Antarctica. Many of the great names in the continent's history—such as Charles Wilkes, Robert Falcon Scott, and Richard Byrd—were naval officers and their efforts received naval sponsorship to at least some degree. Furthermore, the seven stations used by American scientists during the IGY were built by the US Navy during its annual *Operations Deep Freeze*. The drafters of the Antarctic Treaty recognized that for the foreseeable future their respective military establishments would have a monopoly on many of the resources required to support successful operations on the ice, even if the emphasis in Antarctic affairs had shifted from exploration toward scientific research.

Consequently, the treaty allows military personnel and equipment to be used for "scientific research and for

any other peaceful purpose.''[13] As a result, the military
continues to play a major role in Antarctica, performing
"logistical" functions in the Antarctic programs of several
nations. As will be seen in Chapter 5, several hundred
American military personnel perform duties in the Antarctic
during the summer season. These individuals fly aircraft,
operate airfield and communications equipment, provide
weather forecasts, and carry out various and sundry
administrative tasks.[14] Likewise, the Argentine military plays
a major role in its country's Antarctic program.[15]

To help enforce its arms control provisions, the treaty
also establishes a mechanism for enforcing compliance
through on-site inspection. Specifically, the treaty states that

> all areas of Antarctica, including all stations,
> installations and equipment within those areas, and
> all ships and aircraft at points of discharging and
> embarking cargoes or personnel in Antarctica, shall
> be open at all times to inspection.

Additionally, "aerial observation" is permitted "at any
time over any and all areas of Antarctica." Any country
that wishes to conduct an inspection designates its own
observers to perform the task. Finally, parties to the treaty
must inform each other of all expeditions, stations, and
military personnel or equipment in the region.[16] The treaty
thus was one of the very first arms control agreements to
provide for an "intrusive" inspection regime.

In practice, few nations have invoked their right to conduct inspections. New Zealand carried out the first one in
1963, followed by Australia and Great Britain the same year.
The United States mounted its first inspection in 1964, and
since then has been the most active in implementing this particular provision of the treaty. As of the 1988-89 season, the
United States had conducted nine inspections, visiting different locations each time. Happily, the inspections have
never raised any question about compliance with the arms
control tenets of the treaty.[17] The treaty implies, however,

that the inspection system is designed to promote the objectives and ensure observation of the entire treaty, not just its arms control provisions. Thus, in recent years, US inspection teams have reported possible violations of environmental measures adopted by the signatories under the consultative provisions of the treaty.[18]

A CLAIMS SETTLEMENT   In addition to prohibiting military measures that might lead to armed clashes in the Antarctic, the Antarctic Treaty also sought to get at the root cause of conflict in the region: the claims dispute. The Chilean *modus vivendi* proposal and the ''gentlemen's agreement'' provided the basis for the approach adopted. Article IV states that nothing in the treaty will be interpreted as renunciation, diminution, recognition, or non-recognition of any nation's rights, claim, or basis of claim to sovereignty in Antarctica. Furthermore, no acts or activities occuring while the treaty was in force would be allowed to constitute ''a basis for asserting, supporting, or denying a claim to territorial sovereignty'' or creating any rights to such a claim. Likewise, no new claim or enlargement of an existing claim could be asserted while the treaty was in force.[19]

The treaty does not resolve the sovereignty question once and for all. The seven claimant countries could (and still do) assert their pre-1961 claims; non-claimants could (and still do) assert their pre-1961 ''rights'' and non-recognition policies. Article IV, however, does put the issue on hold for the duration of the treaty. Some diplomats had hoped in 1959 that the claims dispute would simply wither away during this extended period, as freedom of access on the continent and shared responsibility for Antarctic affairs replaced nationalistic desires to exercise control over territory in the traditional sense.[20] As discussed later, events have not completely borne out such optimism, for a few claimants still cling tenaciously to their asserted rights in the region.

Even if the rosiest expectations for Article IV have not materialized, its significance should not be underestimated.

Several commentators have in fact labeled Article IV the most important provision within the treaty—for unless the sovereignty issue were defused in some manner, other provisions of the treaty probably wouldn't work. Only by suspending the basic source of potential conflict in the region could the Antarctic remain an open and demilitarized area preserved for scientific research. Critics who label Article IV a temporary "non-solution" to the sovereignty question are technically correct. And, as will be argued in the next chapter, the sovereignty issue ultimately could undo the entire treaty. But, in 1959, Article IV probably was the best solution the conferees could hope to achieve, given the political environment of the day. More importantly, the approach has been remarkably successful—so far.[21]

A SCIENCE COMPACT   The IGY clearly was the model for the Antarctic Treaty. As stated in its preamble and in Article II, one of its central objectives is to continue and further develop the freedom of scientific investigation evident during the IGY. In specific terms, the treaty provides for the exchange of research plans, scientists, and scientific observations and results "to the greatest extent feasible and practicable." The treaty also encourages the "establishment of cooperative working relations" with the United Nations and other international organizations.[22]

Despite the importance attached to science in the Antarctic, the treaty in the end says very little about science, other than to enshrine the principle of free exchange. Treaty nations instead have worked out the details of scientific cooperation through the consultative process established by the treaty, as well as through the good offices of the international Scientific Committee on Antarctic Research (SCAR).

AN ADMINISTRATIVE FRAMEWORK   The treaty establishes mechanisms for carrying out its provisions, admitting new members, handling civil and criminal jurisdiction, and resolving disputes among treaty parties. As such,

Scientists conduct an on-ice research project in the Antarctic. A cardinal objective of the Antarctic Treaty is to promote freedom of scientific investigation throughout the continent and its surrounding waters.

the treaty creates a rudimentary system of international administration for the continent.

Provisions for administering the treaty are very informal, reflecting a definite bias against fixed institutions. In the meetings prior to the 1959 Conference on Antarctica, several representatives expressed an interest in establishing a permanent body to administer the treaty. The prospect of exchanging potentially vast amounts of scientific information or coordinating inspections would seem in the abstract to require a full-time staff dedicated to this purpose. The proposal, however, garnered little support. The Latin Americans, for instance, feared that a supranational Antarctic body gradually would erode their claims to sovereignty in the region.[23]

Instead of creating a secretariat or commission, the treaty simply establishes a process for holding regular meetings among certain parties to the treaty. Article IX directed the original signatories to meet at "suitable intervals and places" to exchange information, consult, and make recommendations to their governments on measures to further "the principles and objectives of the Treaty." The treaty specified a list of issues to be considered in this manner. This list included major provisions of the treaty and added the "preservation and conservation of living resources in Antarctica."[24] The treaty did not exclude any issues from discussion. Presumably, therefore, any topic related to "principles and objectives" of the treaty could be entered on the agendum of the meetings. (The next section of this chapter describes in greater detail how the consultative process has operated and evolved from 1961 to the present.)

The treaty also stipulates the means by which new nations can join the treaty and take part in the consultative process. The first step is for a nation to ratify or accede to the treaty in accordance with its own constitutional procedures, and then notify the depositary government (in this case, the United States) of its actions.[25] The new nation is then bound by terms of the treaty, but is not yet entitled to take part in the consultative process with the original 12 signatories. Neither does the new nation enjoy privileges granted to the original members by the treaty, such as conducting inspections or proposing and approving amendments.

To gain these rights, a new nation must demonstrate (in the words of the treaty)

> an interest in Antarctica by conducting substantial scientific research activity there, such as the establishment of a scientific station or the despatch of a scientific expedition.[26]

This criterion roughly parallels the rationale the United States used in inviting nations to the Conference on Antarctica. The treaty also seems to imply that a nation that has achieved consultative party status but no longer demonstrates this interest may lose its right to participate in the consultative process. This stipulation, however, does not apply to the original 12 signatories, of which Belgium no longer maintains stations in the Antarctic.[27]

The treaty thus created two categories of membership. The *first*—known today as "acceding states" or "non-consultative parties"—includes those nations that have simply acceded to terms of the treaty. The *second*—referred to as "consultative parties"—includes the original 12 signatories and new nations that meet the test of active interest in the Antarctic. As of 1 June 1990, 27 new nations had acceded to the treaty. Of these states, 13 had become consultative parties, bringing the total number to 25. (See Table 1.) Worth noting is the fact that the roster of consultative parties did not expand beyond the original 12 until Poland achieved that status in 1977—16 years after the treaty entered into force. (The next chapter addresses the motives and practical implications of the surge in membership after 1980.)

The treaty also addresses the knotty issue of legal jurisdiction over individuals in the Antarctic. Normally, a state exercising sovereignty over a particular territory also exercises legal jurisdiction over everyone within that territory. (Diplomats granted immunity are an exception.) However, as noted above, the question of sovereignty in the Antarctic was confused and disputed prior to the Antarctic Treaty. The claimant nations, in most cases, had asserted the right to exercise legal jurisdiction over anyone within their sector.[28] Alternatively, those nations refusing to recognize a particular claimant's assertion of sovereignty correspondingly refused to recognize the claimant's right to exercise jurisdiction. Nevertheless, an individual conceivably might commit an act somewhere in the Antarctic that the parties to the treaty could agree required some civil or criminal sanction. But who would have jurisdiction over the case?

The treaty handles the jurisdiction problem by providing that officially designated observers, scientific personnel, and accompanying staff "shall be subject to the jurisdiction of the Contracting Party of which they are nationals in respect of all acts or commissions occurring while they are in the Antarctic." If a disagreement arises between two or more parties, the treaty enjoins them to "immediately consult together with a view to reaching a mutually acceptable position."[29]

This provision by no means covered all possible contingencies. For example, it does not address the treatment of individuals who are not scientists, observers, or staff—such as tourists, businessmen, or adventurers. For this reason and others, international law experts find the treaty's provisions regarding jurisdiction particularly untidy and have devoted considerable attention to possible gaps and loopholes. The consultative parties continue to grapple with the question in their regular meetings. In the meantime, individual parties have handled specific jurisdictional problems on an ad hoc basis.[30]

The treaty also contains procedures for resolving disputes among signatories. According to Article XI, the parties are first obliged to "consult among themselves with a view to having the dispute resolved by negotiation, inquiry, mediation, conciliation, arbitration, judicial settlement, or other peaceful means." If this approach fails to resolve points of contention, then the parties are supposed to refer their dispute to the International Court of Justice for settlement. However, referral to the International Court is not mandatory; rather, all parties to the dispute must consent to this action.[31] As noted earlier, the British government had tried to take its claims dispute with Argentina and Chile to the International Court before the treaty was negotiated, but objections of the Latin American governments blocked this move. To date, no parties to the treaty have invoked Article XI. Instead, they have worked out their differences over the scope and interpretation of the treaty within the consultative process.

Lastly, the treaty briefly addresses the matter of "third parties." Article X requires the signatories to "exert appropriate efforts" to ensure that "no one engages in any activity in Antarctica contrary to the principles or purposes" of the Antarctic Treaty. The treaty does not specify how the signatories are supposed to carry out this responsibility, other than to state that their actions must be "consistent" with the United Nations Charter.[32] Nor does it begin to explore the legal question of whether states can be bound in any way by a treaty they have not signed.[33] Article X nevertheless clearly conveys the impression that the original 12 signatories fully intended to create a regime that applied not only to themselves, but to any other nation performing activities in the region covered by the treaty.

The treaty is, in the final analysis, a political document. Its provisions reflect an effort to achieve compromise and consensus among nations with different political systems and different stakes in the Antarctic. Consequently, the treaty is not a definitive or comprehensive legal formula for settling conflicts in the region. Nor does it address every outstanding problem in the area.[34]

The task of defining a system for managing Antarctic affairs, however, did not stop with the signing of the Antarctic Treaty. Instead, the treaty contains within it provisions for continued consultation, negotiation, and—ultimately—decisionmaking on Antarctic affairs. That process has gradually resulted in a significant expansion in the range and scope of issues the parties to the Antarctic Treaty decide for themselves and (for the time being) the rest of the international community.

Operation and Expansion of the Treaty System

As noted in the beginning of this chapter, the Antarctic Treaty system consists not only of the treaty itself but also several subsequent agreements made by its signatories. These agreements are the product of the consultative process established by Article IX. Since 1961, the consultative parties have regularly met to exchange information, discuss matters of mutual interest, and, most importantly, make recommendations on measures to further principles and objectives of the Antarctic Treaty.

This process has led to a growing body of agreements and laws that have amplified and, in some cases, significantly expanded on the original provisions of the treaty. The most notable achievements so far have dealt with protection of the Antarctic environment. For example, the treaty parties successfully negotiated two separate conventions to conserve living resources in the Antarctic, and, in 1988, provisionally agreed on a regime to govern future mineral resource activities. One particularly important aspect of these agreements has been the creation of new institutions for deciding key technical *and* political issues in the region.

ANTARCTIC TREATY CONSULTATIVE MEETINGS   By far the most important vehicle for the regular consideration of Antarctic matters by treaty parties is the so-called Antarctic Treaty Consultative Meeting. As mandated by the treaty, the Australian government hosted the first consultative meeting in Canberra in July 1961.[35] Since then, the consultative parties have convened 14 consultative meetings at roughly two-year intervals. (See Table 2.) These meetings have rotated among their capitals, though none has yet been held in the Soviet Union or South Africa. Since the treaty makes no provision for a secretariat or staff, the host government for each meeting assumes responsibility for administrative matters, such as circulating papers and publishing reports and recommendations.[36]

According to rules of procedure adopted at the first consultative meeting, participating governments may

Table 2
Antarctic Treaty consultative meetings, 1961-89

Date	Meeting Number	Location
July 1961	I	Canberra
July 1962	II	Buenos Aires
June 1964	III	Brussels
November 1966	IV	Santiago
November 1968	V	Paris
October 1970	VI	Tokyo
Oct-Nov 1972	VII	Wellington
June 1975	VIII	Oslo
Sep-Oct 1977	IX	London
Sep-Oct 1979	X	Washington
June-July 1981	XI	Buenos Aires
September 1983	XII	Canberra
October 1985	XIII	Brussels
October 1987	XIV	Rio de Janeiro
October 1989	XV	Paris

NOTE: Germany has agreed to host the XVI consultative meeting in 1991.

Source: John Heap, ed., *Handbook of the Antarctic Treaty System*, 6th ed. (Cambridge, England: Polar Publications, April 1989), Annex C; and the Office of Oceans Affairs, US Department of State.

choose whomever they wish to represent them at the meetings.[37] The composition of national delegations tends to correspond to the major subject areas under discussion. For example, the American delegation to the 1989 consultative meeting in Paris included officials from the State Department, the Marine Mammal Commission, the National Oceanic and Atmospheric Administration, the US Geological Survey, the National Science Foundation, and the Council on Environmental Quality. In recent years, the American delegation also included advisers drawn from private environmental groups—a reflection of the strong interest the so-called "green lobby" has in Antarctic issues.[38]

The representatives meet for the most part behind closed doors. Thus, an air of secrecy has traditionally surrounded the consultative meetings. Rules of procedure stipulate that all sessions—except for the opening plenary session—are held in private, unless the representatives to the meeting decide otherwise.[39] Moreover, all papers prepared for the meeting are classified and withheld from public dissemination. The only exceptions to this classification rule are the approved recommendations and final report.[40] Secrecy in this case can hardly be justified by traditional concerns about national security. Rather, restrictions on information are said to promote a frank exchange of views among the meeting participants.[41] However, a cost is associated with this secrecy. Specifically, it prevents outside states and interest groups from directly observing the process by which important decisions affecting the Antarctic are made. As a result, their confidence in the oft-professed intention of the consultative parties to make policies for the "benefit of all mankind" suffers.[42]

The Antarctic Treaty consultative parties have been sensitive to repeated complaints—particularly those lodged by Third World countries in the United Nations (see the next chapter)—about secretiveness and have slowly taken steps to open up their deliberations.[43] Final reports from recent consultative meetings, for example, provide far more details on what happened in the private sessions than in the past. Also, starting with the thirteenth consultative meeting in 1985, the consultative parties began to release documents from previous consultative meetings.[44] At the fourteenth consultative meeting in 1987, the representatives decided that all future meeting documents, not specifically labeled otherwise, would routinely be made available to the public. In addition, *all* documents from each consultative meeting would be reviewed for release at the *next* meeting.[45]

In a similar vein, the consultative parties now allow ''outsiders'' to attend their meetings. They invited the treaty's non-consultative parties to send representatives to the 1983 and 1985 consultative meetings. In the latter meeting, they formally recommended that non-consultative parties be allowed to attend as a matter of course.[46] However, under revised rules of procedure, non-consultative parties can only speak and present documents; they may not take part in decisionmaking.[47] At the 1987 consultative meeting, the representatives also approved a change in their rules of procedure to permit observers and experts from international organizations to attend consultative meetings on a case-by-case basis. Representatives from four different, non-treaty organizations participated in the 1987 meeting. The number of outside observers more than doubled at the 1989 meeting in Paris, with nine different organizations represented.[48]

The principal objective of the national delegations to the Antarctic Treaty consultative meetings is to agree on a list of recommendations covering various Antarctic issues. In accordance with the Antarctic Treaty, these recommendations must be submitted to national governments for final approval. Before a recommendation can become binding, *all* consultative parties must approve it.[49] This requirement for ultimate unanimity imposes a corresponding requirement for consensus among the representatives to consultative meetings. In fact, their rules of procedure state that ''recommendations formulated at the meeting shall be approved by all the representatives present.''[50] (The final report, however, requires only majority approval.)[51]

The requirement for consensus and unanimity injects an inherent bias toward delay into the consultative process, with progress being made only at the rate of the slowest member. The above discussion on making meeting documents public is a good case in point. While the consultative parties ''generally agreed'' in 1977 on the need to make meeting documents more available, they did not adopt a specific policy to do so until after 10 years of desultory discussions on the subject. Moreover, as one expert on Antarctic affairs—Peter Beck—has noted, decisions resulting from this tedious process tend to reflect the lowest common denominator of views.[52]

The process of obtaining government approval for recommendations is likewise slow. Antarctic issues compete for attention with a host of more pressing matters on national bureaucratic and legislative agendas. As a result, governments often fail to approve some recommendations within the two years between consultative meetings.[53] Such delays have caused concern among the consultative parties. In response, some representatives to consultative meetings have urged national governments to observe particular recommendations in practice, while formal approval was still pending. In 1987, the United States suggested that the representatives make greater use of the final report, rather than the recommendations, to record agreement on non-controversial items. In this way, the need for subsequent ratification could be avoided. Other nations, however, expressed concern that such an approach might constitute a circumvention of the treaty's provisions on consultation.[54]

Before discussing the actual substance of the meetings' recommendations, one additional point regarding procedure merits attention. While the Antarctic Treaty makes no provision for a secretariat or full-time staff, the consultative process nonetheless has benefited enormously from technical advice and support provided by the Scientific Committee on Antarctic Research (SCAR). During the IGY, the *Comité Spécial de l'Année Géophysique Internationale* had helped coordinate the various national research programs in the Antarctic. When plans were made in 1957 to extend the IGY research efforts for one year as part of the so-called International Geophysical Cooperation program, the International Council of Scientific Unions

(ICSU) chartered SCAR to take over this coordination function.[55]

SCAR has performed this function ever since. According to its constitution, SCAR consists of one scientific delegate from each country with an active research program in the Antarctic, as well as scientists nominated by the ICSU, other scientific unions with interests in the Antarctic, and the World Meteorological Organization. To coordinate scientific activity in the Antarctic (which its constitution defines as the area bounded by the Antarctic Convergence, *not* 60° south latitude), SCAR regularly holds meetings, sponsors seminars, and publishes information on research in the region. A small administrative headquarters at the Scott Polar Research Institute in Cambridge, England, supports these activities.[56]

Though SCAR is a non-governmental body and has no formal status under the Antarctic Treaty, it plays a major role in the operation of the treaty system. At the first consultative meeting, for example, representatives formally recommended that their national governments should encourage SCAR to continue its advisory work and exchange of information.[57] Subsequent consultative meetings have followed this practice, frequently calling on SCAR for particular services. From time to time, some consultative parties have floated proposals to recognize SCAR as a formal part of the treaty system. Others have preferred to preserve SCAR's independence and, thereby, shield it from undue political interference. The dispute is largely philosophical. As author Jeffrey Myhre has noted, whatever its legal status, "SCAR, in practice, is the technical support body of the Treaty."[58]

RECOMMENDATIONS   As noted in the previous section, Article IX of the Antarctic Treaty listed several issues that the treaty parties were supposed to address in the consultative process. Representatives to the consultative meetings generally have stuck to this list. Between

1961 and 1989, they approved 186 formal recommendations, which subsequently were submitted to their respective governments for approval. The recommendations fall into the following three broad catgegories:

First, several recommendations deal with the operation of the Antarctic Treaty system itself. These recommendations include the previously described measures to provide more meeting documents to the public and grant non-consultative parties and observers greater access to consultative meetings. Representatives also have recommended creation of two additional forums for consultation. The 1966 consultative meeting formally sanctioned the so-called "meetings of experts." In these meetings, technical specialists from the consultative parties and other invited organizations discuss "practical problems" and report their findings to the next consultative meeting. To date, "meetings of experts" have been held on logistics and Antarctic telecommunications policy.[59] In 1977, the consultative parties convened a "special consultative meeting" to approve Poland's application for consultative status. In the process, they decided that a "special consultative meeting" would be the venue for considering all such applications in the future.[60] In addition, the consultative parties used "special consultative meetings" to start negotiations for conventions on living resources, as well as on Antarctic mineral resources.[61]

A *second* group of recommendations focuses on measures to facilitate scientific research and cooperation. These recommendations entail efforts to share meteorological data, improve telecommunications in the Antarctic, make common use of transportation, provide assistance in emergencies, and improve the apparently haphazard process of sharing scientific plans and information. In 1972, the representatives recommended creation of so-called Sites of Special Scientific Interest to prevent activities that might jeopardize scientific research in

NSF Photo by Ann Hawthorne

This hut, constructed in January 1911 by Robert Falcon Scott at Cape Evans in the Antarctic, is preserved as an historic monument, under Recommendation VII-9 of the Antarctic Treaty system's consultative process.

particular Antarctic locations. So far, the consultative parties have designated more than 30 such sites.[62]

The *third* group of recommendations deals with environmental issues. Article IX of the Antarctic Treaty lists the "preservation and conservation of living resources" as a topic the consultative parties should address in their regular meetings. From the beginning, the consultative parties have followed this mandate and focused considerable attention on the issue. This attention is largely attributable to the importance a relatively pristine environment holds for research conducted in Antarctica. Likewise, scientists consider the Antarctic environment to be particularly vulnerable to human interference.[63] Since the Antarctic climate is so harsh, a plant or animal species might require decades to recover from serious depletion caused by the side effects of human habitation or

Krill, a tiny, shrimp-like crustacean, is a major source of food for several species of Antarctic animals.

pollution. Moreover, depletion of a particular species could reverberate throughout the entire Antarctic ecosystem with disastrous consequences. For example, a small, shrimp-like crustacean—known as krill*—serves as the major source of food for whales, seals, birds, and other animals in the region. Starting in the mid-sixties, several nations began to fish for krill in the Southern Ocean, raising fears that over-harvesting would directly jeopardize survival of other species as well.[64]

In response to these concerns, the consultative parties have created an ever-widening regime of environmental

---

*Eleven species of euphausid crustaceans, or krill, are found in the Southern Ocean. The most prevalent is *Euphausia superba*. The adult crustaceans are about two inches long (or three inches long if their antennae are included) and are about 15 percent protein.

measures for the Antarctic. At the very first consultative meeting in 1961, representatives recommended establishing internationally agreed measures for protecting living resources in the region. In the interim, they urged their governments to issue general conservation guidelines proposed by SCAR.[65]

Three years later, the third consultative meeting approved a set of environmental provisions—known as the "Agreed Measures for the Conservation of Antarctic Fauna and Flora."[66] Though the Agreed Measures technically are an annex to a formal recommendation, they resemble a treaty in many respects. Fourteen articles define the scope of the agreement, responsibilities of governments, amendment process, and so on. Like the Antarctic Treaty, the Agreed Measures apply to the area south of 60° south latitude and do not prejudice high seas rights. They urge participating governments to enact regulations prohibiting the capture or killing of native animals (except in a few, limited circumstances) and minimizing "harmful interference," such as allowing dogs to run free or disturbing bird and seal colonies during breeding periods. The Agreed Measures also establish Specially Protected Areas. Persons can enter these areas only if they have a permit issued by their governments for a "compelling scientific purpose." As of this writing, 20 Specially Protected Areas had been established.[67] Finally, the Agreed Measures require governments to take steps to alleviate pollution of water adjacent to the coast or ice shelves, and to limit introduction of non-indigenous plants and animals into the Antarctic.

Since the Agreed Measures were part of a formal recommendation, they required subsequent approval by the representatives' governments. Ultimately, all consultative parties formally approved them (except West Germany), though the process was slow.[68] The United States, for example, took seven years to approve the Agreed

Measures, finally codifying them in the Antarctic Conservation Act of 1978.[69]

Since recommending the Agreed Measures, the consultative parties have included a wide range of environmental issues on the agenda of their meetings. For example, in 1966, they discussed for the first time the environmental implications of increased tourism in Antarctica.[70] At the eighth consultative meeting in 1975, they adopted a code of conduct for expeditions and stations that deals with the disposal of solid and liquid wastes and reinforces the Agreed Measures.[71] Representatives to the 1987 consultative meeting called on their governments to require environmental impact statements for major scientific and logistics activities. Finally, the representatives to the 1989 Paris meeting recommended the creation of two new categories of protected areas: One, to preserve areas of outstanding wilderness value; the other, to better manage areas with multiple uses. More significantly, perhaps, they also called for a special consultative meeting in 1990 "to explore all proposals for the protection of the environment," including presumably the joint French-Australian call for a comprehensive environmental protection convention.[72]

While the consultative parties have explicitly recognized the need to strike a balance between environmental protection and freedom of scientific research (a cardinal tenet of the Antarctic Treaty), the overall trend clearly is in the direction of wider, more comprehensive environmental measures.

The Agreed Measures and code of conduct apply only to activities on the continent or adjacent waters. Because the Antarctic Treaty specifically placed the high seas outside its purview, the consultative parties initially balked at addressing conservation measures that apply to the high seas. However, many animals that inhabit the Antarctic coasts and ice shelves—such as penguins and seals—spend a good deal of their time in the water or on floating ice.

Additionally, as noted above, these same animals depend on krill for food. Consequently, the Agreed Measures and code of conduct did not establish a comprehensive environmental regime for the entire Antarctic ecosystem.

The consultative parties recognized that unless environmental protection were extended to the high seas, measures adopted for the coast might have little effect in safeguarding Antarctic species. To rectify the situation, they drafted two conventions: One to protect seals; and the other to protect krill and other marine living resources. Both technically lie outside the purview of the Antarctic Treaty. But both, in reality, demonstrate the flexibility of the treaty system and, at the same time, reinforce the role the consultative parties play in managing Antarctic affairs.

CONVENTION FOR THE CONSERVATION OF ANTARCTIC SEALS   During the nineteenth century, the seal trade took an enormous toll on the six species of seals that live in the Antarctic region. The fur and southern elephant seals, for example, faced extermination through overhunting.[73] As stocks dwindled, interest in Southern Ocean sealing fell off sharply. However, as the number of Antarctic seals rebounded in this century, the possibility of sealing arose once more. In 1964-65, the Norwegian ship *Polarhav* conducted an expedition to the Antarctic to determine the feasibility of harvesting crabeater seals on pack ice. The expedition proved unsuccessful and the promise of profits from sealing once again receded. Nevertheless, the brief flurry of interest in sealing raised fears of a return to unregulated hunting in the Antarctic.[74]

The consultative parties already had taken steps to conserve seals in the Antarctic Treaty area. The Agreed Measures afforded some degree of protection to all native animals—including seals—on land and ice shelves. The Agreed Measures also had designated Ross and fur seals as

NSF Photo by Russ Kinne

A Weddell seal, one of six species of seals that live in the Antarctic.

Specially Protected Species, meaning they could not be killed except for a compelling scientific purpose.[75]

These provisions, however, did not address sealing on floating ice or at sea—commonly referred to as pelagic* sealing.[76] Therefore, in adopting the Agreed Measures at the 1964 consultative meeting, the representatives also recommended that their governments "voluntarily regulate" pelagic sealing south of 60° south latitude to ensure species survival and ecological balance.[77] Two years later, the 1966 consultative meeting went further by recommending interim guidelines governments could use in regulating pelagic sealing. These guidelines were designed to prevent seal harvesting from exceeding the "maximum sustainable

---

*Pelagic refers to animals (or plants) that live in the middle depths and surface water of the open sea, often far from land.

yield'' of a particular species; that is, the yield beyond which normal reproduction would fail to replace animals killed by hunting. The guidelines also suggested that the hunting of Ross seals and the killing of any seals in the water be banned altogether.[78]

Not until 1970, however, did the consultative parties explicitly commit themselves to negotiating an international agreement to regulate Antarctic sealing. Instead of drafting another set of recommendations or Agreed Measures, they decided instead to produce a convention *outside* the consultative process. This approach promised to avoid legal and political problems posed by the geographical scope of the Antarctic Treaty, and to open the new sealing regime to non-treaty states. Representatives to the sixth consultative meeting correspondingly discussed a draft convention in informal sessions.[79] Once agreement was virtually certain, the consultative parties called a conference in London in February 1972 to complete their work. The convention was signed that year, and officially went into effect in 1978, when the required number of ratifications was in hand.[80] (The text of the Seals Convention is included here at Appendix B.)

In reality, the effort to draft a seals convention outside the consultative process represented more form than substance. Only consultative parties took part in negotiations. And only consultative parties have signed the convention—though the convention is open to accession by any state, subject to the consent of the contracting parties. Moreover, the convention contains language that ties it directly to the Antarctic Treaty. For example, its scope is the same as the treaty's scope (60° south latitude)— though the seas are included this time, for obvious reasons. More importantly, parties to the convention must explicitly ''affirm'' the Antarctic Treaty's Article IV provisions on the issue of Antarctic claims.[81]

As for specific conservation measures, the convention forbids the killing and capturing of three species of seal

NSF Photo by Russ Kinne

US scientists tag seals in the Antarctic. "Harvesting" of seals is regulated by the 1972 Convention for the Conservation of Antarctic Seals.

(Ross, southern elephant, and fur) and sets permissible catch limits for another three species of seal (crabeater, leopard, and Weddell). It establishes sealing seasons, sealing zones, and reserve areas. It also obliges contracting parties to provide information to SCAR for research and to prohibit their citizens from killing seals in the water. The convention authorizes the establishment of a commission and an inspection mechanism "*any time after commercial sealing has begun.*"[82]

No one has had reason to invoke this last provision as yet. The first known taking of Antarctic seals in large numbers did not occur until the 1986-87 austral summer, when the Soviets reportedly harvested 4,800 seals for "scientific" purposes.[83] The Convention for the Conservation of Antarctic Seals thus put in place a conservation regime before a potential problem actually surfaced—a bit of prescience that supporters of the Antarctic Treaty system frequently cite with pride. If sealing had indeed actively resumed before the signing of the convention, the issue already might have become too encumbered with political and economic baggage to permit successful negotiation of conservation measures.

CONVENTION ON THE CONSERVATION OF ANTARCTIC MARINE LIVING RESOURCES   Within three years of concluding the seals convention, the consultative parties to the Antarctic Treaty embarked on an even more ambitious approach to conservation in Antarctica.

Starting in the early seventies, several fishing nations began to view the Southern Ocean as a fishery of potential importance. At least two factors prompted this interest. The *first* was a general leveling off, or even a decline, in fishing stocks elsewhere in the world. The *second* was the widespread imposition of 200-mile exclusive economic zones by maritime nations, significantly limiting the operating areas of foreign fishing fleets. As both fish stocks and fishing areas shrank, fishing in the inhospitable Southern Ocean suddenly became more economically attractive.[84] For example, between the 1972-73 and 1973-74 fishing seasons, the total catch of fin fish and krill in Antarctic waters increased more than 785 percent! While the total catch has fluctuated considerably since then, the overall trend is up as growing numbers of ships from several countries—including the Soviet Union, Poland, Japan, Taiwan, Spain, and Germany—fish in the region. Yet, to put the matter in perspective, Antarctic fishing accounts for less than 1 percent of the total world catch.[85]

Nevertheless, increased interest in the Southern Ocean fishery excited fears about the adverse impact unregulated fishing might have in the region. The waters around Kerguelen and South Georgia Islands were heavily fished in the late sixties and early seventies, resulting in serious decline in the stocks of some species of fin fish.[86] A growing interest in krill as a source of protein also was a cause for concern. As noted earlier, krill plays a pivotal role in the Antarctic ecosystem. It is the major source of food for whales, seals, birds, and squid. If future fishing seriously depletes krill stocks, then other species could well be in jeopardy. The precise degree of danger, however, is not known. Much remains to be learned about krill—its life cycle, reproductive rates, total size of the krill population, and so on—and the effects of krill fishing on the ecosystem as a whole.[87]

The first effort by the consultative parties to grapple with implications of increased fishing in the Antarctic, therefore, was to call for more data on the problem. At the eighth consultative meeting in 1975, the representatives urged their governments and SCAR to devote more attention in their national scientific research programs to questions related to Antarctic marine biology.[88] SCAR subsequently organized a cooperative, international program, known as the Biological Investigation of Marine

This Adelie penguin, and other species of animals that feed on krill, benefit from the 1980 Convention on the Conservation of Antarctic Marine Living Resources (CCAMLR).

Antarctic Systems and Stocks (BIOMASS), to conduct research in the Southern Ocean. The first phase took place during the 1980-81 season and concentrated on krill biology. The second phase took place over two seasons (1983-84 and 1984-85) and included research on the relationship between species and ocean structure, as well as further study of krill.[89]

In the meantime, the consultative parties decided to press ahead with steps to impose some constraints on exploitation of krill and other marine living resources in the Antarctic. In 1977, representatives to the ninth consultative meeting recommended interim guidelines that did little more than urge "the greatest possible concern and care" in harvesting Antarctic krill and fish stocks. More significantly, they also recommended negotiations leading toward a "definitive" conservation regime and set late 1978 as the target date for an agreement.[90] The task of drafting the agreement fell to three special consultative meetings held alternately in Canberra and Buenos Aires. As with most major initiatives undertaken within the consultative process, negotiations took longer than planned. They finally ended in a conference in Canberra in May 1980 with completion of the Convention on the Conservation of Antarctic Marine Living Resources (CCAMLR, commomly pronounced "camel are"). The convention ultimately entered into force in 1982.[91] (See Appendix C here for the full text of the CCAMLR convention.)

Like the seals convention, the consultative parties ostensibly negotiated CCAMLR outside the treaty framework. And, once again, form obscured reality. Only the consultative parties took part in special consultative meetings between 1980 and 1982. As with other consultative meetings, documents and debates remained confidential. The final conference in 1982 was open to all parties. But by then the consultative parties already had decided the most controversial issues amongst themselves.[92]

More importantly, the drafters of CCAMLR explicitly tied the convention to the Antarctic Treaty and the treaty system in several respects. For example, parties to CCAMLR must agree—"whether or not they are Parties to the Antarctic Treaty"—to refrain from activities in the Antarctic region that are contrary to "principles and purposes" of the treaty. Parties to the convention also must abide by the treaty's provisions on demilitarization and territorial claims. Additionally, they must observe the Agreed Measures for the Conservation of Antarctic Fauna and Flora, and

> such other measures as have been recommended by the Antarctic Treaty Consultative Parties in fulfillment of their responsibility for the protection of the Antarctic environment.[93]

In short, the very act of acceding to the convention obliges a party to subscribe to core tenets of the Antarctic Treaty and to accept the legitimacy of the consultative process in managing Antarctic affairs, at least as far as environmental matters are concerned.

The Convention on the Conservation of Antarctic Marine Living Resources, however, did represent a departure from the past in terms of the number of signatories, its scope, and the establishment of permanent institutions. Recall that only the original 12 Antarctic Treaty members signed the seals convention, and only three other consultative parties subsequently acceded to it. CCAMLR has fared much better, garnering signatures beyond the small circle of consultative parties. In addition to the 13 consultative parties (the original 12 plus Poland), two (then) non-consultative parties—East and West Germany—also signed the convention in 1980. Since the convention went into effect in 1982, several additional Antarctic Treaty members have acceded to CCAMLR. The convention also provides for "regional economic integration organizations" to accede; the European Economic Community did so in 1982.[94]

Beyond expanding participation in the growing conservation regime, CCAMLR also expanded in one sense the scope of the Antarctic Treaty system. The original treaty and the seals convention included only the area south of 60° south latitude. As one might suspect, the natural range of krill and other marine resources is not limited by an imaginary line, but by the Antarctic Convergence. Imposing conservation measures south of 60° south latitude, while permitting unregulated fishing north of that area, would make little sense. As in earlier negotiations, apprehensions about national rights with respect to sub-Antarctic islands whose ownership was *not* in dispute (France's claims to Kerguelen and Crozet, for example, are widely recognized and accepted) made use of the Antarctic Convergence as a boundary for the regime difficult. Common sense and clever drafting ultimately triumphed over concerns about national rights. CCAMLR thus applies not only to marine living resources south of 60° south latitude, but to the area between that latitude and the Antarctic Convergence as well. Since the precise position of the Antarctic Convergence fluctuates, the convention provides specific geographic coordinates.[95]

The conferees took two actions to satisfy the concerns of nations with recognized claims in the expanded zone. *First*, the Final Act of the conference (a separately negotiated document) also contains language that gives France the final say on whether conservation measures adopted under CCAMLR will apply to waters adjacent to Kerguelen and Crozet. The same understanding applies to other islands ''over which the existence of State sovereignty is recognized by all Contracting Parties.''[96] *Second*, the convention itself adds an additional clause to the original treaty's language on territorial claims. Specifically, Article IV of CCAMLR states that nothing in the convention will prejudice rights or claims ''to exercise coastal state jurisdiction under international law'' within the area to which the convention applies. This provision presumably includes the area around the sub-Antarctic islands. Interestingly, this deliberately ambiguous provision also might permit the seven claimant nations to argue they have the right to exercise coastal state jurisdiction (for example, impose a 200-mile exclusive economic zone) off the coasts of their respective continental claims as well. Non-claimants, of course, can refuse to honor the argument. This deliberate ambiguity is known as the "bifocal" approach, since either side can *see* the issue through either of two, different *lenses*. Fortunately, no claimant has seriously tried to enforce coastal state jurisdiction—yet.[97]

In addition to expanding the scope of the Antarctic Treaty system, CCAMLR also establishes for the first time permanent institutions to manage particular aspects of the Antarctic regime. Drafters of the Antarctic Treaty had shied away from creating a full-time bureaucracy to implement the treaty; the consultative meetings perform this task instead. CCAMLR departs sharply from the bias against formal administrative structures by creating not one, but three organizations.

The *first* is a Commission comprised of one representative from each state that originally signed the convention *and* each acceding state engaged in research or harvesting of marine living resources in the convention area. Regional economic organizations also can join the Commission as long as their members also are entitled to do so. (The Commission also has invited observers from acceding states not represented on the Commission, and from various international organizations interested in the Southern Ocean, to attend its meetings.) The function of the Commission is to "give effect to the objectives and principles" of the convention, including facilitating research, compiling data, instituting conservation measures, and implementing a system of inspection and observation. The Commission must meet at least once a year. Like the consultative meetings, decisions on substantive matters require consensus. Conservation measures adopted by the Commission automatically become binding on all member states within 180 days, unless a particular state notifies the Commission otherwise.

The convention also establishes a Scientific Committee to serve as a consultative body to the Commission and authorizes the Commission to appoint a full-time Executive Secretary and staff to support it and the Scientific Committee. Headquarters for all three organizations—Commission, Scientific Committee, and Secretariat—is Hobart, Australia.[98]

The convention actually says little about specific conservation measures other than to set forth basic principles. According to CCAMLR, conservation includes "rational use." Thus, harvesting is not ruled out altogether. Instead, parties to the convention must prevent harvesting that threatens stable population levels in the harvested species or other species in the ecosystem. The convention is thus said to adopt an "ecosystem approach," rather than the "maximum sustainable yield" approach common to other fisheries.[99] The convention leaves specific conservation measures to the Commission. Since CCAMLR entered into force in 1982, the Commission has adopted proposals prohibiting fishing in certain areas, defining the mesh size of nets, and protecting different species of fish.[100]

CCAMLR is still in its early days. The first few meetings of the Commission dealt primarily with procedural issues. Still remaining to be seen is how the convention will operate in practice. Some governments and interest groups already have raised concerns that CCAMLR, to quote environmentalist Barbara Mitchell, "is famous for its sweeping environmental purview and infamous for its lack of teeth to back it up." Particularly troublesome to critics is the requirement for consensus in decisionmaking, which might allow a state intent on unrestricted fishing to delay effective conservation measures.[101] As a matter of fact, the Commission has not yet devised a conservation strategy to implement the standards set forth in the Convention.[102]

An Appraisal of the System

In the nearly three decades since the Antarctic Treaty entered into force, the system for managing Antarctic affairs has evolved and expanded considerably. The basic principles expressed in the treaty remain the foundation of the system—peaceful use of the Antarctic, demilitarization, suspension of territorial claims, free access for scientific research, and consensus in major decisionmaking. Nevertheless, significant change has occurred. The consultative process has opened up, albeit slowly. The circle of consultative parties has grown from the original 12 signatories to 25 countries. With the addition of Brazil, China, and India, the consultative parties now represent more than two-thirds of the world's population.[103] The roster of acceding states likewise continues to expand, as does their degree of involvement in the consultative process. At the same time, the consultative parties have allowed more information about their activities out and brought more parties into their deliberations. The *trend* is clearly in the direction of greater participation and less secrecy in decisionmaking.

Through the consultative process, treaty members also have expanded the range of issues falling under the purview of the treaty system. The Antarctic Treaty consultative meetings have resulted in some 186 formal recommendations on a host of issues ranging from procedural matters to conservation measures. In ratifying these recommendations, member states have created a substantial body of common laws and regulations on Antarctica.

The entry into force of two conservation conventions, in particular, has had far-reaching implications for the Antarctic Treaty system. Both expanded the scope of the system: First, to the high seas, and then to the Antarctic Convergence. Both displayed an ability to tackle complex issues in a pragmatic, non-polemical fashion. Finally, the Convention on the Conservation of Antarctic Marine Living Resources created new institutions that pointed the way for the management of other aspects of the Antarctic system, such as mineral resources (as discussed in the next chapter).

Supporters of the treaty system—including the US Government—refer to measures adopted in the consultative process with considerable satisfaction. Special mention usually is made of efforts to set regulatory regimes in place before, rather than after, problems fully manifest themselves.[104]

Other observers are less enthusiastic about the track record to date, particularly with respect to environmental measures. For example, Barbara Mitchell has concluded that this record is

> only fair: The outposts are seriously overcrowding certain areas that provide a home for seals, penguins, and other birds.... And the stations' power generators produce gases, heat, dust, and noise that interfere with scientific study of the area's 'pure' environment.[105]

Likewise, environmentalist James Barnes has criticized the treaty system because it "lacks any centralized environmental review body or regulatory authority." Consequently, Brown said, "interpretation and enforcement" of the environmental guidelines recommended through the consultative process are "left to each country."[106] For this reason, some experts have called for better coordination among the growing number of institutions and organizations that have interests in the region.[107]

These criticisms aside, the Antarctic Treaty system has proven thus far to be a workable and—given its limited aims—successful approach to managing Antarctic affairs. Treaty members have in fact kept Antarctica peaceful, promoted international cooperation, developed institutions that meet the need for consultation, and responded to criticisms (like secretiveness) and new problems (like growing worldwide interest in Antarctic resources). While progress may have been slow at times and not as extensive as some may have liked, cautions inherent in the system have protected individual national interests in the region and thereby prevented defections and a relapse into the international free-for-all that marked the pre-treaty period.

Despite its modest successes so far, not all is well in the Antarctic Treaty system. Pressures from within and outside the system threaten to disrupt the continuing political compromise that the Antarctic Treaty represents. As a result, the continuing viability of the treaty system—as it currently exists—is in question. As 1991—the first year a consultative party can request a review conference—approaches, this question grows more pressing.

3

Challenges to the Antarctic Treaty System

THE ANTARCTIC TREATY DID NOT RESOLVE ALL the existing (much less looming) issues associated with the region. Instead, it waffled on some critical matters and ignored others altogether. For example, the treaty is virtually silent on the question of resource development. The only mention of resources is in Article IX, which simply states that the treaty's signatories should address "the preservation and conservation of living resources" in their consultative meetings. The treaty says nothing at all about "non-living" resources—such as oil and minerals.

Another area of deliberate ambiguity concerns the apparent mismatch between stated applicability and actual procedure. The treaty and subsequent recommendations from consultative meetings make reference to the interests of "all mankind" and to the "purposes and principles" of the United Nations. However, as discussed in the previous chapter, the consultative parties have arrogated the right to take part in decisionmaking on Antarctic affairs unto themselves, in effect excluding nations that may have an interest in the region, but lack the wherewithal to mount major expeditions.

Drilling granite cores in New Victoria Land in the Antarctic.

Finally, the Antarctic Treaty does not actually end the basic conflict that gave rise to it in the first place—the dispute over territorial sovereignty. Instead, Article IV essentially shelves the matter for the indefinite future.

For several years, the political compromises and resultant ambiguities in the treaty lay dormant. Indeed, the treaty and the consultative process provided for a remarkably workable system of cooperation among those countries with active interests in the Antarctic.

However, political and economic developments of the past decade have focused increasing attention on soft spots in the treaty and, in effect, linked them to one another. In a nutshell, treaty and non-treaty nations alike have expressed keen interest in the potential living and non-living resources of the Antarctic as scarcities have developed at home. Yet, resource exploration and exploitation entail various technical and commercial matters—for example, licensing, regulation, profit distribution, and taxation—that by their very nature require that someone or some body be able to make legally binding decisions. In other words, someone has to exercise something akin to sovereignty. As noted in the previous chapter, the treaty members instituted a new system to regulate the harvesting of living resources in 1982. This precedent paved the way to negotiations on a system for managing mineral developments as well. Yet, just as this process got underway, several non-treaty nations objected in principle to the creation of any resource regime that excluded them from any benefits or profits that might someday come out of the Antarctic.

The current challenges facing the treaty system can thus be characterized as a triangle of three interrelated issues: resources, participation in the decisionmaking process, and sovereignty. The paramount question for the next several years, then, is whether the existing treaty system can accommodate these challenges by establishing an effective resource regime that preserves the principles embodied in Article IV of the Antarctic Treaty, protects the Antarctic environment, *and* satisfies the rest of the world community—all at the same time.

If not, the system could undergo significant transformation or collapse altogether. Should that happen, American policymakers then would be forced to redefine US goals in the region, as well as the strategy and presence required to achieve them.

Antarctic Resources

The prospect of bountiful resources in Antarctica has long excited the human imagination. Even before the continent's discovery in 1820, men speculated about the great wealth of a continent whose existence had only been predicted on the basis of highly questionable scientific logic. In 1772, Yves-Joseph de Kerguelen-Tremarec (discoverer of Kerguelen Island) wrote, "No doubt wood, minerals, diamonds, rubies and precious stones, and marble will be found [in the Antarctic continent]."[1]

Though most explorers who actually sailed through the Southern Ocean ultimately formed more pessimistic views about the promise of Antarctic riches, the history of the region continued to be closely tied to the quest for resources of one sort or another. The lucrative seal trade, in fact, drew many explorers to the region and led to the first sightings of the continent. Several decades later, whaling interests in the Southern Ocean prompted nations to assert formal claims to Antarctic territory. Later, Argentine, British, and Chilean desires to protect resource options helped fuel the conflict that simmered in the region after the Second World War.

The reality of Antarctic resources has failed to live up to more optimistic expectations. Obstacles to finding, much less exploiting, resources in the region are enormous. Most of the continent is covered by an ice sheet almost two miles thick in places. Even in ice-free areas, extreme cold, harsh winds, and the long winter darkness make prospecting a daunting task. Assuming abundant resources could be found, the costs of extracting and then transporting them to markets probably would far exceed the economic returns for doing so—at least as long as alternative sources were available in northern climes. Perhaps for this reason, Dr. Laurence Gould—geologist and Antarctic explorer—testified in 1960 that he "would not give a nickel for all the mineral resources I know in Antarctica."[2]

By the seventies, however, interest in Antarctic resources returned. During this turbulent decade, the inhabited world suffered from a severe economic malaise brought on by oil shortages and dramatic price increases. Respected analysts and popular writers alike offered dire predictions about imminent shortages in other resources as well, including food, water, and strategic minerals. Government officials in many countries correspondingly devoted increasing attention to the politics of scarcity and the search for alternative sources of important commodities. At the same time, the program of scientific investigations underway in the Antarctic since the IGY began to offer provocative evidence that important living and non-living resources might be found in the region after all.

As discussed in the previous chapter, the harvesting of krill and fin fish in Antarctic waters rose sharply in the early seventies. Since krill plays a pivotal role in the region's food chain, the Antarctic Treaty nations grew concerned about the potential impact of unregulated krill harvesting on the entire Antarctic ecosystem. In 1977, they decided to negotiate a separate convention regulating Southern Ocean fishing. Subsequent talks encountered a host of difficulties centered largely on the issue of sovereignty (particularly over the issue of coastal state jurisdiction), illustrating the seriousness with which several countries approached their claims in the region and the extent to which sovereignty disputes could intrude into resource questions. Like the Antarctic Treaty, the resulting Convention on the Conservation of Antarctic Marine Living Resources (CCAMLR) never actually resolved the principal issue. It merely provided clever language that allowed both sides to the dispute to read whatever they wanted into the convention. Some claimants have in fact enacted legislation that presumes the right to exercise coastal state jurisdiction in Antarctica, though none has actually tried to enforce such jurisdiction.[3]

At the moment, no compelling reason can be seen to take such a step. As noted earlier, harvesting in the Southern Ocean accounts for less than 1 percent of the world's total catch. While environmental concerns remain, the level of fishing activity in the region does not yet threaten any claimants' presumed economic rights. Additionally, krill and fin fish are not restricted to any one sector of the Southern Ocean, but are distributed around the entire continent.

Thus, the claimant states are not likely to jeopardize benefits currently enjoyed under the Antarctic Treaty just to reap modest economic gains, or merely to prove a point. If, however, a state did attempt to enforce a 200-mile exclusive economic zone adjacent to its claims south of 60° south, the fundamental compromise on which the entire Antarctic Treaty system is constructed would be undermined.

The prospect of exploiting oil and mineral resources in the region presents the treaty system an even more difficult problem in terms of reconciling worldwide interest in tapping alternative sources of supply with the special political and environmental circumstances of the Antarctic. The actual potential for extracting non-living resources from the area is subject to varying predictions, based either on speculation or tentative results from scientific research largely conducted for reasons other than prospecting.

The speculative element revolves around the theory that the Antarctic was once part of the supercontinent *Gondwanaland.** (See Map 5.) The apparent similarities between geological formations in the Antarctic and the Bushveld in South Africa and the Gippsland Basin in Australia suggest to some experts that the rich deposits of important minerals or oil found in the latter two regions also may be present in Antarctica.[4] Others, however, have questioned the validity of speculating from the *Gondwanaland* hypothesis, noting, for example, that the physical processes that produced oil in some known fields may have occurred *after* the breakup of the supercontinent and, therefore, might not have affected what is now Antarctica.[5]

In addition to speculative theories, some limited empirical evidence indicates that important deposits of oil and minerals may in fact exist in the Antarctic. Since the IGY, some nations have conducted seismic, gravity, and magnetic surveys that have identified several thick segments of sedimentary rock that are usually associated with oil deposits beneath the ice sheets and continental shelves.[6] In 1973, the US research vessel *Glomar Challenger* drilled a series of holes in the Antarctic continental shelf and discovered small amounts of hydrocarbon gases.[7] More recently, New Zealand researchers drilling in the Ross Sea in late 1986 discovered hydrocarbon residue in

---

*In his hypothesis on continental drift, outlined in 1912, Alfred Wegener (1888-1930), German geologist and meteorologist, envisioned that the world's continents at one time formed part of a single supercontinent known as *Pangaea*. This original land mass began separating during the Mesozoic Era, Wegener believed, and split into two large continents: *Gondwanaland*, which included South America, Africa, India, Australia, and Antarctica, was the southern half; the northern half is known as *Laurasia*. Bearing out Wegener's theory, rock strata, known as the Gondwana System in India, for example, contain geologic evidence of a former land connection.

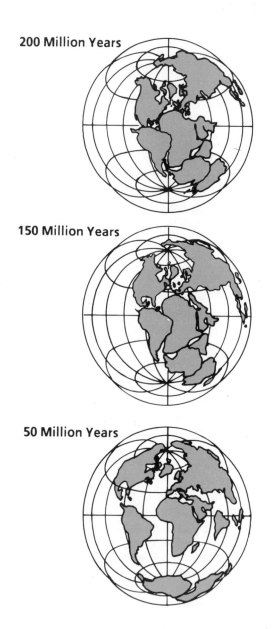

200 Million Years

150 Million Years

50 Million Years

Source: The Times, *Atlas of the World*, 6th ed., 1980

Map 5. Gondwanaland

sedimentary rock, suggesting that oil had been present once.[8] Likewise, geologists have found occurrences of several different minerals on the continent, including iron, copper, nickel, chromium, uranium, coal, and other minerals.[9]

The scanty data on oil and mineral deposits in the Antarctic spawned some rather optimistic assessments of the region's resource potential in the seventies. In 1975, the US Geological Survey predicted that as much as 15 billion barrels of recoverable oil might be found in the West Antarctic continental shelf.[10] During preparations for an Antarctic Treaty consultative meeting, American representatives suggested that "the Antarctic continental shelf could contain potentially recoverable oil in the order of a magnitude of tens of billions of barrels," compared to the 8 billion or so barrels thought to lie beneath the Alaskan North Slope.[11] In 1979, Dr. James Zumberge—then US delegate to the Scientific Committee on Antarctic Research (SCAR)—concluded that the prospect of finding large amounts oil in the Antarctic was "based more on inference than fact," but the circumstantial evidence nevertheless was "fairly impressive."[12]

In contrast to this early enthusiasm, today's predictions on oil and mineral resources in the Antarctic are generally conservative and carefully hedged. Most experts stress that the occurrences of hydrocarbon gases in continental shelf drillings or of various minerals in exposed rock formations do not yet imply that non-living resources will be found in commercially viable quantities. More data is needed before any meaningful estimates of oil or mineral resources can be made.

The experts also point out the enormous difficulties of discovering and then recovering oil or minerals in the Antarctic environment. Since ice covers 98 percent of the continent, exploration essentially is limited to exposed rock outcrops. The task of getting at these outcrops entails major logistical problems of transporting researchers and provisions to remote areas. Even when minerals are discovered in exposed areas, they may or may not be indicative of the actual frequency or distribution of minerals throughout the region. Actual mining operations also would require the production of energy, a source of melted water, and the means and facilities for transporting ore back to civilization.[13]

Drilling for oil on the continental shelf also would present major technological challenges. The continental shelf surrounding the Antarctic is generally deeper than anywhere in the world. (This phenomenon probably is due to the depression of the continent caused by the enormous weight of its ice sheet.) Moreover, the seas above the shelf are covered with ice 9 to 10 months out of the year. Drilling rigs would have to contend with mammoth icebergs and routinely high winds. Wellheads on the ocean floor would be vulnerable to bottom-scouring icebergs.[14] Despite these obvious difficulties, however, oil companies overcame different, though equally demanding, challenges in Alaska and the North Sea. Thus, one is forced to conclude that the technology needed to explore and exploit Antarctic oil (assuming it exists) certainly could be developed if financial incentives to do so ever materialized.[15]

Nevertheless, the prospect of oil or mineral resource development at any time in the near future is remote. Because of the lack of data, technical obstacles, and financial costs required to overcome them, a 1983 US Geological Survey report concluded that

> it is doubtful ... that any metallic or non-metallic mineral resources in Antarctica will be exploited for many years, unless world economic or political conditions change drastically.[16]

The US Geological Survey currently considers off-shore oil to be the only mineral resource in Antarctica likely to be exploited in the next two to three decades, and then *only* if drilling technology suitable to the unique conditions of the Antarctic becomes available and market conditions make it economically attractive to do so. A more recent (1989) report by the US Congress's Office of Technology Assessment echoes this conclusion, predicting that the development of Antarctic mineral resources of any kind "is probably about three decades away under the most optimistic scenarios, and it may possibly never occur."[17]

Even though exploitation of non-living resources in the Antarctic was hardly close at hand, the Antarctic Treaty nations began to worry in the early seventies about the environmental and political ramifications of unregulated drilling and mining. The United Kingdom formally raised the issue in 1970, and the consultative parties subsequently placed it on the agenda of the seventh consultative meeting in 1972. According to then Assistant Secretary of State Dixy Lee Ray, "the issue [at the 1972 meeting] was still highly charged and agreement was reached only to postpone discussion."[18]

At the next consultative meeting, several nations argued in favor of a moratorium on any mineral resource activity until potential problems of resource development were thoroughly understood. The United States opposed a formal ban on such activities because it felt, in the words of R. Tucker Scully of the State Department, that "a moratorium was not so much a delay to permit rational calculation as a decision not to examine the issue at all."[19] With the 1973 embargo by the Organization of Petroleum Exporting Countries (OPEC) still fresh in the national memory, the United States was not willing to rule out any approaches to identifying alternative sources of oil. Instead of a moratorium, the American delegation proposed the negotiation of an international agreement that would establish procedures for deciding whether, and under what conditions, resource activities would take place.[20] Even though the United States was in the minority, the consensus rule precluded adoption of a moratorium. By way of compromise, the consultative parties agreed to voluntarily refrain from mineral exploration and exploitation "while seeking timely agreed solutions" to the minerals problem.[21]

The consultative parties continued to discuss the mineral issue at their biennial meetings for the remainder of the decade. They invited SCAR to continue to coordinate geological and geophysical research in the region.[22] They also commissioned two groups of experts to assess current technology for resource exploration and exploitation, as well as the possible environmental impact of such activity.[23] However, not until 1981 did the consultative parties formally recommend that a "regime on Antarctic mineral resources should be concluded as a matter of urgency."[24]

One could fault the consultative parties for seeming to procrastinate on the issue. However, as already suggested, scientific data on the entire minerals question was minimal at best and, consequently, requirements for a regime were not entirely clear. At the same time, the consultative parties may have wanted to wait and see how negotiations for a living resources regime turned out before tackling another, more complicated issue. The decision to proceed toward a minerals regime in fact came during the first consultative meeting after CCAMLR was concluded. Finally, the consultative parties probably are justified in citing with pride that they initiated negotiations for a minerals regime well before serious prospecting had even begun. Motives for pressing ahead were obvious. As with living resources, negotiating a minerals agreement would be far more difficult if undertaken after, rather than before, exploitable deposits were found and requisite technology for Antarctic operations had been developed.[25]

The consultative parties were mindful from the outset that a failure to regulate mineral activities could jeopardize the entire Antarctic Treaty. As the State Department's Tucker Scully testified in 1979,

> the questions of dealing with mineral resource development in Antarctica go right to the heart of the questions relating to sovereignty and the differences over sovereignty.[26]

For one thing, access to oil and mineral supplies is a matter of strategic importance to virtually every nation. Guaranteeing access to sources of supply is generally considered a vital national interest. At the same time, control over important resources confers undeniable economic benefits to those nations fortunate enough to exercise it. Thus, for strategic and economic reasons, claimant countries are not likely to cede control over a potential Antarctic bonanza within their respective sectors to any nonclaimants. For their part, non-claimant countries have a vested interest in perpetuating the Antarctic Treaty's principle of open access to the continent for peaceful activities (such as drilling and mining).

Given these powerful political pressures, some observers feared that either a claimant or a non-claimant nation might begin resource development in the absence of an agreement to preempt measures that might somehow constrain access to Antarctic resources or give advantage to other nations in the region.

The seemingly inevitable showdown between resource development and unresolved questions of sovereignty presumably could have waited until the day of actual development drew closer. Unfortunately, resource development by its very nature typically requires the resolution of title (or, in this case, sovereignty) disputes before it actually starts. The costs and risks of exploration generally are so high that few companies are willing to begin even prospecting unless the rules of the game and their stakes in the enterprise can be assured up front. The

Environmentalists fear that oil development in the Antarctic would threaten the region's fragile ecosystem, endangering native species, such as the skua (above) and the emperor penguin (below).

absence of any clear authority over mineral questions in the Antarctic eventually could have the effect of, 1) discouraging active exploration altogether *or*, 2) prompting one or more claimants to assert their presumed rights in the region by granting licenses and promulgating regulations.[27]

In addition to problems associated with sovereignty, the consultative parties also expressed great concern about the potential environmental impact of resource development. As discussed previously, the Antarctic environment and ecosystem are considered very fragile. Moreover, the relatively pristine conditions found on the continent are important to several areas of scientific inquiry. As a result of well-publicized ecological disasters in the developed world, the prospect of widespread drilling or mining in the Antarctic quite naturally conjures up images of oil well blowouts, tanker spills, and huge ore tailings.

Indeed, some experts contend that the likelihood of environmental accidents and the ability to recover from them are magnified by unique conditions in the region. For example, oil drilling platforms would require the capability to rapidly disconnect from wellheads if a large iceberg approached. Failure to do so properly could result in a major spill. If the spill occurred near the end of a summer season, cleanup operations might be delayed for half a year. Additionally, extreme water temperatures would retard natural degradation. Oil would jeopardize not only large mammals and birds, but the plankton and under-ice algae that constitute important elements in the food chain.[28]

Even routine mining would pose risks to the environment. The production of energy and water required for mining operations probably would require burning large amounts of oil or coal that might increase atmospheric pollution in the area. It might even alter the amount of solar energy reflected by the surrounding ice sheet (its "albedo")* and cause it to melt.[29]

In short, mineral resource exploitation in the Antarctic surely would have some impact on the environment. The degree of impact in turn would be a function of the processes involved and the frequency of accidents. More ardent environmentalists have concluded that risks of even limited exploitation are so great that mineral resource activities ought to be prohibited outright. Others fear that measures to regulate resource development simply would not be observed. For example, undersea explorer Jacques-Yves Cousteau has asserted that

> miners are miners the world over. To think they are going to put on gloves and clean shoes before going to work in the Antarctic is just wishful thinking.[30]

Because of these concerns, some environmental groups have proposed that the Antarctic be designated a world park. The consultative parties have, for the most part, rejected this approach, preferring instead a scheme that would permit development, but minimize environmental risks through strict regulation and enforcement. (However, in late summer 1989, two claimant nations—France and Australia—formally proposed that Antarctica be turned into an international wilderness reserve.)[31]

Concerns about sovereignty and the environment both found expression in the guidelines that the consultative parties adopted for negotiating a mineral regime. The guidelines dealt with the sovereignty question by stating that "the provisions of Article IV of the Antarctic Treaty should not be affected by the regime." Additionally, they said any agreement on mineral resource development should "be acceptable and without prejudice" to claimant

---

*Reflective power; the fraction of electromagnetic radiation or incident light reflected by a surface or body, as a cloud or the moon.

and non-claimant countries alike. As for environmental concerns, the guidelines stressed that

> protection of the unique Antarctic environment and of its dependent ecosystems should be a basic consideration.

Finally, the guidelines emphasized that the consultative parties "should continue to play an active and responsible role in dealing with the question of Antarctic mineral resources," and they should take care not to prejudice "the interests of all mankind" in the process. Most importantly, the treaty should be maintained "in its entirety."[32] In other words, the consultative parties had no desire to follow the example of such fora as the United Nations Conference on the Law of the Sea, and open up negotiations to the entire community of nations. The treaty nations intended to maintain their unique role in managing Antarctic affairs.

As one might expect from the foregoing preconditions, the negotiation of a minerals regime proved to be a long and arduous task. The consultative parties first convened the Fourth Special Consultative Meeting for this purpose in June 1982 in Wellington, New Zealand. Representatives from the parties subsequently met in 10 different sessions and 9 different locations in an attempt to hammer out an agreement.[33] Their efforts did not meet with success until six years later, when negotiators adopted a Convention on the Regulation of Antarctic Mineral Resource Activities (CRAMRA) by consensus in June 1988.

The minerals convention was formally opened for signature on 25 November 1988. Before it can enter into force, 16 of the 20 consultative parties* that took part in the final session of the special consultative meeting must ratify the document. Moreover, the list of 16 ratifying

---

*The Antarctic Treaty currently has 25 consultative parties. However, at the time the minerals convention was initialed, only 20 countries enjoyed this status.

countries must include *all* seven claimants, plus the United States and the Soviet Union.[34] Until the convention enters into force, the so-called Final Act (a separately negotiated document) of the meeting enjoins the prospective parties to the convention from engaging in any mineral resource activities "pending its timely entry into force."[35]

The minerals convention itself (included here as Appendix D) sets forth basic principles, establishes an institutional framework, and outlines procedures for managing mineral resource activities in Antarctica. It defines "mineral resources" as "all non-living natural non-renewable resources, including fossil fuels, metallic and non-metallic minerals."[36] This definition conceivably could be applied to ice and icebergs, which some observers have suggested may one day serve as a source of fresh water for drought-stricken regions. However, the Final Act explicitly states that the convention does not apply to ice and suggests that the consultative parties should consider the issue at their next regular meeting.[37] "Resource activities" are defined as prospecting, exploration, or development, but do not include basic scientific research covered under the Antarctic Treaty.[38]

Like the earlier convention on marine living resources, the minerals convention provides for a policymaking commission. Membership is to be comprised of a representative from each party to the convention that also was a *consultative party* to the Antarctic Treaty on the date the convention was opened for signature. (See Table 1 for the 22 nations to which this rule applies.) The basic composition of the commission thus ensures that the consultative parties will continue to exercise a predominant influence over the region's affairs. The minerals convention, however, does expand participation in Antarctic policymaking somewhat by allowing certain parties to the convention to join the commission, even if they are not parties to the Antarctic Treaty. Specifically, those parties to the convention that engage in substantial research related to Antarctic mineral resources, or who sponsor resource exploration or development, may become members of the commission for the period of time they meet either of these two criteria. If such prospective commission members are not already parties to the Antarctic Treaty, they must nevertheless agree to abide by the formal recommendations promulgated in the Antarctic Treaty's consultative process, a measure obviously designed to ensure the continued leadership of the consultative parties in setting policy.[39] The minerals convention authorizes the commission to appoint a full-time executive secretary and secretariat staff. The commission also can establish a permanent headquarters, which (according to the convention) must be located in New Zealand.[40]

In addition to the commission, the convention also creates two advisory groups: the Scientific, Technical, and Environmental Advisory Committee; and the Special Meeting of the Parties. Both entities are open to all parties to the convention. Moreover, both can admit observers to their proceedings. While the convention expects the commission to take cognizance of the advice tendered by both groups, neither the Advisory Committee nor the Special Meeting of the Parties has any formal decisionmaking power.[41]

The most novel and potentially the most important institution created by the convention is the so-called regulatory committee. A separate regulatory committee is to be formed each time the commission approves an application to have an area of Antarctica officially identified for possible exploration or development. The regulatory committee established for a particular identified area will include 10 members determined by and drawn from the commission. Four of these members must represent claimant nations, including any nation (or nations) that assert rights or claims in the identified area in question. The other six members of the regulatory committee can be representatives of any non-claimant nation, except that the two countries that (in the words of the convention) "assert a basis of claim in Antarctica"—namely, the United States

Marine resource research is important part of US Antarctic program.

and the Soviet Union—must always be included. In filling
out the roster of the regulatory committee, the commission
chair is to include any nations that are conducting significant research in the identified area, and at least three
developing countries. Finally, those parties sponsoring
applications for exploration or development also are admitted to the regulatory committee while those activities are
ongoing.[42]

The function of a regulatory committee is, as its name
implies, to regulate exploration and development activities
in the identified area.* To this end, the committee is to
divide the identified area into blocks, adopt guidelines and
requirements for conducting resource activities in the area,
examine applications for exploration and development permits, and approve a "management scheme."[43] A management scheme essentially is a contract that prescribes "the
specific terms and conditions for exploration and development of the mineral resources concerned within the relevant block." As such, it is to cover, among other things,
the duration of the permit, safety measures, performance
requirements, liability, financial guarantees, insurance,
and "payments in the nature of and similar to taxes, royalties or payments in kind."[44] In other words, the regulatory
committee is to exercise the powers traditionally associated
with a mining commission or board at the federal or state
level, subject to the principles set forth in the convention
or adopted by the commission, as well as the advice tendered by the Advisory Committee.

Any assessment of the Convention on the Regulation
of Antarctic Mineral Resource Activities can at this point
only be tentative. As of this writing, the convention has
not yet entered into force. Nations must still ratify the

---

*Prospecting can take place under the convention without formal
approval by the commission or a regulatory committee, but prospectors
must adhere to the principles on environmental protection, non-
interference, liability, and so on, as enumerated in the convention.

convention according to their individual constitutional procedures and, in some cases (such as the United States),
enact implementing legislation.

Two claimant countries—Australia and France—have,
in fact, publicly indicated that they do not intend to sign the
minerals convention and, as noted above, have recommended Antarctica become an international wilderness
reserve and called for a comprehensive environmental protection convention. Additionally, in February 1990, New Zealand announced it was setting aside ratification of the
CRAMRA. The official explanation offered for this reluc-
tance to complete a new minerals regime suggests that concerns remain about the ability of any such agreement to
protect the Antarctic environment. These concerns were
greatly exacerbated by two ecological disasters occuring at
opposite ends of the globe in 1989—the grounding and subsequent oil discharge from the Argentine supply ship *Bahia
Paraiso* near the Antarctic peninsula, and from the tanker
Exxon Valdez in Prince William Sound, Alaska. For many
observers, both events merely confirmed the direst warnings
about the dangers posed by resource exploitation in the polar
regions. Under the terms of the minerals convention, all
claimant countries must ratify the document before it can
enter into force. Thus, if the claimant countries continue to
object to the CRAMRA, it will never formally take effect.[45]

Even if the convention eventually enters into force, the
members of the commission are obliged to negotiate a further
agreement—namely, a separate protocol elaborating rules
and procedures regarding liability and responses to accidents.
Until this protocol is agreed, no party can apply for an
exploration or development permit.[46]

Finally, the types of resource activities that would trig-
ger the creation of a regulatory committee may not take place
for many years (if ever). In short, the final verdict on the
minerals convention is still a long way off. However, a few
observations are in order.[47]

First, the convention clearly reflects a concern for protecting the Antarctic environment and ecosystem, and for

ensuring that mineral resource activities do not intrude unduly on other activities in the region, such as scientific research. While the most ardent environmentalists are dissatisfied with the convention because it does not prohibit resource development outright, the convention nevertheless requires the commission and various committees to assess the environmental implications of each and every step of any resource activity. The ultimate test of the convention with respect to environmental concerns then will be the effectiveness with which its institutions apply and enforce the environmental standards and principles listed in the convention or in any subsequent commission decisions.

Second, for reasons elaborated below, the convention is sensitive to the interests of the developing countries in any mineral resource activities in the region. For example, in assigning particular areas for exploration or development, the commission and regulatory committees are supposed to give priority to cooperative ventures that involve developing country participation.[48] Additionally, the commission is required to use any surplus resources to help fund research projects, particularly those involving developing country parties.[49] Finally, as noted above, each regulatory committee formed by the commission pursuant to an application for exploration or development is supposed to include 3 developing countries among its 10 members.

Third, the convention attempts to deal with the "ownership" issues that inherently accompany mineral resources activities by relying on the time-tested political compromises manifested in the original Antarctic Treaty. For example, it repeats the major clauses of Article IV (on claims) almost verbatim. Thus, no activities taking place under the convention are supposed to "constitute a basis for asserting, supporting or denying a claim to territorial sovereignty." Neither will they be interpreted as "renunciation or diminution" of any right, claim, or basis of a claim.[50]

The scope of the minerals convention and the Antarctic Treaty are virtually the same, though (as was the case with the living resources convention) certain caveats have been added to protect the interests of nations with undisputed claims to sub-Antarctic territories. The convention's area of application is "the continent of Antarctica and all Antarctic islands, including all ice shelves, south of 60° south latitude and in the seabed and subsoil of adjacent offshore areas up to the deep seabed."[51] The wording here is basically similar to that provided in the original treaty, with the exception of explicit references to Antarctic islands and the seabed and subsoil of adjacent offshore areas (where oil exploration and development would most likely occur). Also, as stated in the Final Act, the convention does not extend to "any continental shelf appurtenant" to islands located *north* of 60° south latitude.[52]

Like the treaty, the convention also provides for an intrusive inspection regime. Indeed, "all stations, installations and equipment related to Antarctic mineral resource activities in the area in which these activities are regulated by the convention, as well as ships and aircraft supporting such activities at points of discharging or embarking cargoes or personnel" are subject to inspection. Nations thus can determine for themselves whether their presumed rights are being protected in the actual implementation of the convention.[53]

Finally, the interests of both claimant and non-claimant nations in any resource activities are further safeguarded by such provisions as the required composition and voting procedures of the regulatory committees and the commission. As noted above, at least 4 of the 10 members of the regulatory committee must be claimant parties. Additionally, while regulatory committee decisions are taken on the basis of an overall two-thirds majority, a simple majority must exist within the group of claimant nations on the committee, as well as a simple majority within the group of non-claimant nations.[54] On the commission, many matters of substance can be decided by a two-thirds majority; however, decisions regarding budget and financial matters (such as the levying of fees), non-discrimination, and identification of an area for exploration or development all require a consensus.[55] Therefore, on those issues most central to actual resource development, a single nation—claimant or non-claimant—can block action in much the same way a single nation can block progress within the Antarctic Treaty consultative process.

In the end, the minerals convention itself does not really come to grips with the sovereignty issues that could bedevil or be exacerbated by mineral resource activities in the Antarctic. Rather, it establishes a set of principles and a complex set of institutions and procedures to resolve these issues as they arise. In designing a regulatory regime, the drafters of the minerals convention attempted to ensure that the various competing interests—claimants, non-claimants, developed countries, developing countries, environmentalists, scientists, developers, and so on—all have an opportunity to take part in the decisionmaking process if and when mineral resource activities begin in the Antarctic. It remains to be seen, however, whether this elaborate mechanism can in practice fairly and effectively balance those interests. It also remains to be seen whether individual countries or groups will be satisifed with the decisionmaking process and its outcome and, if not, what actions they are prepared to take in an attempt to achieve their objectives.

Participation in
Antarctic Policymaking

The signatories of the Antarctic Treaty were not the only countries to focus attention on the continent's potential resources. The prospect of oil and mineral development also drew the interest of several countries outside the treaty system as well. This interest eventually led to a small flurry of diplomatic activity over the Antarctic, starting in the early eighties and continuing to the present.

Specifically, several Third World nations—led principally by Malaysia—object to the alleged exclusivity of the Antarctic Treaty system, in general, and to the emerging minerals regime, in particular. These critics charge that the treaty nations are not, as they frequently claim, acting for the benefit of all mankind; rather, the critics say, they are simply carving up the resource pie among themselves. Thus, a number of developing countries argue that a United Nations (UN) committee ought to be given cognizance over Antarctic resources in addition to—or, for that matter, in lieu of—the existing treaty system.

Attempts to involve the UN in Antarctic affairs are by no means new. As noted in the first chapter, the US State Department initially considered placing Antarctica under UN trusteeship as one means of resolving troublesome territorial disputes among its allies. The British, however, torpedoed the idea, ostensibly because UN involvement would provide the Soviets a tailor-made opportunity to meddle in Antarctic matters.[56] In 1956, the prime minister of one claimant nation—New Zealand—proposed that the continent be put under UN administration as a "world territory."[57] That same year, and again in 1958, the Indian government also tried to enroll the "question of Antarctica" on the UN General Assembly agenda, claiming that the issue was of "great importance" to the entire international community.[58]

The New Zealand and Indian initiatives came to naught. By 1958, those nations already active in the region were well on their way to creating a more limited system for managing Antarctic affairs. While the drafters of the Antarctic Treaty did have sufficient political sensitivity to insert various references to the United Nations in their text, the treaty (in the words of one Antarctic affairs expert, Peter Beck) nevertheless "assigned the UN to a virtual non-role in the affairs of about 10 percent of the world's land surface."[59]

In the years that followed, UN agencies and representatives occasionally attempted to address Antarctic issues that might conceivably fall under their purview. For example, in the mid-seventies, the United Nations Environment Program toyed with the notion of creating environmental guidelines for resource development on the continent.[60] During the same period, the UN's Food and Agriculture Organization addressed the fishery potential of the Southern Ocean, ultimately proposing a major program to further develop fishing in the region.[61] In both cases, the treaty nations acted in concert to stymie initiatives—however modest and well-intentioned—that dealt with subjects they felt belonged within their special competence and jurisdiction, as defined by the treaty.

The Antarctic Treaty parties' ability to thwart encroachments on their supposed turf was due in part to the diplomatic clout they collectively wielded within the United Nations and its various organizations, and to a general lack of interest in Antarctic matters. Indeed, the absence of any strenuous objection to the Antarctic Treaty system was viewed by some of its members as conferring legitimacy on the system and their self-professed role in managing Antarctic affairs on behalf of all mankind.[62]

By the late seventies, however, interest in the continent was increasing because of speculation concerning its potential resources. At the same time, changes in the composition and general ideological tenor of the United Nations itself had created the conditions necessary for a major diplomatic challenge to the treaty nations' virtual monopoly over Antarctic issues. When the UN was first created in 1945, it had 51 members. By 1975, membership had grown to 138 nations, with most new members being developing countries that had only recently emerged from colonialism. Thus, in terms of sheer numbers alone, the ability of the consultative parties to control the UN agenda through their collective voting power and influence was diluted by the growth in membership. In addition to possessing strength in number, many new members tended to be skeptical of institutions that appeared to perpetuate the dominant position of the industrialized nations in the world economy. They used their voting power in the UN to push for a ''new international economic order'' (NIEO) based on the principle that all states—including countries of the Third World—had an equal right to take part in decisions affecting the international community.[63]

Closely allied to this notion was the concept of ''common heritage,'' which postulated that areas beyond the reach of state jurisdiction belonged to all mankind, and, therefore, all nations should share equally in economic benefits derived from those areas. The common heritage idea had in fact already found expression in some internationally negotiated documents. The United Nations, for example, wrote this concept into the 1967 Outer Space Treaty (which states that exploration of the moon and other celestial bodies ''shall be carried out for the benefit and interest of all countries . . . and shall be the province of all mankind'') and the subsequent Moon Treaty of 1979 (which explicitly defines ''the moon and its resources'' as ''the common heritage of mankind'').[64] Third World states had succeeded in bringing the ''common heritage'' concept a little closer to earth by adopting it as one of the underlying principles in the treatment of deep sea mining in the Third United Nations Law of the Sea Conference (UNCLOS III).[65] Thus, by the early eighties, proponents of the common heritage principle boldly asserted that it had become a widely accepted norm of international relations.

For many Third World statesman, the ''common heritage'' idea applied to more than just the moon and the deep blue sea. In 1975, Shirley Amerasinghe of Sri Lanka linked the notion directly to the question of Antarctica, claiming that

> Antarctica is an area where the now widely accepted ideas and concepts relating to international economic cooperation, with their special stress on the principle of equitable sharing of the world's resources, can find ample scope for application.[66]

Two years later, another Sri Lankan, Christopher Pinto, argued that any economic benefits derived from Antarctica should take place within the "framework of the new international economic order."[67]

Yet, aside from these and a few other similar statements from Third World diplomats, the developing countries did not press the United Nations to address the existing system of managing Antarctic affairs in the context of the NIEO ideology. One plausible explanation for this apparent reticence was that they placed a higher priority on successfully concluding a Law of the Sea convention and feared that raising the Antarctic question in the UN would only undermine any hope of winning the support of the treaty countries in UNCLOS.[68]

As negotiations for a Law of the Sea Convention drew to a close in 1982, however, a war of words against the Antarctic Treaty system soon broke out. The Malaysian Prime Minister—Mahatir Mohamad—fired the opening volleys during a UN General Assembly speech in September of that year. He noted, "Henceforth all the unclaimed wealth of this earth must be regarded as the common heritage of all the nations," and said the UN should convene a meeting "to define the problem of uninhabited lands." According to Mahatir, the Antarctic continent clearly qualified for such consideration and, not withstanding the merits of the current Antarctic Treaty, should be governed by a "new international agreement."[69]

The following year, Malaysia—joined by the government of Antigua and Barbuda—lobbied for support at

meetings of the Non-Aligned Movement and other Third
World regional groupings. As a result of these efforts, the
UN formally addressed the "Question of Antarctica" for
the first time in its history during the fall of 1983.[70]

The ensuing discussions of Antarctica in the UN's
First Committee, and then in the General Assembly,
revealed a sharp division of opinion between members of
the Antarctic Treaty system on the one hand and its Third
World critics on the other.

For their part, the critics argued that the common
heritage concept ought to be applied to the Antarctic. In
their opinion, the existing Antarctic Treaty system mili-
tated against an equitable distribution of the continent's
resources. Because of its alleged exclusiveness and
secretiveness, the treaty system was in effect a rich man's
club that made decisions for its own benefit, rather than
for the benefit of the world community. In addition to
issues of economic equity and full participation in decisionmaking, several African nations also raised objections
to the inclusion of South Africa within the treaty's ranks
and called for that country's immediate expulsion from the
system.

Recommendations offered by the critics, however,
varied. The Malaysians urged that the UN should create an
entirely new international regime for the Antarctic. The
Antiguans, by way of contrast, adopted a less radical
approach that called for reforming rather than replacing the
existing arrangement.[71]

Supporters of the Antarctic Treaty system countered
by pointing to the success the treaty had already achieved
in demilitarizing the region, promoting international cooperation, and prudently managing environmental and other
problems. In response to the common heritage argument,
some pro-treaty delegates denied that the concept had the
force of international law or (even if one accepted the concept at face value) that it actually applied to the Antarctic,
since—unlike the deep sea bed or the moon—territorial

claims had in fact been made and a regime for managing its affairs was already in place. In rebutting charges of secretiveness and exclusivity, treaty proponents correctly pointed out that the Antarctic Treaty was open to accession by all nations. Moreover, any attempt to replace the existing regime would, in their opinion, be resisted by claimant countries and might lead to a reassertion of territorial claims and the very conflict everyone agreed must be avoided. Finally, from a purely practical point of view, its supporters claimed, a regime controlled by the United Nations (rather than the smaller group of consultative parties) would prove unwieldy and inefficient.[72]

In short, supporters of the existing system argued that the existing system was not broken and, therefore, did not need fixing. Indeed, tinkering with the system could undermine cooperation in the region and give rise to new and more serious difficulties.[73] Thus, they concluded, the UN should quite simply refrain from playing a direct role in Antarctic affairs. As Australian Foreign Minister Bill Hayden noted in a speech to the General Assembly, the purpose of the UN was "to solve problems, not create new ones."[74]

The first UN debate—as well as discussion in subsequent years—failed to bridge the gap between critics and supporters. In 1983, the UN General Assembly adopted a resolution calling on the Secretary General to produce

> a comprehensive, factual, and objective study on all aspects of Antarctica, taking fully into account the Antarctic Treaty system.[75]

The study set the stage for the 1984 debate on the question of Antarctica, which resulted in a restatement of positions and a fairly innocuous resolution thanking the Secretary General for his study and inscribing the topic on the 1985 General Assembly agenda.[76] The following year, critics forced a General Assembly vote on three resolutions: (1) requesting the Secretary General to update the study on

Antarctica, (2) expressing concern about the restrictive and secretive nature of the negotiations for a minerals regime, and (3) urging the consultative parties "to exclude the racist apartheid regime of South Africa" from their meetings. Though the treaty nations refused to vote on the resolutions, all three still passed with substantial majorities in both the UN First Committee and the General Assembly.[77]

This pattern of charge and countercharge has repeated itself every fall since then, as the UN General Assembly has adopted resolutions criticizing the negotiations on minerals, calling for expulsion of South Africa, and urging consultative parties to include the UN Secretary General in their meetings.[78]

The resolutions adopted by the United Nations to date have had little impact on the formal structure of the existing Antarctic regime. The treaty system is still very much intact.

Nevertheless, the diplomatic assault on the Antarctic Treaty and growing international interest in the region have had some impact on the treaty system. As noted in Chapter 2, the consultative parties have taken slow, but nonetheless significant, steps toward less secrecy and greater openness in the consultative process. Beginning in 1983, they invited non-consultative parties to their meetings and permitted them to present documents and make comments. In 1987, they also changed their procedures to permit observers from international organizations to attend consultative meetings on a case-by-case basis. The consultative parties also have adopted measures to make more of their documents available to the public. Finally, the minerals convention initialed in 1988 has a number of "sunshine" provisions (such as permitting observers to attend meetings and requiring public disclosure of reports) specifically designed to permit outsiders to follow developments within the new resource regime.[79]

Another change wrought by all the diplomatic attention focused on the Antarctic has been the dramatic increase in the number of consultative parties, which started in 1981. Before then, only 1 country (Poland) had joined the original 12 signatories in this privileged circle. (See Table 1.) Since 1981, an additional 12 countries have attained this status. Significantly, the new members included several nations outside the industrialized world: India, Brazil, Uruguay, and the People's Republic of China. During the same period, several more nations acceded to the treaty. This sudden rush to join the treaty system resulted no doubt from a hardheaded decision that—Third World solidarity aside—the most effective way for governments to take part in decisionmaking on Antarctic resources was to work within the existing regime, rather than sniping at it from the outside.

In any event, the addition of Brazil, China, and India to the consultative parties effectively robbed Third World critics of potentially powerful support in their campaign to create a UN-centered regime. Indeed, proponents of the treaty seized on the increase in membership by arguing that a system encompassing more than two-thirds of mankind could hardly be deemed exclusive, unrepresentative, or unaccountable to world opinion and interests.[80]

If the recent growth in treaty membership does indeed reflect a desirable increase in representativeness and accountability, a potential downside nevertheless exists. From a purely practical point of view, a proliferation of members could overwhelm the ability of the current system to keep up with the administrative details of implementing the treaty and recommendations emanating from the consultative process. The system's existing administrative procedures can at best be described as rudimentary, ad hoc, and already strained to the limit. At least one member government has candidly admitted that "the distribution of information on Antarctica by Consultative Parties has not always been as effective as it might have been."[81] As the number of consultative parties increases and the participation of non-consultative parties widens, the number of documents and inquiries likewise will expand.

For this reason, the United States has urged the consultative parties "to consider a more formal structure for the treaty consultative mechanism," such as a "secretariat."[82] Some consultative parties have objected to a secretariat because they fear that an international body of this sort inevitably would assume certain powers and functions traditionally associated with the exercise of sovereignty and, thereby, undermine existing territorial claims. However, this taboo already has been breached to some extent. Both the living resources and the new minerals conventions provide for a secretariat. Recognizing the political sensitivities involved, the United States suggests that the establishment of a secretariat for the treaty itself "proceed in modest fashion."[83] In any event, as membership continues to grow in response to heightened international interest in the region, the consultative process clearly needs a more regular and permanent administrative structure. Otherwise, an already ponderous system may grind completely to a halt.

A less tangible but equally important challenge posed by rapid growth in membership is the increased potential for a breakdown in the consensus that has characterized the treaty system to date. In the short run, criticism directed toward the treaty system has produced a remarkable degree of unity among existing treaty members. Statements presented in the United Nations by representatives from these countries indicate a common set of assumptions about the value and importance of the Antarctic Treaty and the consultative process. Even new consultative members from the Third World have espoused the benefits of the treaty system and have not, as some older members may have once feared, served as stalking horses for the critics. Additionally, several observers report that during the early eighties, delegates to consultative meetings and mineral negotiations consistently maintained a cooperative attitude despite, in some cases, strained relations elsewhere in the world. (Examples include the Anglo-Argentine war in the South Atlantic or tension between the United States and the Soviet Union early in the Reagan administration.)[84]

In this respect, the treaty has achieved its goal of preserving peace in the Antarctic, and also has provided fora in which countries with very different political goals and systems can continue a dialogue and work toward common purposes. Whether this degree of consensus will continue in a larger, even more heterogeneous group is open to question. As one scholar, Christopher Joyner, puts it, "The more policy-making players there are, the more difficult it plainly will be to obtain consensus on issues," thus increasing the risks for "disagreement, dissension, open conflict, and maybe even dissolution of the treaty regime."[85] It is worth remembering in this context that, under the terms of the Antarctic Treaty, it takes only one disaffected consultative party to call for a review conference after 1991.

To summarize, while Malaysia and its allies have not achieved their professed goal, the political pressure they engendered has forced important changes in the composition and political perceptions of the system they so vehemently criticized. Moreover, they set in motion forces that may eventually result in substantial restructuring of the existing Antarctic regime. For the moment, however, the critics' prospects of garnering enough diplomatic strength to forge a UN alternative to the current regime are remote. Quite simply, they do not have the requisite support either inside or outside the treaty system to force major changes in that system. The recent accession of large developing countries to consultative status diminishes even further the chances of marshaling sufficient support at any time in the near future.

The battle, however, apparently is not over. The "question of Antarctica" has become a perennial item on the United Nations' fall calendar—despite the treaty members' contention that the issues have all been aired by now. Moreover, after passing relatively benign, consensus resolutions in 1983 and 1984, critics have more recently won approval of resolutions that make explicit calls for changes in the existing regime. Even if these resolutions have had no direct impact on the operation of the treaty system, they have at least kept the issue of Antarctica and resource development alive within diplomatic circles. Given a scenario in which the current treaty breaks down for some reason, its critics already may have laid the foundation for an entirely new and different international arrangement for managing the continent's affairs.

The Sovereignty Time Bomb

The ultimate challenge to the current Antarctic Treaty system is the very problem which gave rise to the treaty in the first place—the possibility that rival claims on Antarctic territory might someday lead to armed conflict. When they first drafted the treaty in 1959, some of its authors expressed the hope that disputes over sovereignty eventually would wither away as individual nations grew more and more accustomed to cooperating—rather than competing—with each other in the region. In this respect, many observers viewed the Antarctic Treaty as a model approach to conflict resolution. Unfortunately, the optimistic expectation that the treaty might somehow undo the age-old tendency of nation states to squabble over territory has not been realized—at least not yet.

After nearly 30 years, sharp differences of opinion on the question of "who owns the Antarctic" remain.[86] None of the original seven claimant nations has renounced its claim to sovereignty. The United States and the Soviet

Union continue to assert that they too have sufficient grounds to stake a claim based on their respective activities in the region before the treaty entered into force. Additionally, other nations—for example, Brazil—have broadly hinted that they also have a right to make claims to Antarctic territory, and might in fact do so if the treaty ceases to function.

In short, the potential for conflict over rival territorial claims has not withered over time. If anything, the sovereignty issue is even more complicated now than before the treaty was signed.

The intensity with which claimants continue to insist on their sovereign rights in the region varies. By far the most insistent are Argentina and Chile. As Professor Jack Child has pointed out in his studies on the potential for conflict in South America, both nations consider maintenance of their Antarctic territories to be a vital national interest. This assessment stems from the perceived importance of Antarctica to exercising control over the Drake Passage and, hence, the southern tip of South America. The resource potential of the region also raised Latin American interest in the Antarctic. Finally, for both countries, their respective Antarctic territories are intimately bound up with the less tangible but highly emotive factors of patriotism and pride. This last element has become especially important to Argentina since it lost a war to the British over the Falklands/*Malvinas* Islands in 1982. Significantly, the Argentines viewed British policies leading up to the conflict as intended to deny the Argentines not only their claims to the Falklands/*Malvinas*, but also their Antarctic claims as well.[87]

Even though Article IV of the Antarctic Treaty states that no action taken by signatories will be considered a basis for a claim, the Argentines and the Chileans apparently have attempted to reinforce their positions through a highly visible presence in the region and through acts designed to symbolize the exercise of sovereign power. For example, both countries maintain a large number of bases in (and only in) their claimed sectors. In recent years, the Argentines have operated seven year-round stations, while the Chileans have operated up to three. (See Map 6.) Likewise, both countries have printed maps, stamps, and textbooks that clearly depict "their" Antarctic sector as part of their respective national territory. Heads of state from both nations have made trips to Antarctica to underscore the importance each country attaches to the region. In 1973, the Argentine president and cabinet traveled to *Marambio* base, which was declared the Argentine capital for the day.[88] In 1977, Chilean President Pinochet visited Marguerite Bay, where he deposited an urn with soil from all regions of Chile to signify unity between continental Chile and the Chilean Antarctic Territory.[89] Perhaps the most publicized and dramatic display of "presence" occurred in 1978, when an Argentine woman gave birth to the first child born on the continent. Today, families (including children) from both countries live on the continent.[90]

On the diplomatic front, both Argentina and Chile usually have been the most vocal in their opposition to initiatives that might appear to detract from "national" sovereignty in the area, such as the establishment of a permanent secretariat to administer the treaty.

The foregoing examples certainly suggest that both countries have absolutely no intention of ever renouncing their claims to Antarctic territory, and seem determined to take whatever measures permitted by the treaty to shore up their existing claims.

The Australian government likewise attaches considerable importance to its Antarctic claim, though its style is generally more low key than that of either Argentina or Chile. In 1979, its Antarctic Research Policy Advisory Committee characterized the preservation of Australian sovereignty over the Australian Antarctic Territory, including rights over offshore areas, as the principal objective of

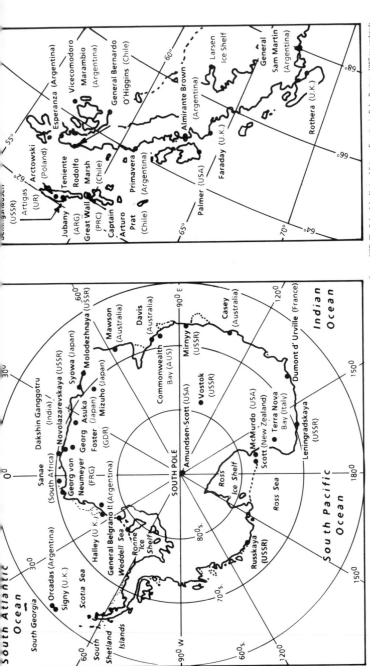

Source: NSF, *The Role of the National Science Fountion in Polar Regions,* 1987 (as updated)

Map 6. Year-round Antarctic stations

the Australian program of scientific research and exploration in the region.[91] The current Labour Government—which first came to power in 1983—has continued to stress the primacy of the sovereignty issue.[92] For example, in 1985, Foreign Minister Bill Hayden noted that "Australia's sovereignty is an expression of national interests in the continent, interests which are substantive and which it intends to maintain."

These interests have included preventing conflict in the region, protecting the environment, conducting scientific research, and "being informed about and being able to influence developments in an area close to Australia."[93] Much like the Argentines and Chileans, the Australians traditionally have voiced concern about the geopolitical significance of Antarctica, lying as it does astride the southern approaches to their homeland, and the possibility that an adversary might gain control of the region and thereby threaten Australian security.

To back up its overall policy toward the Antarctic (including maintenance of its claim), the Australians operate three year-round stations and additional summer camps within the so-called Australian Antarctic Territory. The Labour Government initially expressed a desire to expand Australian activities on the ice; however, fiscal constraints and political realities have precluded any quick change in the Australian presence and even led to withdrawal from their planned participation in one phase of an international study of the Southern Ocean fishery.[94] The government nevertheless is reportedly pursuing plans to renovate its existing bases, purchase a supply and research icebreaker, and ultimately institute regular air transportation into Mawson station.[95]

Despite (or perhaps because of) its continued insistence on sovereign rights on the continent, the Australian government has emerged as one of the staunchest defenders of the existing treaty system. Australian diplomats, for example, served as spokesmen and coordinators for the treaty states during the recent UN debates on the system.

London's attitude toward its claim to British Antarctic Territory changed substantially in the eighties. During the previous decade, some Britons had toyed with the notion of downplaying British claims to facilitate greater international cooperation in the area, such as in negotiations for a minerals regime.[96] The British government also had kept funding for the British Antarctic Survey at constant levels during the seventies which, given growing logistics costs, actually resulted in a net decline in British activities on the ice. Finally, in 1981, the Ministry of Defence decided to withdraw the ice patrol ship HMS *ENDURANCE* from service in the Southern Ocean. Many observers interpreted this last action—both at the time and in hindsight—as an unfortunate signal of diminishing interest in the region, one that may in fact have contributed to the Argentine decision to invade the Falklands.[97]

The subsequent war in the South Atlantic led the British to reassess their policy in the entire region, including the British Antarctic Territories. Indeed, in the minds of some Britons the Argentine attack on the Falklands was actually part of a larger effort to secure all Argentine claims in the area (in other words, a mirror image of Argentine views on the connection between the Falklands and the Antarctic for the British). Thus, following the end of the war in June 1982, the British government reversed its decision to withdraw HMS *ENDURANCE* and, *inter alia*, increased the overall budget for the British Antarctic Survey by 70 percent for the 1983-84 period.[98] Today, it continues to maintain five full-time stations in the Antarctic, all within the British claimed sector. In short, while the British are not as publicly insistent as some claimants on their rights in the area, they have nonetheless taken a far more serious view of the political implications of their presence and the potential for conflict in light of recent events.

The French always have been very adamant about their territorial claims in the Southern Ocean region, particularly with respect to Kerguelen and Crozet islands. As noted in a previous chapter, during the negotiations leading to the living resources convention, the French refused to accept any limitations on their presumed rights to exercise coastal state jurisdiction off their sub-Antarctic islands.

The French support their territorial claims by maintaining an active presence in the region, operating one year-round station within their narrow sector. In recent years, they have made plans to upgrade the *Dumont d'Urville* facility by constructing a runway. The proposed airfield raised the ire of environmental groups, who argued that the location of the strip and French construction practices threatened local bird colonies. In 1984, a government-appointed committee of experts conducted an inquiry in response to the criticism and reportedly sided with the environmentalists. However, the French apparently intend to continue with the project, despite construction delays imposed by budgetary constraints.[99]

Of all the claimant nations, New Zealand and Norway probably have been the most ambivalent about their claims to Antarctic territory. New Zealand continues to operate a major year-round station at Scott Base and, as noted in the next chapter, provides logistical support to the US Antarctic program. Historically, New Zealand diplomats have been the most willing to explore various proposals to "internationalize" the region, including the idea of designating the continent a "world park."[100]

For their part, the Norwegians until recently did not maintain any stations in the region, though the government always was quick to point out that Norwegian scientists took part in other nations' research programs in the region. The Norwegian government also periodically declared its intention to uphold its sovereignty claims in the region, while at the same time expressing an interest in "broadening the constructive international cooperation under the Antarctic Treaty."[101]

The Norwegian government's approach to maintaining its position in the Antarctic, however, may be undergoing a significant change, in response to growing interest in the region's resource potential. During the 1989-90 summer season, Norway launched an impressive sailing expedition to Antarctica, with plans to inspect other countries' stations (as permitted by the Antarctic Treaty) and to build a permanent base for future projects. Norwegian officials have made no secret of the broader political purposes of this ambitious undertaking. According to Olav Orheim, the expedition's leader, "If Norway wants to help determine the future, we have to be established in the region."[102]

In addition to views of the seven claimant nations, the status of the sovereignty question also hinges on positions taken by the two most important non-claimants—the United States and the Soviet Union. Views of the superpowers in this respect have changed very little since the early fifties. They still refuse to recognize any existing claims to territory. They also continue to assert that their pre-treaty activities in the region form the basis for a territorial claim as strong—if not stronger—than those advanced by existing claimants. Both countries maintain an active and visible presense in the region, in part to maximize their influence in Antarctic diplomacy and in part to protect their options in the event the treaty system collapses.

Chapter 5 describes the extensive American presence in considerable detail. Its most salient features are its impressive logistics reach—headquartered at McMurdo—and the prominent position the United States currently occupies with its South Pole station.

Though different in many respects, the Soviet presence in Antarctica is equally impressive. The Soviets currently occupy seven year-round stations on the continent and several summer stations (compared with three year-round and three summer for the United States). Significantly, the Soviets have located their stations in ring-like fashion around the entire continent. Except for territory claimed by New Zealand, the Soviets have placed a station in every sector, including the unclaimed territory around Marie Byrd Land. Geopolitical considerations must have played a large part in the Soviet authorities' decisions on where to site their stations, since some are located in the most austere and inaccessible regions of the continent.

Like the Americans, the Soviets also have sophisticated and multifaceted Antarctic logistics systems. However, while the American system has remained essentially the same for the past two decades, the Soviets have continuously expanded and improved their capability to deliver personnel and supplies throughout the continent. They currently can land large, wheeled aircraft at *Molodezhnaya* station and plan to provide airlift support to all their stations after 1990. Since the early seventies, they have regularly sailed three to four research vessels to the region. In late 1987, they deployed a new icebreaking flagship—*AKADEMIK FEDOROV*—for the Antarctic. Moreover, as journalist Deborah Shapley has pointed out, because of a large infrastructure for operations in its native Arctic regions, the Soviet Union has a large fund of manpower, equipment, and ice-worthy ships that it can draw on for the Antarctic. The Soviets thus have the potential to expand their Antarctic operations greatly should they decide that political or resource considerations in the region warrant a larger presence. No other nation can match the ''surge'' capability of the Soviets in this regard.[103] Indeed, because the United States has reduced its Coast Guard icebreaker fleet (discussed later), its relative ability to project influence on the continent unquestionably has diminished vis-a-vis the Soviets.

For the moment, the Soviet presence cannot be considered inimical to American interests in the region. The

Soviet government continues to champion the Antarctic Treaty system—even in the face of the challenge mounted in the United Nations by countries it might otherwise be inclined to support for political reasons. Likewise, the consultative process continues to be an arena in which American and Soviet representatives traditionally cooperate on the basis of shared interests, regardless of whatever else may be happening in superpower relations. Nevertheless, if the treaty system for some reason collapsed, the Soviet Union, by virtue of its presence in the region, would be in a very good position to exert a strong influence over affairs of the region, and eventually could stake a claim. The relative strength of that position in large part would be measured by the level and nature of US activities in the region at the time.

Finally, in addition to existing claimants and "old" potential claimants, "new" potential claimants have emerged in recent years to cloud the sovereignty issue even further.

The new potential claimant with the highest profile is Brazil. In recent years, Brazilian writers have discussed a new concept for assigning sovereign rights in the Antarctic. According to their so-called "frontage theory" or "facing principle," every South American nation has a right to control an Antarctic sector corresponding to the eastern and westernmost meridians that bound its national territory and do not encompass any other South American nation. (See Map 7.) Under this scheme, Brazil, Uruguay, Peru, and Ecuador would gain a claim to Antarctic territory, while the Argentine and Chilean sectors would be reduced in size, and the British would be shut out altogether. While the frontage theory apparently enjoys no official sanction within Brazilian government circles, Brazil has still acted very much like a nation with possible territorial ambitions in the region— mounting research expeditions since the 1982-83 season, becoming a consultative party in September 1983, and operating a base on the Antarctic peninsula.[104]

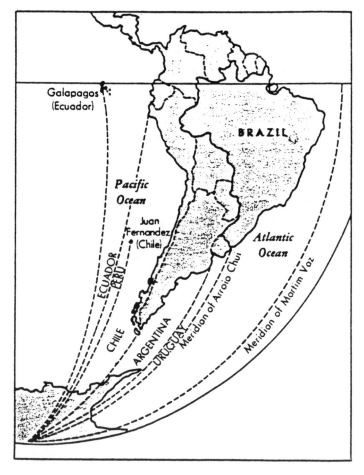

Source: Jack Child, "Geopolitical Conflicts in South America," 1989.

Map 7. The frontage theory

The other potential beneficiaries of the frontage theory also have been active in Antarctic affairs. Uruguay gained consultative status in October 1985 and maintains a station on the peninsula. Peru conducted two scientific expeditions to the Antarctic (in 1987-88 and 1988-89) and in October 1989 became a consultative party to the treaty. Ecuador also has informed the United States (as depository government for the Antarctic Treaty) that it too wants to be granted consultative status.[105]

Some observers have interpreted the actions of these Latin American countries as laying the foundation for a territorial claim in the event the treaty unravels.[106] Doing so, however, would bring them into direct competition with their Argentine and Chilean neighbors (not to mention other countries with interests in the region), thus leading at least one scholar to conclude that

> the conflict over control of Antarctica is potentially the most complex, wide-ranging, and dangerous of all the conflicts involving the South American nations.[107]

Moreover, if the Brazilians ever felt confident enough to advance a claim on the basis of a novel geopolitical concept and a few expeditions, one can only imagine the response of those nations who also have sent expeditions or maintained stations on the ice for many years—like the Federal Republic of Germany, Japan, Poland, India, the People's Republic of China, and South Africa.

In the final analysis, the sovereignty issue simply will not go away. Moreover, it also grows more complex over time. The original seven claimants cling to their assertions of sovereign rights in the region. Their insistence in this regard manifests itself both in governmental pronouncements and in positions taken in negotiations over Antarctic issues, most particularly those on living and mineral resource development. Meanwhile, the list of potential claimants continues to grow. In the absence of any clearly defined standards for perfecting title in the Antarctic, their arguments to support a claim ultimately may carry as much (or as little) political weight as some of the existing claims.

For the present time, Article IV of the Antarctic Treaty precludes making and enlarging a claim *for those nations party to the treaty*. Likewise, nations continue to join and adhere to the treaty because it continues to suit their individual self interests to do so. The danger is that the lure of resources, rivalries outside the Antarctic, or old-fashioned nationalism eventually might lead one of these nations to calculate that its interests would be better served by trying to enforce a territorial claim. Such action could ultimately cause a complete breakdown of international cooperation in the region and a return to unregulated competition for a piece of Antarctic territory.

Such competition would increase the potential for conflict in the region. Prior to 1959, incidents of actual hostilities growing out of rival claims were few and relatively benign. At that time, Antarctica was a distant region and relatively unknown in terms of economic potential. Today, technology has made the continent more accessible and the prospect of resource development has excited the interest of the entire world community. Lest one conclude that no nation would ever consider Antarctica worth fighting for, it is useful to remember the deadly ferocity with which two claimant nations recently fought over sovereign rights in the nearby Falklands/*Malvinas* islands.

The breakdown of the Antarctic Treaty and armed conflict in the region arising from disputed sovereignty surely represent a remote and worst-case scenario. Nevertheless, the prudent American planner must always bear this eventuality in mind in designing a US strategy toward the region for 1991 and beyond.

4

US Interests in the Antarctic

T HE ANTARCTIC TREATY SYSTEM ESTABLISHES THE context in which the individual policies of treaty nations—including the United States—operate. As described in Chapter 2, that system encourages various expectations and imposes certain constraints on national activities in the region. Within this context, however, nations are free to pursue their own interests and programs. As one might expect, these interests and programs vary considerably from country to country.

In articulating US policy toward the Antarctic, senior American officials have maintained considerable continuity over time. With the exception of a more explicit emphasis on environmental concerns and potential resources in the region, objectives pursued today differ little from goals pursued in the period immediately before the Antarctic Treaty was signed in 1959.

As with other issues in the American political system, policies toward the Antarctic do not spring fully formed from the head of Zeus, but result instead from the political ''push and pull'' among different agencies and groups with different perspectives and stakes in the Antarctic. A complete understanding of current policy, as well as the

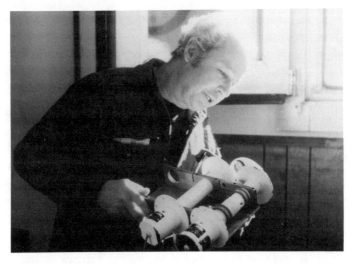

NSF Photo

A scientist at the South Pole Station adjusts a pyrheliometer, an instrument for measuring the total intensity of the sun's energy radiation.

opportunities for and limits to change, requires a thorough understanding of organizational interests and biases inherent in making that policy.

Current US Policy

American policy toward the Antarctic is strongly influenced by its historical roots. Before the Antarctic Treaty came into being, US officials pursued several broad objectives in establishing policy toward the region. Specifically, successive administrations attempted to protect American interests in, and access to, Antarctica by, 1) steadfastly refusing to recognize territorial claims made by other countries and, 2) publicly and privately insisting that the United States reserved certain "rights" in the area— including the right to assert claims of its own.

Immediately after the Second World War, Washington also took the lead in searching for a formula that would prevent territorial rivalries in the region from erupting into armed hostilities among important allies. To this end, American officials explored various proposals for "internationalizing" the southern continent with the claimant countries.

At the same time, American officials, particularly within the Defense Department, wanted to preclude potential adversaries from using the Antarctic as a military base in the event of a major war. In fact, the US Government hoped to exclude the Soviet Union from the Antarctic altogether. When this objective ultimately proved to be totally unrealistic, Americans sought instead to contain Soviet ambitions on the ice by seeking an agreement that would perpetuate the "gentlemen's agreement" forged during the International Geophysical Year.

These broad themes eventually found expression in the American proposal to negotiate an Antarctic Treaty in 1958. As President Eisenhower noted at the time, the United States was dedicated to the principle that Antarctica should be used only for peaceful purposes, did not want the region to become an object of political conflict, and proposed that Antarctica be open to all nations for scientific and other peaceful purposes.[1] The subsequent treaty satisfied each of these principles and, therefore, represented the achievement of every major American policy objective toward the region.

As several observers have noted, American policy toward the Antarctic has been remarkably consistent since the signing of the Antarctic Treaty.[2] Every presidential administration since 1959 has conducted one or more major reviews of Antarctic policy and has come to the same basic conclusions. As a result, six very different US presidents have said very similar things about the Antarctic, including expressions of strong support for the Antarctic Treaty, the need to prevent conflict and promote cooperation, and the requirement for free access to the continent.[3] Presidents also have been fond of referring to the Antarctic Treaty as a model for other multilateral arms control agreements.[4]

Despite a high degree of continuity, the emphasis placed on particular aspects of Antarctic policy has shifted somewhat over time. In keeping with developments in the consultative process, American officials have devoted progressively more attention to environmental and resource issues in their public pronouncements on US policy. For example, in 1965, President Johnson stated that the United States supported "the preservation of unique plant and animal life there" and hoped that peaceful cooperation in Antarctica "will yield resources which every nation needs and every nation can use."[5] In 1970, President Nixon also stressed the need "to protect the Antarctic environment and develop appropriate measures to ensure the equitable and wise use of living and non-living resources."[6] In the wake of the 1973-74 oil crisis and mounting interest in the possibility of finding oil and gas formations in the Antarctic, American officials began to stress the importance of guaranteeing "nondiscriminatory access" to any part of the region (except specially protected areas) to exploit such resources.[7]

Current US policy toward the Antarctic is an amalgam of all these elements. American officials usually define this policy in terms of five clusters of related interests: political, security, environmental, scientific, and resources.[8]

The publicly stated *political and security interests* differ little from interests articulated during the pre-treaty era. According to the US State Department, these interests include reserving the region for peaceful purposes, preventing the Antarctic from becoming the scene or object of discord, continuing the ban on military measures and nuclear weapons, assuring American access to all areas, and preserving "any basis for a U.S. claim to territorial sovereignty in Antarctica which existed prior to the entry into force of the Antarctic Treaty.''[9] A 1983 Office of Management and Budget report to the Congress on the US Antarctic program describes the last item as a hedge against "future contingencies," which presumably would include a breakdown of the current Antarctic Treaty system.[10]

The *scientific and environmental interests* noted by officials reflect the same concerns expressed in biennial consultative meetings and in agreements resulting from that process. These interests include maintaining and protecting the Antarctic environment (including the continental and Southern Ocean ecosystems), gaining a better understanding of the Antarctic environment and its impact on global processes, conducting research that benefits from the Antarctic's relatively uncontaminated condition, and maintaining freedom of and cooperation in scientific research.[11]

In recent years, American officials also have expressed an interest in better regulation of what they regard as a new threat to the Antarctic environment: private expeditions and tourism. As any avid reader of *National Geographic* knows, private explorers continue to follow in the footsteps of Scott, Amundsen, and other heroes by testing their mettle in the Antarctic continent or surrounding seas. The same spirit of adventure also has attracted an increasing number of tourists to the region, starting with the first commercial venture in 1966.[12] At the end of 1988, at least five operators had entered the Antarctic tourism market, offering trips ranging from cruises around the Antarctic peninsula to skiing expeditions on the continent.[13]

The National Science Foundation (NSF)—which exercises a monopoly over all official American trips into the Antarctic region—takes a rather dim view of the upswing in private activities on the ice. For one thing, visits to American stations by tour groups can be disruptive. The obligation to brief and escort visitors takes away from the already limited time available for research. American officials also are concerned about the obvious dangers associated with travel in the remote and forbidding region, as well as the difficulties of rescuing stranded explorers and tourists. One disaster already has occurred— the fatal crash of a New Zealand DC-10 into Mount Erebus in 1979. Finally, large tour groups can adversely affect the environment in a more traditional sense, particularly if visitors fail to exercise caution in nesting and breeding areas, or if passenger ships discharge oil or garbage into coastal waters.[14]

The Antarctic Treaty consultative meetings have touched on the problems posed by private expeditions and tourism in a rather desultory way since 1966.[15] Officials within the US Government (particularly the NSF) feel the subject merits greater attention and they urge the adoption of an international code to regulate non-governmental activities in the region.

American *resource interests* for the moment can best be described as a general desire to protect US options to develop living and non-living resources in the Antarctic, should that prove economically feasible or necessary in the future. To this end, American officials stress the need to increase our knowledge about potential resources, conserve Antarctic species, minimize the impact of resource activities on the environment, and (most importantly) guarantee ''non-discriminatory access to all areas of Antarctica in which mineral resource activities may be determined acceptable.''[16]

According to administration officials, the broad range of American interests described above can best be met by following two general courses of action.

The *first* is to support and maintain an effective Antarctic Treaty system. The State Department's position on this system is unequivocal:

Mt. Erebus, which rises out of the Ross Sea in the Antarctic, was the site of a crash of a New Zealand DC-10 aircraft in November 1979; all 257 tourists and crew members on board were killed in the crash.

> It [the Antarctic Treaty] is a strong, responsive
> framework for conducting activities in Antarctica in
> a peaceful, cooperative, and environmentally sound
> fashion.[17]

Thus, as noted earlier, the United States has recommended a variety of measures to improve the operation of the existing Antarctic Treaty system—such as the creation of a permanent secretariat. American officials also have strongly endorsed ratification (both at home and abroad) of the new Antarctic minerals convention, as a means of bolstering the treaty system, in general, and furthering US resource and environmental interests, in particular. Not surprisingly, Washington has taken strong exception to Third World proposals to overhaul existing arrangements for managing Antarctic affairs.

The *second* way to satisfy American interests, according to officials, is for the United States to continue to exercise a major leadership role in Antarctic research and within diplomatic circles of the Antarctic Treaty system. This role in turn requires, in words used by President Reagan in 1982, "an active and influential presence in Antarctica."[18] Consequently, administration officials generally have resisted efforts to cut the scope of scientific and logistical activities on the ice, despite periodic temptations within both the executive and legislative branches to do so.

Organization for Policymaking

Like the policy itself, the organization for formulating US policy toward the Antarctic and for managing the US Antarctic program has remained relatively stable over the past 20 years—though some changes have occurred at the margin. In the jargon of contemporary political science, this organization consists of a "policy network" formed by various offices within the executive bureaucracy, relevant congressional committees and subcommittees, and several different interest groups and consultants.[19]

THE BUREAUCRACY   The basic organization for Antarctic policymaking within the executive branch first took shape in 1965. In that year, President Johnson established the interagency Antarctic Policy Group (APG) and gave it the task of "guiding our Antarctic policy and helping develop the US program in that region."[20] According to the Office of Management and Budget publication that assigned responsibilities for Antarctica within the executive branch (OMB Circular A-51), the APG was in charge of developing policy guidance "for the totality of U.S. activities under the Antarctic Treaty."[21] The group formally consisted of the heads of the three agencies most directly involved in Antarctic affairs and the US Antarctic program: the Secretary of State (who also served as chair), the Secretary of Defense, and the Director of the National Science Foundation. In addition, the chair could invite representatives from other agencies to participate on an ad hoc basis.[22] Each member could, and usually did, delegate participation in the APG to a lower ranking official within the organization. Thus, the APG convened at the assistant secretary level for almost its entire history—when it convened at all. In reality, the APG rarely ever met. Instead, a working group under the APG, comprised of "action officers" from various agencies with interests in the Antarctic, shouldered the bulk of the APG's workload.

The only specific task assigned to the APG was to review the annual operations plan for the Antarctic. In practice, the APG working group devoted much of its attention to coordinating positions taken by American delegations to regular meetings of consultative parties, the Convention for the Conservation of Antarctic Marine and Living Resources (CCAMLR) Commission, and negotiations associated with the recently concluded Convention on the Regulation of Antarctic Mineral Resource Activities.

In 1989, at the start of the Bush administration, the formal structure for developing Antarctic policy was changed somewhat by a general reorganization of inter-agency coordination procedures in Washington. The role previously played by the Antarctic Policy Group now is performed by the Antarctic Policy Working Group, which officially meets at the Assistant Secretary level. Despite the change in name and level of authority, the basic process for formulating Antarctic policy within the executive branch remains basically the same as it has been since the mid-sixties. The State Department still chairs the process; the principal agencies involved continue to be the State Department, the NSF, and the Department of Defense; and, at the working level, the "action officers" are essentially the same people.

In addition to chairing the interagency process, the State Department's own particular role with respect to Antarctic affairs is to handle diplomatic matters associated with US interests in the region. The State Department is the focal point for formulating the US position on bilateral problems that arise from time to time, as well as broader multilateral issues—such as issues directly associated with the consultative process. The State Department also is responsible within the executive branch for legal matters related to the interpretation and implementation of the Antarctic Treaty.[23] Similarly, the State Department performs formal and informal duties that attend the special status of the United States as depositary government for the Antarctic Treaty—such as responding to queries from other governments concerning requirements for accession.

The State Department has no Antarctic office or "desk" that focuses exclusively on Antarctic matters. Rather, the Office of Oceans Affairs, within the Bureau for Oceans and International Environmental and Scientific Affairs (OES), monitors events, drafts cables, and prepares memoranda related to the region. State Department officials generally constitute the largest single group on US delegations to the biennial Antarctic Treaty consultative meetings. For example, the American team in 1989 was headed by the director of the Office of Oceans Affairs and included another officer from that same office.[24]

While the State Department generally takes the lead on "high policy" with respect to the Antarctic, the focal point for actual American operations in the region is the National Science Foundation (NSF). Under *OMB Circular A-51* and subsequent White House directives, the NSF was made "responsible for *all* aspects of developing and implementing an integrated US program for the Antarctic." The Foundation's specific functions include funding and managing the entire Antarctic program, including logistics, as a "single package." Thus, while the military services and the Coast Guard may provide manpower and equipment for Antarctic operations, the NSF pays for them out of its own budget. In addition, the Foundation develops scientific goals for the Antarctic and funds university, other non-Federal, and all Federal scientific research programs in the region. It serves as a clearinghouse for official and unofficial information and documents on the Antarctic. Through its senior representative in Antarctica, the NSF also provides on-site management for field programs. Finally, in conjunction with the State Department, the Foundation arranges for cooperative research and logistics efforts with other Antarctic Treaty nations.[25]

By virtue of its preeminent role in operations on the ice and, more importantly, its control over the budget for the US Antarctic program, the NSF obviously has a major say in forming American policy toward the Antarctic. Officials within the NSF's Division of Polar Programs actually carry out this role on a day-to-day basis.

The Department of Defense traditionally has had the responsibility to plan and carry out logistic support for operations in the Antarctic, as requested by the National

Science Foundation or the interagency process.[26] All three US military departments (Army, Navy, and Air Force) share in this role to one degree or another.* The US Navy, however, exercises overall control of military logistics on the ice through its US Naval Support Force, Antarctic.[27] The department is generally represented at interagency meetings on Antarctica by an official from the Office of meetings on Antarctica by an official from the Office of the Assistant Secretary of Defense (International Security Policy). Despite the importance of the military's logistics role, no offices within any of the military service head-quarters or the Joint Chiefs of Staff deal exclusively with Antarctic policy.

Though it did not sit on the old Antarctic Policy Group, the Department of Transportation nevertheless has had significant responsibilities to the US Antarctic pro-gram. Specifically, the Coast Guard provides icebreaker services as requested by the NSF. As is the case with the military logistics support, the Foundation pays for Coast Guard icebreaking operations in the Antarctic from its own budget.[28]

Finally, several other executive agencies have inter-ests in the Antarctic arising from their functional respon-sibilities. For example, the National Oceanic and Atmospheric Administration (NOAA), under the Depart-ment of Commerce, maintains a two-person weather sta-tion at the South Pole to measure elements in the atmosphere that may have an impact on the global climate. The NOAA (along with the NSF and the National Aero-nautics and Space Administration, NASA) has been at the forefront of research on the depletion of the ozone layer over the Antarctic. Likewise, the NOAA funded research by the National Marine Fisheries Service as part of the international Biological Investigations of Marine Antarctic

---

*The next chapter describes the nature and scope of logistical support provided by the military and the Coast Guard.

Systems and Stocks (BIOMASS) described in an earlier chapter. It also has a congressionally mandated responsibility for continuing research both on living resources in the Southern Ocean and, more generally, on hard minerals found on the deep seabed.[29]

The Marine Mammal Commission (MMC) is concerned with conservation and protection of the 15 species of mammals found in Antarctica, as well as other aspects of the ecosystem that impact on them. The Scientific Program Director of the MMC has served as the US representative to the Scientific Committee established by the Convention for the Conservation of Antarctic Marine Living Resources.[30]

The US Geological Survey, under the Department of the Interior, has published studies on mineral, oil, and gas resources in the region. The Interior Department also had a major interest in the recent negotiations for an Antarctic minerals regime.[31]

It is worth noting that officials from the NOAA, MMC, and US Geological Survey served on the American delegation to the 1989 Antarctic Treaty consultative meeting in Paris.[32]

CONGRESS   Congressional interest in Antarctic policymaking can at most be described as modest. Antarctica simply does not rank high on the crowded list of issues that compete for the legislators' limited time. A few senators, representatives, and staff members have visited the region at the invitation of the National Science Foundation. Most of them come away impressed with what they see and enthusiastically support the US Antarctic program. However, no legislator has yet emerged as an outspoken champion or recognized spokesperson for Antarctic issues. As a result, the executive branch is clearly in the driver's seat as far as defining American interests and objectives in the region is concerned.

Reasons for the general congressional disinterest in the Antarctic are relatively clear cut.

First and foremost, senators and representatives have virtually no electoral incentive to pursue Antarctic issues. Simply put, ''penguins don't vote'' and constituent interest in the region is minimal. The maximum number of Americans who work in the Antarctic is about 1,000 in any given year, and they hail from many different districts and states. The only interest groups actively engaged in the region are the environmentalist and scientific communities, and the Antarctic is only one of many issues on their respective political agenda. Moreover, the amount of money devoted to the Antarctic program is relatively small—only about one-hundredth of 1 percent of the total Federal budget. Consequently, the US Antarctic program cannot be viewed as a major threat to more highly prized programs, nor does it provide many opportunities for traditional ''pork barrel'' politics. Finally, a broad consensus exists in both houses and on both sides of the political aisle, indicating that the current American program is necessary and sufficient to achieve widely shared views on US interests in the region.

Despite the relatively low priority attached to Antarctica on Capitol Hill, Congress nevertheless plays an important role in policymaking for the region. It routinely addresses Antarctic issues in fulfilling three of its most basic constitutional roles: budgetmaking; ratifying and implementing agreements made by the executive branch with foreign governments; and overseeing operations of executive agencies. In these contexts, members of Congress express their views and preferences on Antarctic issues, and, in the process, set parameters for US activities there.

Congress regularly addresses costs of US Antarctic programs each year as part of the annual budget process for the Federal government. The process of establishing a budget for a particular agency or program involves actions by both the executive and legislative branches.

On the executive side, individual departments and agencies prepare budget requests for the coming fiscal year. These requests are reviewed and very often revised by the Office of Management and Budget (OMB), which then consolidates them and forwards the package to the President. The President resolves differences between the OMB and the departments, and then sends a formal budget submission to Congress.[33]

On the legislative side, the Congress first passes an authorization bill which, according to congressional scholar Walter Oleszek, "establishes or continues an agency or program and provides it with legal authority to operate ... (and) may recommend funding levels for programs and agencies."[34] Within both houses of Congress, jurisdiction over a particular agency usually belongs to a single authorizing committee, which in effect becomes the policy "expert" on the various issues affecting that agency. Congress then must pass an appropriations act, which authorizes an agency "to make financial commitments up to a specified amount that eventually result in the spending of dollars."[35] Details of a particular agency's budget usually are worked out in the Appropriations subcommittee that has jurisdiction over the agency.

As this basic description of the budget process suggests, several different groups are directly involved in determining an agency's budget; and, therefore, individual policymakers or groups have many opportunities to affect the final outcome.

Since the National Science Foundation has responsibility for funding the entire Antarctic program, Congress considers the Antarctic program budget in the context of determining the size of the larger NSF budget.[36] The House authorizing committee for the NSF is the Committee on Science, Space, and Technology. In the Senate, two different committees share jurisdiction over the Foundation authorization: the Committee on Labor and Human Resources *and* the Committee on Commerce, Science, and

Transportation. The provision for serial jurisdiction resulted from a political compromise in 1981 on the part of two committee chairs who felt strongly that the NSF ought to fall within the purview of their respective committees.[37] The unusual arrangement has proven awkward and untidy. For example, both committees conduct separate hearings each year and report bills on the NSF. This duplication of effort contributed in part to a failure in Congress to pass an authorization act for the NSF for the first four years after serial jurisdiction went into effect. As a result, the House and Senate subcommittees with jurisdiction over NSF appropriations—the Subcommittee on Veterans Affairs, Housing and Urban Development, and Independent Agencies (in both chambers)—have tended to exercise a greater say over NSF and Antarctic policy than might otherwise be the case.

The authorizing and appropriations committees in both houses generally have endorsed the executive branch's budget requests for the US Antarctic program. In fact, formal committee reports on authorization and appropriations bills occasionally cite "strong" and "long-lasting" support for the Antarctic program as "the principal expression of national interest and policy" in the region.[38] However, during the Reagan administration, final dollar amounts appropriated by Congress fell short of the President's original requests each fiscal year (FY), except for FY 1984 and FY 1987. (See Table 3.) The reductions (with exceptions noted below) do not appear to have resulted from any fundamental disagreements between the executive branch and Congress over the size and scope of the Antarctic program. Rather, they reflect a more general concern about Federal spending and the budget deficit, or (in some cases) the forced sequestering of funds mandated by the Gramm-Rudman-Hollings Act. In the end, however, the budget for the US Antarctic program has increased every year since the late seventies.

Table 3
US Antarctic program budget requests and appropriations

Fiscal Year	Administration's Request	Actual Appropriation
1982	$ 70,100,000	$ 68,500,000
1983	86,400,000	83,200,000
1984	102,100,000	102,100,000
1985	115,000,000	110,830,000
1986	120,100,000	110,151,000
1987	117,000,000	117,000,000
1988	143,000,000	124,800,000
1989	141,000,000	131,000,000

(Source: Various published reports of the House and Senate Authorizing and Appropriating Committees on the NSF budget from 1981 to 1989.)

Despite general support from the authorizing and appropriations committees, one major point of contention has surfaced repeatedly in these committees over the past several years. Specifically, some legislators have expressed concern about the relative size of the two basic components of the total Antarctic budget request: the research program, and operations support. The former is typically only about one-tenth of the latter, since the direct costs of actual research projects are far less than the costs of the bases and logistics structure that support the entire research effort. For example, in the FY 1989 budget submission, the administration requested $15.5 million for the research program, compared with $125.5 million for operations support.[39] Much like the debate over the proper "tooth-to-tail ratio" for the American armed forces in the seventies, the apparent lopsidedness of support costs has caused a raised eyebrow or two, despite National Science Foundation assertions that such costs inevitably will be high when conducting research in a remote and inhospitable locale.

Operations support, consequently, has been a favorite target for potential cuts. In 1982, the Senate Appropriations Committee limited the amount of money the NSF could spend for support in FY 1983, in hopes of freeing up more funds for other NSF research.[40] That same year, the House-Senate conference committee report on the NSF appropriations bill took note of "the increasing costs to the Foundation of logistical and support activities" for the Antarctic program, and requested the Office of Management and Budget (OMB) to study alternative funding procedures, such as making other Federal agencies bear some of the budget burden. OMB subsequently reaffirmed its support for continued NSF funding of the entire Antarctic program, but added that all Antarctic program requirements would be grouped together as a single item in the NSF budget request.[41]

In 1985, the Senate Committee on Labor and Human Resources voted to cut $10 million from the administration's FY 1986 request for operations support.[42] In considering the FY 1988 budget request, the same committee endorsed a substantial (22.1 percent) increase in support as being "vital for the Nation if it is to adequately support the research programs." The Committee's report, however, also noted that it expected an "increased emphasis on the actual research" in subsequent years.[43]

That same year, the House Committee on Science, Space, and Technology voted to cut $25 million from the US Antarctic program, since it felt that "present priorities within the overall range of NSF programs" did not justify a large increase in operations support. The committee chose instead to redirect the money to the Foundation's science and engineering education program.[44]

The apparent unease with which some members of Congress view the Antarctic operations support budget has important implications for the size and nature of the American presence in Antarctica. The NSF continues to be under pressure to hold down the costs of Antarctic

NSF Photo

This seismic station is located on Abbott Peak, Mt. Erebus, in the Antarctic. By its very nature, scientific research in the region involves substantial logistics costs.

logistics. As a result, it has actively considered alternative ways of funding and procuring services currently provided by the Navy and Coast Guard, including ''contracting out'' these services to a civilian company. While this approach may have merit from a cost effectiveness perspective, it also may have an adverse impact on the Antarctic program and the American position in the Antarctic over the longer term, as discussed later. At the same time, congressional concern with the operations support budget also would appear to rule out any substantial increases in American logistics capabilities in the region (such as the oft-discussed possibility of building a year-round airfield on the continent) unless political or economic rationales for an American presence in the region change significantly.

While the budget process serves as the principal vehicle for regular and routine congressional consideration of the US Antarctic program, other committees also have focused on specific aspects of the program or American policy toward the region from time to time. Tables 4 and 5 list congressional hearings on Antarctic issues over an 11-year period. As the list indicates, congressional interest in the region outside the budget process appears to be a function of two factors.

One factor is the requirement to pass legislation that implements or ratifies agreements reached by the executive branch through the consultative process of the Antarctic Treaty system. For example, the Senate Foreign Relations Committee and three committees in the House held hearings on the Antarctic Conservation Act, which implemented the Agreed Measures on the Protection of Antarctic Flora and Fauna concluded at the third consultative meeting of the Antarctic Treaty parties. Ratification of the new minerals convention also will require Senate approval, and the entire Congress must enact implementing legislation if the convention is ever ratified.

A second factor that heightens congressional interest in the Antarctic is those issues that occasionally lead to wider-than-usual public concern about the subject. A spate of ''oversight'' hearings have been held recently, for instance, on the depletion of the ozone layer in the atmosphere, a phenomenon that is most dramatically evident in the Antarctic region.

An analysis of the content of special congressional hearings dealing with Antarctic issues does not reveal any glaring biases or noticeable trends in congressional attitudes toward the subject. As in the budget process, the legislators generally support American policy objectives in the region as expressed by State Department and NSF officials. However, as interest in the resource potential of the region has risen since the late seventies, questions have been raised whether the American research program places sufficient emphasis on resource matters.[45] Overall benefits and costs of the program likewise have been the subject of

Table 4
House hearings on Antarctic issues, 1977-88

COMMITTEE Subcommittee	Issue	Year

APPROPRIATIONS
  HUD and Independent
  Agencies
	NSF appropriations	Annual

SCIENCE, SPACE, AND TECHNOLOGY*	Ozone depletion	1987
Science, Research, and Technology	NSF authorization Oversight	Annual 1979
	State Department role in environmental affairs**	1980

Environment and the
  Atmosphere
	Nuclear power plant in
	  Antarctica
		1977

	Antarctic Conservation Act of 1977**	1977

Natural Resources,
  Agriculture Research,
  and Environment
	State Department role in
	  environmental affairs**
		1980

	Carbon dioxide and climate**	1982

Investigations and
  Oversight
	Carbon dioxide and
	  climate**
		1982

MERCHANT MARINE
AND FISHERIES
  Fisheries & Wildlife
  Conservation &
  Environment
	Antarctic Conservation
	  Act of 1977**
		1977

	Negotiations on Antarctic marine living resources	1977

	Polar Living Marine
	  Resources Conservation
	  Act
		1978

(continued on next page)

Table 4—Cont'd
House hearings on Antarctic issues, 1977-88

COMMITTEE Subcommittee	Issue	Year
	Antarctic biological research	1983
	Antarctic Marine Living Resources Convention Act	1983
Coast Guard and Navigation	Coast Guard icebreaker requirement	1984
FOREIGN AFFAIRS Human Rights and International Organizations	Antarctic Marine Living Resources Convention Act	1984
ENERGY AND COMMERCE Health and the Environment	Ozone depletion	1987
JUDICIARY Immigration, Citizenship, & International Law	Antarctic Crimes Act of 1977	1977

*Previously known as Committee on Science and Technology.
**Joint hearing with another subcommittee listed in table.

NSF = National Science Foundation; HUD = Department of Housing and Urban Development.

(Source: Congressional Information Service and Congressional Record)

discussion. For example, in 1979, Rep. Toby Roth (R-Wis.) wondered if, after several years of American activities in the region, ''we probably know everything there is to know about the area.''[46] But, in the end, Antarctic issues can hardly be said to arouse strong passions one way or the other within congressional circles.

Thus, for the time being, the initiative for policymaking in the region clearly resides in the executive branch. Congress occasionally casts a parsimonious eye on the budget for the Antarctic program—particularly with the operations support account—but has never acted as a serious brake to a program that enjoys wide, if sometimes disinterested, support on Capitol Hill. Congress nevertheless is sensitive to major topical issues emerging from the Antarctic, as recent hearings and congressional reports on minerals, ozone, and the environment suggest. If these issues or others were to grow more salient, congressional interest in the region no doubt would increase and the legislators might very well play a more prominent role in Antarctic policymaking.

INTEREST GROUPS   Just as the Antarctic does not figure prominently on the congressional agenda, few interest groups devote attention to the Antarctic. Once again, the reasons are not hard to discern. Quite simply, Antarctica does not impact the lives and livelihood of very many people. As of the late eighties, for example, American fishermen had shown almost no interest in the Southern Ocean and no American companies or consortia were seriously prepared to explore for oil or minerals in the region.[47] Thus, the economic motivation for interest group activity is almost totally lacking.

Two major groups, however, have expressed interests in the area and sought to influence American policy there.

By far the most visible non-governmental organizations associated with Antarctic affairs are the environmental groups that take positions or develop programs on the

Table 5
Senate hearings on Antarctic issues, 1977-88

COMMITTEE Subcommittee	Issue	Year
APPROPRIATIONS		
HUD and Independent Agencies	NSF appropriations	Annual
LABOR AND HUMAN RESOURCES*		
Health and Scientific Research	NSF authorization	Annual
COMMERCE, SCIENCE, AND TRANSPORTATION	Negotiations on Antarctic marine living resources	1978
	Marine Mammal Protection Act	1984
Science, Technology, and Space	NSF authorization Oversight	Annual 1984
Merchant Marine	Coast Guard icebreaker operations	1984
ENERGY AND NATURAL RESOURCES	Scientific research and resources	1979
FOREIGN RELATIONS		

Arms Control, Oceans,
  and International
  Environment
	Exploitation of Antarctic
	  resources
		1978

	CCAMLR ratification	1981
ENVIRONMENT & PUBLIC WORKS		

Subcommittees on
  Environmental
  Protection; and
  Hazardous Wastes and
  Toxic Substances
	Ozone depletion	1987/1988

*Previously known as Committee on Human Resources.

NSF = National Science Foundation; HUD = Department of Housing and Urban Development.

(Source: Congressional Information Service and Congressional Record)

region. Their number has grown since the early seventies, as worldwide interest in Antarctic resource development and its potential environmental implications have both increased. Specific concerns vary from organization to organization. For example, groups dedicated to the protection of whales have expressed a particular interest in efforts to manage the Southern Ocean fishery since krill is a major source of food for baleen whales. Likewise, tactics also vary: From staging public demonstrations, to publishing newsletters, to organizing expeditions and establishing a station in Antarctica (such as Greenpeace International has done), to lobbying legislators and executive branch officials.[48]

Representatives of some environmental groups also have had an opportunity to take part directly in formulating American policy toward the region. For example, Lee Kimball (of the World Resources Institute), Dr. William Brown (of the Environmental Defense Fund), and James Barnes (who helped found the Antarctic and Southern Ocean Coalition) have regularly testified in congressional hearings on legislation dealing with the Antarctic—such as the Antarctic Environmental Protection Act of 1978—and special oversight hearings. Both Kimball and Brown (in addition to representatives from industry and science) have worked with the Antarctic Section of the State Department's Advisory Committee on Oceans and International Environmental and Scientific Affairs in recommending US positions in talks on living and mineral resources. Since 1977, a representative of an environmental group has served on the US delegation to the Antarctic Treaty consultative meetings. Lee Kimball, for example, served as an adviser with the American delegation to the 1987 meeting in Brazil and the 1989 meeting in Paris. In short, as Kimball herself has concluded, the United States affords more access to interest groups in the Antarctic policymaking process than any other country in the treaty system.[49]

Not all members of the environmental lobby, however, are satisfied with this level of participation.

Barnes, for instance, has criticized the closed and secretive nature of the consultative mechanism and urged the US Government to take a more assertive stance in opening up the process to more direct involvement by non-governmental organizations.[50]

The influence and impact of the environmental lobby on the policymaking process are difficult to gauge. On one hand, several proposals adopted by some environmental groups—such as turning Antarctica into a "World Park" or creating an Antarctic Environmental Protection Agency—command little support among nations still protective of their presumed territorial "rights" in Antarctica and historically reticent to create supranational organizations with jurisdiction over the region. (Though, as noted earlier, the "World Park" concept received a big political boost with the 1989 joint French-Australian proposal to designate the Antarctic as an "international wilderness reserve.") On the other hand, the US Government clearly takes responsible environmental spokesmen seriously, as evidenced by their advisory role in the executive and legislative branches. Moreover, the attention given to environmental concerns within the treaty's consultative process and within US implementing legislation obviously reflects a significant influence—even if progress has not been as rapid or as extensive as some environmentalists might like.

Scientists with professional research interests in the region represent another group with special concerns in the Antarctic. As described in the next chapter, the Antarctic is an enormously important location for conducting research in several different disciplines. A number of scientists regularly return to the region to pursue their investigations. However, as several officials interviewed for this study stated, scientists with interests in the region represent only a small fraction of the American scientific community. Moreover, the "Antarcticans" generally are not disposed nor particularly well organized to lobby on behalf of their particular interests.

The principal input into the US policymaking process from the scientific community thus has come principally from governmental and quasi-governmental advisory boards. Over the past decade, the Polar Research Board (PRB) of the National Research Council—which serves as the US national committee under the international Scientific Committeee on Antarctic Research (SCAR)—has published several reports on the current state and future of research in the Antarctic.[51] These reports frequently are cited in official documents and congressional testimony, suggesting that the efforts of the PRB do in fact contribute to internal deliberations of policy. The National Science Board (NSB)—which sits as an official advisory board to the NSF—also serves as a more-or-less independent source of views from the scientific community. For example, the NSB commissioned a 1987 study on the National Science Foundation's role in polar research that drew on comments from scientists who were supportive and critical of the current US Antarctic program.[52] Finally, congressional committees occasionally have invited prominent scientists to testify in hearings on the Antarctic. Dr. James Zumberge, for example, made several trips to Capitol Hill when he served as president of SCAR.[53]

The Policymaking Process

Before addressing the substance of the current US Antarctic program, two comments about the organizational structure for policymaking described above are in order.

First, the Antarctic is not a high-profile issue even within departments, agencies, and legislative committees that have major responsibilities for the region. In the National Science Foundation, as well as the State and Defense Departments, policymaking essentially is confined to division-level offices—three or four tiers below the top. And, within those offices, the Antarctic may be only one of several issues that fall within their respective bailiwicks. In congressional hearings, out of the hundreds of pages of testimony and statements on the NSF's budget, a mere fraction deal with the Antarctic program. In fact, Antarctic issues typically engage the attention of senior policy-makers only when major problems affecting some other aspect of US policy arise—such as the difficulties with New Zealand in the mid-eighties over the access of American naval vessels to its ports.

While officials who deal with the Antarctic on a day-to-day basis are highly skilled and dedicated, the lack of regular high-level attention devoted to the region poses the danger of Antarctic policy being developed without reference to other dimensions of US foreign, security, and resource policy. Moreover, policy also may suffer from the natural tendency of lower-level, functional offices to focus on programmatic and budgetary issues of the moment, at the expense of considering longer-range policy matters.

Second, bureaucratic perspectives and normal operating procedures of agencies involved in Antarctic policymaking induce inherent biases into the process. For example, the principal function of the National Science Foundation is to provide governmental support for scientific research and education by providing grants to individuals and organizations.[54] This approach has served the advancement of science research within the American academic and political context quite well. What it means for the US Antarctic program, however, is that even though American interests in the region ostensibly are very broad, the actual expression of those interests (such as the US program on the ice) is defined almost entirely by the nature of and unique requirements for conducting scientific research.

The isolated pursuit of this objective conceivably could jeopardize other interests. For example, the NSF (as discussed below) has considered sharply reducing Navy and Coast Guard roles in providing logistics support by making greater use of contractor services and vessels. While this approach may make sense if the only consideration is reducing the costs of conducting scientific research (a proper and legitimate institutional concern of the Foundation), it also may conflict with broader political-strategic interests in the region—such as tacitly demonstrating an ability for American military forces to operate in the high southern latitudes should the Antarctic Treaty system ever collapse.

Concern also is evident in some quarters that the kind of science sponsored by the NSF on the ice has not kept pace with American interests in the area. Some observers have in fact faulted the NSF for failing to support aggressively resource-related research. As a result, critics contend, the United States is not in a strong position to exercise influence in areas that are now becoming the principal focus of Antarctic diplomacy.

The predisposition toward basic science is in large part a function of the NSF's charter and modus operandi. Since its creation in 1950, the principal purpose of the NSF has been to support *basic*, as opposed to applied, research. The current structural organization of the NSF continues to reflect this orientation. Moreover, the NSF does not pursue a research strategy in the Antarctic per se; rather, it relies on unsolicited proposals (which are subjected to a process of peer review) to structure the research agenda for any given fiscal year. Thus, the initiative for determining the quality and direction of the Antarctic research program rests primarily on the shoulders of individual scientists and academic institutions, *not* the NSF. According to critics, these factors have resulted in an Antarctic science program that is fragmented, preponderantly focused on traditional disciplines, and lacking in a long-term view of the future.[55]

The foregoing discussion is by no means intended to suggest that an emphasis on basic scientific research has undermined American interests in the Antarctic. In the author's opinion, this emphasis is entirely appropriate for the current time and situation. Nevertheless, in crafting a US strategy toward the region in the future, the decision-maker must recognize that (for good or ill) the current structure for policymaking does have inherent biases that will tend to channel decisions in a particular direction. More importantly, any attempt to alter US policy in light of possible changes in political, economic, or security conditions affecting the Antarctic must account for the inevitable tendency of institutions involved to implement policy in accordance with those biases.

In the final analysis, the most important manifestation of American policy toward the Antarctic is what we actually do "on the ice." The United States has maintained a permanent presence in the region since the International Geophysical Year of 1957-58. The size and scope of that presence—including the kind of scientific research performed, number and location of stations, and dimensions of logistics support—reflect and define the range of American interests there. The central question then in evaluating the efficacy of US policy toward the Antarctic is whether the US Antarctic program is properly designed to meet current and future American interests in the region.

5

The US Antarctic Program

IN HIS NOVEL *THE MASTERS*, C.P. SNOW WRYLY observes that the first rule of politics is to be present. This rule applies as much to Antarctic diplomacy as it does to the selection of a Cambridge college master.

As noted in Chapter 1, the United States played a decisive role in the successful negotiation of the Antarctic Treaty in the late fifties. The ability of US diplomats to influence Antarctic affairs in this instance owed much to their country's unique role as leader of the Western World. But, perhaps more importantly, they could speak with authority on Antarctic issues precisely because the US Government previously had supported expeditions and constructed installations on the continent with the conscious aim of promoting American influence in Antarctica.

The presumed relationship between presence and influence has characterized the conduct of US policy toward the region ever since. American administrations have consistently held that the United States must have an active presence in Antarctica to support the country's varied interests there.[1] In other words, the ability of the United States to achieve its objectives in the region is said

NSF Photo by Russ Kinne

A helicopter lands on the deck of the US Coast Guard Icebreaker
***POLAR SEA* during operations in the Antarctic.**

to be a function of both the nature and scope of American activities on the ice.

If one accepts this premise (and the author does), then a major aspect of formulating US policy toward the region is to decide how much is enough with respect to the US Antarctic program.

Since the early sixties, successive White House directives have answered this question by stating that "an active and influential presence" requires three elements: The conduct of *scientific activities* in major disciplines, year-round *occupation of the South Pole and other stations*, and the availability of *logistics support*.[2] On the basis of this guidance, the United States has pursued a program in the Antarctic matched only by the Soviet Union in terms of its size and reach.

Ironically, this program has changed very little over time. American activities on the ice are basically the same today as they were three decades ago. Yet, during that same period, the tenor of Antarctic politics has changed considerably as a result of growing interest in Antarctica's resource potential. Thus, one must wonder (as several observers have) whether the US Antarctic program—as currently structured—can adequately support future American interests in the region.[3]

The answer depends in large part on developments that cannot be predicted with certainty. If resource development and the conflicts inherent in Antarctic politics can be managed within the parameters of the existing Antarctic Treaty system, the current American program on the ice may well provide sufficient presence to achieve US objectives. If, however, that system fundamentally changes or collapses altogether (as a result of causes discussed in chapter 3), the United States may well require a very different kind of presence on the ice to remain an influential player in Antarctic diplomacy and, thereby, ensure that US interests there are well served.

Scientific Activities

Scientific research has been the principal American activity in the Antarctic at least since the International Geophysical Year in 1957-58.[4] The American science program in the Antarctic currently is the largest in the region. It generally involves about 300 scientists and 80 different research projects during a 120-day summer season. The National Science Foundation (NSF) funds each project. To gain approval and support for research, individual scientists, universities, and Federal agencies annually submit proposals to the Foundation for consideration. The NSF then evaluates the proposals in terms of scientific merit and logistical feasibility. On average, the NSF approves about 60 percent of the proposals it receives each year.[5] In the past, the NSF-funded research program has tended to emphasize basic research in the fields of glaciology,* biological sciences, earth sciences, atmospheric sciences, and ocean sciences. In fiscal year (FY) 1989, this program cost slightly more than $131 million, of which about 10 percent was for actual research and 90 percent was for the facilities and logistics required to support that research on the ice.[6]

The justification for this public investment in Antarctic research is twofold.

First, scientific research in the Antarctic is important not only for gaining a better understanding of the region itself, but for expanding the existing body of knowledge on significant global phenomena as well. Several unique features of the Antarctic make it an ideal location for research having implications that extend well beyond the continent.

Many scientists now believe that Antarctica was once at the center of a large, prehistoric continent (called *Gondwanaland*) that linked the land masses of what is now the Southern Hemisphere. This supercontinent eventually separated into discrete elements through the process of continental drift. Thus, geological and paleontologic evidence gathered in the Antarctic may provide clues not only to the region's past, but to the history of South America, Africa, South Asia, and Australia as well.[7] (See Map 5, Chapter 3.)

The Antarctic's relatively pristine environment also makes it a good place to measure environmental changes elsewhere in the world. By taking core samples from the Antarctic ice sheet, scientists have been able to chart variations in the levels of pollution, carbon dioxide, and

---

*The scientific study of snow and ice on the earth's surface, with specific concentration on regimes of active glaciers, glacier flow and its mechanics, and the interrelation between ice and climate.

other contaminants over several centuries. Likewise, scientists can detect more immediate changes in the composition of the atmosphere by continuously taking air samples at Antarctic stations. This kind of data is particularly relevant to studying such developments as the so-called "greenhouse effect" and the gradual, global warming trend it has apparently produced. Additionally, the study of changes in the Antarctic ice and glaciers could provide vital data on the wider implications of the greenhouse effect, such as potentially calamitous changes in sea level.[8]

The Antarctic also is an important "platform" for collecting data on the earth's upper atmosphere and making astronomical observations. Because of the long daylight hours of the austral (southern) summer, scientists can make uninterrupted measurements of the sun and its effects on man and the environment. Indeed, one motive for nineteenth century expeditions to the Southern Ocean region was to observe the transit of Venus across the face of the sun. Moreover, because the earth's magnetic field lines intercept the ionosphere and the earth's surface at the poles, the Antarctic is an excellent site for studying solar winds and magnetospheric effects* that affect civilian and defense-related communications. In addition, studies of seasonal decreases in stratospheric ozone levels over the Antarctic may yield valuable information on causes of ozone depletion and the implications of subsequent increases in ultraviolet radiation for human health.[9]

Finally, the Antarctic exerts a major influence over global weather patterns and ocean currents because of its extreme cold and the interaction of ice and sunlight.

---

*The magnetosphere is a comet-shaped bubble around the earth, carved in the solar wind. It is formed because the earth's magnetic field represents an obstacle to the solar wind, a supersonic flow of plasma blowing away from the sun. The solar wind flows around the earth, confining it and its magnetic field into a long cylindrical cavity with a blunt nose.

Ice ablation study underway in "dirty ice" near Dailey Island.

Manned and remote meteorological observations in the Antarctic have substantially improved data on global weather trends. Moreover, as noted in a 1987 report to the National Science Board, a better understanding of the impact of the polar regions on the composition and dynamics of the atmosphere is a key to solving problems such as acid rain.[10]

This brief synopsis of the unique opportunities for scientific research in the Antarctic by no means exhausts the range of possibilities. Neither does it do justice to the past accomplishments and continuing work performed by researchers from the United States and other nations in the region. The bottom line nevertheless can be stated quite simply: Scientific research conducted in the Antarctic is diverse, timely, and (in many cases) directly relevant to the study of critically important global phenomena. This fact alone is powerful justification for a substantial investment of resources in Antarctic science.

Still, the benefits derived from scientific research may not—in and of themselves—be sufficient to convince executive branch officials or members of Congress to fund a large American scientific presence in the region. Some legislators have questioned the wisdom of allocating scarce budgetary resources to Antarctic research in lieu of aid to scientific and technical education in the United States. Consequently, supporters have resorted to a second rationale for a sizable scientific program: namely, to show the American flag. A 1983 OMB report to Congress spelled out this point quite clearly:

> In the special circumstances of Antarctica, research program size is important not only for the scientific results it produces but as a measure of national presence and influence.[11]

In other words, science is not the only reason for the research program. In fact, some officials might argue that it is not even the primary reason for our being there.

NSF Photo

Weather balloon is launched at South Pole Station.

If presence (and, ultimately, diplomatic influence) is indeed a major justification for a robust American scientific program in the region, does it make a difference what kind of science the United States pursues in the Antarctic? Basic research dominates the American scientific effort on the ice because, one, the basic research performed there is intrinsically important and, two, the National Science Foundation is not institutionally geared to support other kinds of research. Yet, retaining a position of leadership in Antarctic affairs would intuitively seem to require a research program that also addresses the most pressing issues of the region and, at the same time, keeps pace with the activities of other nations.

The attention devoted by the world community to the potential resources of the region (as well as environmental implications of resource development) would seem to suggest that the United States ought to be at the forefront of research explicitly devoted to ascertaining the oil and mineral wealth of the region. Even if the Antarctic never yields a dollar of oil or mineral wealth, leadership in Antarctic affairs in the coming decade certainly will require a commanding knowledge of the region's resources. American scientists and engineers have played this role in virtually every other corner of the world; they certainly could do the same in the Antarctic if appropriately motivated and supported by the US Government.

Antarctic Stations

While some scientists perform research aboard ships or aircraft based outside the Antarctic, the bulk of American scientific research in the region is conducted in or around three year-round stations and several smaller, temporary stations and camps on the continent.[12]

The largest American station in the Antarctic is McMurdo, located on Ross Island at the edge of the Ross

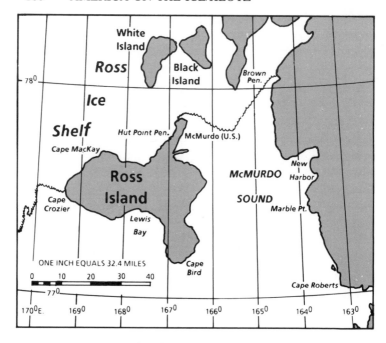

White Island

Ross

Black Island

Brown Pen.

78⁰

Ice

Shelf

Hut Point Pen.

McMurdo (U.S.)

Cape MacKay

Ross

New Harbor

McMURDO

Island

SOUND

Cape Crozier

Marble Pt.

Lewis

Bay

ONE INCH EQUALS 32.4 MILES

0   10   20   30   40

Cape Bird

Cape Roberts

77⁰

170⁰E.   169⁰   168⁰   167⁰   166⁰   165⁰   164⁰   163⁰

Source: National Geographic Society/Defense Mapping Agency, Jet Navigation Chart

Map 8. McMurdo Sound (including Marble Point)

Ice Shelf. (See Map 8.) McMurdo Station is frequently described as the logistics "hub" of the US Antarctic program, because most American personnel, equipment, and supplies destined for the South Pole and other inland research sites pass through the station. It has a harbor capable of handling Navy and commercial resupply ships. It also has aircraft landing strips on sea ice and the ice shelf within two and seven miles, respectively, of the station. McMurdo serves as operating "headquarters" for the senior NSF Antarctic representative and the US Naval Support Force, Antarctica. More than 1,000 people work and conduct research there during the summer; the population falls to about 180 in the winter. The station has about

100 buildings, of all sorts and descriptions, including temporary wooden buildings and Jamesway shelters (canvas-covered, tent-like structures).[13] One writer—Deborah Shapley—has likened the ambience at McMurdo to that of a frontier mining town.[14]

The National Science Foundation currently is implementing a long-range development plan to improve facilities at McMurdo Station. As originally conceived in the late seventies, the plan included construction of a new electric power plant, a water desalination plant, new dormitories, and a replacement science laboratory.[15] After construction began, replacement of a heavy equipment maintenance facility destroyed by fire became necessary. (Fire is a constant hazard in the very dry Antarctic climate.) The NSF also has sought funds to replace obsolete or worn-out radars, communications gear, and other support equipment.[16]

The second American coastal station is Palmer Station, named after the first American reputed to have sighted Antarctica—Nathaniel Palmer. It is located on Anvers Island off the west coast of the Antarctic peninsula. Palmer is considerably smaller than McMurdo in population and size. The number of people at the site ranges from a low of 10 in the winter to a high of over 40 in the summer. Palmer has two major buildings and several smaller ones which support a wide range of scientific activities. The station is perhaps most closely identified with its research on Antarctic marine life, particularly krill. It is accessible by helicopter and ship. The NSF constructed a new aquarium building there in accordance with its long-range development plan and intends to upgrade other facilities as money becomes available.[17]

Though seldom mentioned, the location of Palmer Station is geopolitically significant. The station establishes a year-round American presence in the very area where the pre-1961 claims of Argentina, Chile, and Great Britain all overlap. If the Antarctic Treaty system were to collapse,

McMurdo Station, at the edge of the Ross Ice Shelf, is the logistics hub of the US Antarctic program.

and clashes reminiscent of the early fifties were to occur in that particular area again, the United States presumably would have more at stake in the conflict, as well as greater leverage to force a peaceful resolution, than previously was the case.

The American station at the South Pole is named after the first two men to establish a "station," albeit temporarily, there—Roald Amundsen and Robert Falcon Scott. The United States first built a station at the South Pole during the International Geophysical Year, and has been there ever since. The most distinctive feature of the Amundsen-Scott Station is the large geodesic dome that encloses smaller buildings and equipment. An adjacent ice landing strip can accommodate ski-equipped LC-130 transport aircraft, the main sources of resupply. The station population varies from 20 to 80. As an official NSF information pamphlet rather matter-of-factly notes, "The station is isolated from mid-February to early November."[18] In more recent years, however, Air Force C-141 transport aircraft (supported by Strategic Air Command in-flight tanker aircraft) have dropped supplies by parachute to the adventurous few who occupy the site during the long, dark Antarctic winter.[19]

The American station at the South Pole is politically important. Since six of the seven claimed sectors converge at the pole, that one station establishes a highly visible American presence in each claimed territory. Additionally, the polar station serves as an important jumping off point for activities throughout the continent's interior. For these reasons, a 1983 OMB report to Congress asserted that the South Pole "symbolically and politically is the most important location for a U.S. station."[20]

Several American officials interviewed for this study believe that the site is so intrinsically valuable from a strategic point of view that the Soviet Union would immediately occupy it if the United States ever left.[21] While no plans call for abandoning Amundsen-Scott, the NSF has

NSF Photo

The Amundsen-Scott Station, with its characteristic geodesic dome, establishes the US presence at the South Pole.

indicated that the current facilities eventually will need replacs by the mid-nineties. The costs involved may well lead to a reexamination of American assumptions regarding the importance of a South Pole station. The status of the Antarctic Treaty system at that time clearly will be an important factor in any discussions of the level of investment required to maintain a significant American presence at the South Pole.

In addition to these three year-round stations—McMurdo, Palmer, and Amundsen-Scott—the US presence on the ice also includes several temporary stations. For several years, the United States operated Siple Station at the base of the Antarctic peninsula on a full-time basis. The station currently is used "as needed." The United States also uses two regular summer camps (Byrd Surface Camp and Dome C) and establishes temporary camps with wooden huts, Jamesway shelters, or tents at various sites to support specific research projects.[22]

Logistics Support

Each station described above depends on a logistics system that provides for the transport of personnel, equipment, and supplies to and from the Antarctic, as well as within the region. While perhaps not as glamorous as conducting research in a remote Antarctic location, logistics support nevertheless is the key to maintaining an effective science program and continuing presence in the region. The logistics system includes air, sea, and land elements.

The *air element* consists of aircraft and their associated landing and support facilities. Three types of aircraft operate between the primary staging point at Christchurch, New Zealand, and Williams Field at McMurdo.

Air Force C-141 *Starlifter* transports begin operations to and from Christchurch at the start of the austral (southern) summer in October. They usually end, however, in mid-November—well before the research season is over—because the C-141 is a wheeled aircraft and cannot land on the ice runway after the warmer weather softens its surface. The Air Force makes about 20 flights each year. For example, during the 1989-90 summer season, 22 C-141 flights lifted more than a thousand passengers and a million pounds of cargo from Christchurch, New Zealand, to McMurdo. As noted above, the C-141 also drops supplies from the air at the McMurdo and South Pole stations during the mid-winter.[23]

During the 1989-90 summer season, the Air Force's C-5 *Galaxy*—the largest US transport aircraft—was employed for the first time in operations on the ice, with two flights in and out of Williams Field. Because of its ability to lift large, out-sized cargo, the C-5 could become a regular feature of the US Antarctic program in the years ahead.

The third aircraft involved in resupply missions between the Antarctic and Christchurch is the LC-130

Three sledging parties enjoy their first meal at West Base in the Antarctic after many weeks on the trail during the 1939-41 US Antarctic Expedition. The base leader, Dr. Paul A. Siple (standing), gets a first-hand account of their discoveries. Siple Station is named after this American scientist and explorer.

transport. The National Science Foundation owns a fleet of seven operational LC-130s. The planes are flown and maintained, however, by the Navy's Antarctic Development ment Squadron 6 (VXE-6), permanently based at Point Mugu, California. The LC-130 carries less cargo than the C-141 or C-5, but has the advantage of being able to land at McMurdo throughout the summer season by using ski-equipped landing gear. Because of this unique feature, the LC-130 has become the workhorse of the Antarctic, delivering people and goods to stations throughout much of the continent. At least one of the planes is specially equipped to do double duty as a research platform. LC-130 operations begin in mid-August when the first group of workers fly in to McMurdo to assist the winter party in preparing the station for summer operations. The most active phase of flying takes place between October and February. During the 1989-90 season, the relatively small LC-130 fleet conducted more than 400 missions for over 3,000 hours of flying time. That same year, two New York Air National Guard LC-130s provided additional airlift support, flying missions either in, or to and from Antarctica.[24]

The NSF LC-130 fleet clearly is showing signs of age. Its three "F" model aircraft were built in the fifties; the other four "R" models were acquired in the mid-seventies. Some of the electronic equipment on board still uses vacuum-tube technology. The NSF currently is in the midst of a multiyear program to retrofit the fleet with solid-state navigation and communications gear, and to increase its fuel efficiency.[25]

Whatever improvements are made, flying in the Antarctic will continue to be a risky business, demanding the utmost in skill and professionalism. An extremely cold climate, combined with unpredictable winds and often poor visibility, have taken their toll. For example, in December 1987, an NSF LC-130 crashed in the Antarctic, killing two Navy men and injuring 11 others. Ironically, the plane was on a mission to repair another LC-130 that had crashed at the same spot in 1972.[26]

In addition to the LC-130s, the United States also has used a leased Twin Otter aircraft and several UH-1N helicopters for transportation within Antarctica. The helicopters are owned, operated, and maintained by the Navy's VXE-6. The helicopters can carry up to five passengers. The Navy also uses them for search and rescue missions.[27]

As noted above, the major staging base for air operations into the Antarctic is Christchurch, New Zealand. The US Antarctic program uses Christchurch under the terms of a 1958 cooperation agreement.[28] Virtually every American agency involved in activities on the ice (such as the NSF, VXE-6, and the Air Force) has representatives there.

NSF Photo by Ann Hawthorne

Ski-equipped LC-130 transport aircraft is the workhorse of the US Antarctic program.

Christchurch has proven to be an ideal location from which to mount US aerial resupply missions. The flying distance between Christchurch and the major American station at McMurdo is 2,065 nautical miles. At this range, the LC-130 aircraft can make a one-way flight either to or from McMurdo. Except for Hobart, Australia, no other major airfield in the Southern Hemisphere is as close to McMurdo as Christchurch.

Moreover, New Zealand has a substantial Antarctic program of its own, including a station near McMurdo. Not surprisingly, the United States and New Zealand have supported one another's Antarctic programs in many different ways. For example, the Royal New Zealand Air Force regularly flies C-130 missions to and from McMurdo as part of an ongoing mutual support agreement between the two countries. Additionally, New Zealand military personnel assist in cargo handling and other duties at McMurdo Station.[29]

Thus, the dispute between the United States and New Zealand in the mid-eighties over port visits by nuclear weapon-capable vessels (which eventually led to the unraveling of cooperation in certain military activities) led to fears within the US Antarctic program that use of Christchurch might also be in jeopardy.[30] The reason for concern was obvious. Any detailed analysis of alternative staging bases or resupply methods essentially boils down to one, simple point: There is no quick, low-cost substitute for Christchurch as a staging base for flights to and from the Antarctic. From the perspective of promoting US interests in the Antarctic, the most prudent policy for the United States in the short term was to insulate the various components of its bilateral relationship with New Zealand from each other, so that difficulties in one area did not spoil other, equally important aspects of the total relationship.

Over the longer term, however, the United States might need to develop one or more alternatives to Christchurch—in case it becomes either unavailable or grows inadequate in meeting American transportation requirements in and out of the Antarctic.

One possibility would be to equip the C-141 (or a future long-range transport aircraft) with skis similar to those mounted on the LC-130. With such a capability, the C-141 conceivably could take off anywhere in the world, refuel in mid-air, and land on an ice runway in the Antarctic *anytime* during the summer season. Some feasibility studies already have been done in this regard. They reportedly indicate that the per-unit costs would be high, given the small number of aircraft to be modified. The agencies that would have to foot the bill are naturally reluctant to do so, without a compelling political or strategic reason.

Another alternative to reliance on Christchurch would be to construct a landing site in Antarctica that could accommodate C-141s or other long-range aircraft at all times. The United States has long considered the possibility of constructing an airfield near McMurdo that would permit year-round use by large, wheeled transport aircraft. In January 1958, Admiral George Dufek and Sir Edmund Hillary made the first solid-ground landing in Antarctic history on a strip of beach prepared by Navy Seabees at Marble Point (about 50 miles across McMurdo Sound from McMurdo Station). (See Map 8.) At that time, the Navy—with a strong endorsement from the House Committee on Interstate and Foreign Commerce—conducted a two-year survey to determine the feasibility of constructing a permanent runway there.[31] The NSF's 1979 long-range development plan also addressed the possibility of building a year-round airport, a new science station, and support facilities at Marble Point.*[32] And, in 1987, a report prepared for the National Science Board noted that

> One of the greatest future needs on land is a year-round hard-surface runway and accompanying base, the cost of which would be between $500 million and $1 billion.[33]

Therein lies the rub. The costs associated with building an airfield at Marble Point have always precluded a decision to do so, however advantageous a year-round airport might appear to be. In FY 1988, the NSF spent just over $111 million on operations support. Estimated costs for a Marble Point facility alone exceed that amount five- to tenfold. A decision to invest such sums in Antarctic construction thus would seem to require a major change in the status quo, such as the loss of Christchurch or a decision to expand the American capability to project its presence on the continent to keep pace with political or economic developments (for example, an upsurge in resource activity).

---

*Marble Point currently serves as a helicopter refueling station and as a cargo staging area for research conducted at inland camps.

One possible, less-costly alternative to constructing a solid-ground runway for wheeled aircraft would be to use so-called "blue-ice" runways. At various locations on the continent, weather conditions have resulted in the formation of ice of sufficient density and surface strength to permit wheeled aircraft to land throughout the research season. Though some preparations are required for safe flight operations, the use of blue-ice runways would be far less expensive than building a solid-ground facility. An NSF LC-130 made a landing on a blue-ice runway in January 1990. The feasibility of using such surfaces will be pursued further in the coming years. According to the NSF, it is conceivable that one day a C-5 *Galaxy* could operate out of a blue-ice runway near the South Pole to transport the equipment and supplies needed to renovate the Amundsen-Scott Station.

The *sea component* of the Antarctic logistics system consists of Coast Guard icebreakers and various military and civilian supply ships and tankers. Each season (usually in late December or early January), one of two *POLAR*-class icebreakers in the Coast Guard fleet breaks a channel through the ice in McMurdo Sound to permit resupply ships (normally two a year) to reach the station. The icebreaker also provides escort service for these ships. Additionally, the NSF has employed Coast Guard icebreakers to resupply Palmer Station and (until the 1987-88 season) to serve as platforms for research on or near the pack ice and the Antarctic coast. The Coast Guard also has provided transportation to American observers during the periodic inspections performed under Article VII of the Antarctic Treaty.[34] As noted earlier, the NSF reimburses the Coast Guard for operating costs associated with the use of its icebreakers for the US Antarctic program. In some years, the NSF has been the largest single user of icebreaker time, thus paying a bigger share of costs than even the Coast Guard. Indeed, a former Coast Guard Commandant once described his service as a "minority stockholder in its own fleet."[35]

US Coast Guard Icebreaker *POLAR SEA* is one of only two icebreakers that support US operations in the Antarctic region.

The future of the Coast Guard oceangoing icebreaker fleet, as well as the Coast Guard's role in the US Antarctic program is uncertain. The size of the fleet has dropped sharply in recent years. At the start of 1987, it consisted of five vessels. However, in October of that year, the Coast Guard decommissioned its icebreaker GLACIER because of its deteriorating condition. In early 1988, the Coast Guard decided to decommission its two WIND-class icebreakers because of age (both were constructed during the Second World War) and a lack of funds to maintain them. The Coast Guard icebreaker fleet currently consists of only two vessels, POLAR SEA and POLAR STAR.

The Coast Guard has long looked to the users of its fleet—principally the National Science Foundation and the Defense Department—for support in obtaining funds necessary to maintain the existing fleet and to construct modern replacement vessels. The NSF, however, has never been completely satisfied with the icebreaker support it has received. The perceived needs of science and the perceived needs of operating a multi-mission icebreaker do not always coincide. Thus, some scientists conducting research aboard icebreakers occasionally have criticized the Coast Guard for failing to provide services they apparently expected. Moreover, NSF officials have stated that they believe Coast Guard icebreakers are ''not quite optimized for our Antarctic mission and, as a consequence, may cost us a bit more than would be the case if they were optimized.''[36]

The NSF thus has sought to develop alternatives to reliance on the Coast Guard, particularly in the area of direct research support. Since 1985, the NSF has leased an ice-strengthened research vessel—POLAR DUKE—for its Antarctic science program and logistics, and intends to continue using this particular ship for several years to come.[37] Moreover, a 1987 report to the National Science Board recommended ''a research vessel with icebreaking capability be acquired for the US Antarctic program.'' The

NSF subsequently arranged for the construction of such a vessel, and plans to lease it for Antarctic operations starting in 1992.[38] Still, as NSF officials have noted, the US Antarctic program will continue to need separate icebreaking services to open the channel in McMurdo Sound.[39]

Not surprisingly, the Coast Guard thinks that the NSF's preference for a dedicated research vessel with icebreaking capability undercuts its case for modernization, particularly because the NSF's status as a major user of the fleet gives it an important say in determining the future of that fleet.[40] Likewise, members of Congress repeatedly have expressed concern about the apparent inability of the two agencies to come to an agreement on the future needs of the American icebreaking fleet.[41]

For the future, however, the size of the Coast Guard icebreaker fleet would seem to depend principally on factors other than US operations in the Antarctic. American interests in the strategically more important Arctic region most likely will be the determining factor in justifying a fleet of a given size. Indeed, the widely publicized efforts to free several trapped whales in Alaska and the *EXXON VALDEZ* oil spill focused unprecedented national attention on American capabilities for operating in the Arctic, and correspondingly led to increased concern within Congress about the parlous state of the American icebreaker fleet. When the administration's efforts to include funds for an additional polar icebreaker in the Coast Guard's FY 1990 budget were defeated in the committees with jurisdiction over the Coast Guard, several senators succeeded in putting funds in the Department of Defense appropriations bill for *the Navy* to build an icebreaker with antisubmarine warfare capabilities, which the Coast Guard would operate in peacetime.

The NSF probably will continue to call on the Coast Guard for the annual McMurdo operation for several years to come. One concern, however, is what will happen if one or both of the existing icebreakers are not available because of maintenance downtime or higher-priority national missions. Another concern is whether the diminished US icebreaker capability would be sufficient to support an expanded American presence in the Antarctic if US national interests ever required it. For the moment, NSF officials contend that such contingencies could be covered by commercially leased vessels. However, the availability of civilian ships for government operations never can be guaranteed under all political and market conditions—a problem that has long concerned US Navy planners.

Managing the Logistics Program

While the NSF exercises overall responsibility for the US Antarctic program, the US Navy manages most of the logistics component as part of its annual *Operation DEEP FREEZE*. The organization in charge of *Operation DEEP FREEZE* is the Naval Support Force, Antarctica (NSFA). The NSFA is "home ported" at Port Hueneme, California, and maintains a full-time detachment at Christchurch.[42] Its specific tasks include operation and maintenance of McMurdo Station; scheduling the movement of people and cargo to and from, as well as within, Antarctica; and chartering Air Force aircraft and supply ships. In addition, the Navy's Antarctic squadron VXE-6 "chops" (changes operational control) to NSFA when engaged in Antarctic operations.[43] Several hundred personnel are assigned to the NSFA. In addition, elements of other military services—such as the Army's transportation corps—regularly augment the NSFA during the summer season. NSFA personnel account for about 65 percent of McMurdo's summer population.[44]

Though the Navy has headed up the American logistics effort for Antarctica since 1956, its future role is not altogether certain. Some officials within the Navy reportedly feel that even though the NSF reimburses the Navy for personnel costs, people assigned to Antarctic duty could be better used in more traditional Navy missions. If military personnel ceilings continue to decline as they have in recent years, pressure to transfer personnel authorizations out of the Antarctic could mount.

At the same time, some officials within the scientific community would not be altogether unhappy if the military's role in Antarctica diminished somewhat. Several writers have commented on difficulties inherent in the division of responsibilities in the Antarctic between the Senior NSF Representative and the Commander of NSFA. While the former theoretically is in charge of operations on the ice, the latter has command authority over his assigned logistics elements and is subject to norms, rules, and operating procedures associated with the military.[45]

Aside from the opportunity to clean up the lines of authority, some civilian officials believe that private contractors could deliver logistics services more cheaply than the Navy, thus freeing up more funds for construction or additional research projects. The National Science Foundation already employs a civilian contractor (currently ITT/Antarctic Services Inc.) to perform specialized logistics projects, including operation and maintenance of the South Pole, Palmer, and Siple stations, as well as the *POLAR DUKE* research vessel.[46] A 1987 report to the National Science Board in fact recommended that the Antarctic Development Squadron VXE-6 remain an "integral part of the U.S. Antarctic Program," but that the

> remaining support functions currently provided by the US Naval Support Force, Antarctica be reviewed by NSF management for possible transfer to civilian contractors, as suggested by the US Navy, if such transfer proves to be the most efficient and cost-effective option.[47]

While contracting out the logistics function may ultimately prove to have some cost advantages, it has some very real drawbacks from a policy perspective.

First, it would virtually eliminate any expertise within the Defense Department for Antarctic operations. Though the primary reason for a military role in the US Antarctic program continues to be support of science and an American presence in the region, the military's involvement nevertheless provides knowledge, skills, and experience that could prove invaluable if the current Antarctic regime collapses for some unforeseen reason and national security interests become more salient. While such a contingency may be remote at present, the current military role in the Antarctic is a relatively modest price to pay for having a cadre of uniformed "Antarctic hands" around which a more substantial military organization could be built should the need arise. The Navy's activities in the postwar period and in preparing for the International Geophysical Year clearly added to the influence the United States exercised in Antarctic diplomacy. The same is no doubt true today, particularly when viewed from the perspective of those nations in which more traditional national interests—as opposed to scientific or environmental concerns—dominate the formulation of Antarctic policy.

Second, while the Navy's absense would leave the NSF clearly and solely in charge of Antarctic operations, the NSF ultimately might rue the day it lost the active participation of the military on the ice. The Navy, and ultimately the entire Defense Department, command budgets that dwarf the funds allocated to the National Science Foundation, in general, and to the US Antarctic program, in particular. As long as the military has a stake (even if relatively minor and peripheral) in what goes on in the Antarctic, the NSF can count on the support of key military officials in the annual "battle of the budget." Without this support, the NSF (and more particularly, its Division of Polar Programs) would be forced to go it alone. As the Coast Guard learned with its icebreaker program, in an age of budget austerity, one needs all the allies one can get. Thus, while the NSF ought to search for more cost-effective ways to provide for specific logistics services, total elimination of direct military involvement in the Antarctic program may in the mid- to long-term exacerbate rather than alleviate the overall problem of budgeting for it.

Finally, a continued active military role in Antarctica ensures that the US Antarctic program does not become the captive of a single interest or agency. To the extent a single organization controls the funding and operation of a particular activity, the norms, operating procedures, and bureaucratic perspectives of that organization will dominate. If the only reason for an American presence on the ice were to conduct scientific research, then greater NSF control over the entire program would not only be reasonable and appropriate, it probably would be less expensive as well. However, presidential pronouncements on Antarctic policy consistently state that US interests in the region are clearly broader, and include political, security, resource, and environmental dimensions quite apart from the unique requirements of conducting and supporting scientific research. The most practical approach to guaranteeing these interests receive due consideration is not to consolidate the entire US Antarctic program within a single organization, but to ensure that all relevant agencies take part in an active and meaningful way—which in Washington usually means having some stake in the resources involved.

Thus, as a matter of policy, the US Government ought to keep the Department of Defense (DOD) (including all three military services) and the Coast Guard fully engaged in logistically supporting the US Antarctic program. If the Navy's commitment to the Antarctic does indeed impose an unsustainable burden in terms of personnel, the White House could call on DOD to spread the

NSF Photos by Russ Kinne

Not all American Antarctic research is conducted from the relative comfort of the main US stations. Scientists often must live in tents at remote research sites.

burden more equitably across the services by creating a *joint* Antarctic support force to replace the Naval Support Force, Antarctica. As noted above, elements from all three military departments already take part in the logistics program on a regular basis. A number of functions currently performed by naval personnel (for example, command, flying, scheduling, public affairs, and engineering) also could be performed by personnel from other services.

As an added benefit, placing military support directly under the Office of the Secretary of Defense or the Joint Chiefs of Staff, rather than under a single service, also might provide Antarctica with the visibility and attention within the national security community that it needs, but does not enjoy.

Maintaining an Influential American Presence in the Years Ahead

A principal objective of the US Antarctic program has been to provide an active and influential presence in the region. The program has performed this function remarkably well over the past three decades. The size and broad scope of the American scientific research effort places the United States at the forefront of what for now is the most important human activity in the region. Its three year-round (and several temporary) stations are capable of supporting more than 1,000 scientists and support personnel during the peak summer season. Its logistics system has an unrivaled capability of reaching into almost any part of the continent by air. By establishing a preeminent position on the ice, the United States has been able to exert considerable influence within the Antarctic Treaty system.

Despite its notable successes, the current US Antarctic program has come under fire. Some observers fault the NSF for placing an inordinate emphasis on basic research at a time when Antarctic diplomacy is increasingly preoccupied with resource questions. Environmental groups likewise call for more ecological research, and greater attention to the potentially deleterious impact of man's presence on the Antarctic environment. And, even though the total budget for the Antarctic program is relatively modest, congressional committees question the rising costs of logistics support.

If no change is made in the status quo, then surely there is no compelling reason to alter the US Antarctic program—including its purpose, its size, or its management—in any significant way.

If, on the other hand, either the American stake in the region or the present treaty system undergoes a major transformation, then business as usual may no longer serve US interests there. As recent developments clearly suggest, some change in the status quo may be in the offing. Thus, a prudent strategy for achieving American objectives in Antarctica after 1991 must provide for sufficient capability and flexibility to keep pace with changing circumstances.

As noted at the outset of this chapter, a central question in making decisions about the nature and size of the American presence in the region is "how much is enough?"—that is, how much presence is required to maintain the influence needed to achieve US policy objectives. This question, unfortunately, has no "right" answer. Sane and reasonable people are likely to differ on the details, particularly as government officials haggle over the budget for Antarctic operations.

Perhaps a good place to start in defining the proper size and scope of the US Antarctic program is to assert that the American presence on the ice should be (as it always has been) at least as large as any other nation's. The underlying assumption here is that influence in Antarctic diplomacy is directly proportional to presence. Thus, if the United States wants to retain a strong voice in the region's politics, then its stations, activities, and logistics

infrastructure must match those of the most active countries in the region. Conversely, if the United States allows
its presence to decline, compared to other nations, then it
can expect its influence in Antarctic diplomacy to decline
as well.

At the moment, the US presence fulfills this basic siz-
ing criterion.

However, America's preeminent position in the
region cannot be taken for granted. Indeed, recent
developments suggest a slight downward trend in the relative size of the US presence. For example, in the mid-
eighties, the United States decided to change the operation
of Siple Station (at the base of the Antarctic peninsula)
from a year-round to an "as-needed" base. At roughly the
same time, the ability of the United States to project people and equipment into the area dropped somewhat as a
result of a 60 percent decline in the Coast Guard's oceangoing icebreaker fleet.

Meanwhile, other nations are expanding their Antarctic presence, or are poised to do so in the near future. The
Latin American presence in and around the important
Peninsula region dwarfs that of the United States in terms
of the sheer number of stations concentrated there. The
French and Australians have made (or are making) provisions for regular air transportation to and from their
respective sectors. The Norwegians plan to build their first
permanent base in recent times on the continent. And, the
Soviet Union has opened additional summer stations and
improved both the sea and air components of its Antarctic
logistics system. Moreover, the Soviet Union probably
could expand its presence rather quickly by shifting
resources from its Arctic operations.

What the United States needs to do, then, as a mini-
mum, is to hold the line on the current level of resources
committed to the Antarctic. To achieve this end, the existing number of stations in the region should be maintained.
Doing so, however, will require sufficient funds to repair

and modernize the facilities and equipment needed to conduct meaningful scientific, environmental, and resource-related research.

The first major test of US resolve could be the need to renovate the Amundsen-Scott Station before the turn of the century. The costs could be substantial—given the obvious difficulties of transporting equipment and personnel to the South Pole. Nevertheless, the United States must remain at this politically significant site if it is at all serious about exercising a major say in Antarctic affairs in the years ahead.

The existing logistics system also must be maintained at its present level. The decline of the icebreaker fleet due to age and lack of funds provides a ready example of the relative ease (and speed) with which an important Antarctic resource can slip away. The LC-130 air transport fleet also is growing old. Though efforts currently are underway to update the aircraft's capabilities, the day eventually will come when this venerable workhorse also will require replacement. The ability to reach into the most important areas of the continent by air is the hallmark of the current US logistics program. Without this reach, the US presence would not be nearly as impressive nor influential as it is now.

Beyond simply holding the line, the United States also may need to develop a capability to ratchet up its presence in the Antarctic—either to match significant changes in the activities of other countries or to respond to a sooner-than-expected rush for resource development. In practical terms, this expansion capability might entail building a more robust fleet of government-owned ice-breaking and ice-capable ships, and constructing a year-round airfield on the Antarctic continent. With this infrastructure in place, the United States would be in a better position to increase its facilities and personnel in relatively short order. Without such a capability, the United States might not be able to respond to changing circumstances in sufficient time to influence decisively the course of fast-breaking events. Even if it never became necessary to do so, the ability of the United States to expand its Antarctic presence would significantly affect other nations' perceptions of US seriousness and interests there.

At first blush, the options for developing a rapid expansion capability appear inordinately expensive and, therefore, politically unrealistic. The construction costs of a hard-surface runway at Marble Point might run as much as several times the annual budget of the entire US Antarctic program at the moment. Icebreaking vessels likewise come with hefty sticker prices.

Yet, when viewed in a broader context, the expense is not as large as it might first appear. The impact on the US Antarctic program budget for individual years could be reduced by spreading out the costs over the total number of years required to develop additional logistics assets. The costs also could be shared with other national programs since resources developed for Antarctic operations—such as icebreakers or transport aircraft—could be used to further American interests in other regions—such as the strategically important Arctic.

But perhaps the most important consideration is the potential ''costs'' of not making a prudent, up-front investment in Antarctic capabilities. If the United States maintains a dynamic presence in the region (and, thereby, maintains its traditional leadership role in Antarctic affairs), the current treaty system—which benefits from strong US support—stands a better chance of weathering challenges to its continued existence. In this case, the territorial rivalry and nascent conflict that characterized the pre-treaty period most likely would remain under control. If, however, the United States fails to maintain its preeminent presence in the region and, thereby, relinquishes much of its influence over Antarctic affairs, then the treaty system might not fare as well, and might even collapse altogether. In that event, conflict might ensue, important alliances might be subjected to strain, and, in a worst-case scenario, the United States might feel compelled to deploy military forces to the region to help keep the peace. The costs of renewed rivalry in Antarctica could well amount to far more than the costs of maintaining a robust network of research stations and logistics capabilities.

Persuading the American public and senior officials of the need to spend funds for a large, continuing US presence—particularly in a period of increasing budget austerity—will not be easy. Americans pay scant attention to the region. While the level of interest in the continent's affairs is sufficient to sustain the US Antarctic program at current levels, it is not strong enough to push through major increases in funding.

Thus, an effort to enhance American flexibility in the Antarctic will require coordinated leadership throughout the government. The Department of State and the National Science Foundation have strong institutional interests in the region and accordingly devote a reasonable amount of attention to Antarctic affairs—though some "Antarcticans" surely would welcome more interest on the part of senior department officials. The Department of Defense, however, is not doing all it could to advance US policy objectives in the region. Even though the DOD sits on the Antarctic Policy Working Group, the national security community's interests in the region are minimal. Indeed, as noted earlier, some military officials favor curtailing the Navy's present role in the US Antarctic program.

This benign neglect is, in part, a product of the success of American policy to date. Simply put, the Antarctic never has become the scene or object of major conflict. Consequently, it has only rarely captured the attention of military planners. Yet, it is worth remembering that Antarctica is a peaceful place because of the Antarctic Treaty and the political accommodations it represents. The United States was able to play a leading role in negotiating, and subsequently implementing, the treaty precisely because of the part the Navy and the other services played in opening the region to Americans.

The final chapter of Antarctic history is far from finished. Though the region has remained peaceful for nearly 30 years, conflict could return under the wrong set of circumstances. For this reason, the national security community still has an important role to play in ensuring that US political and security interests in the region are met. To perform this task, the American military certainly *must* be prepared to devote a reasonable share of its resources, talent, and attention to the last continent in the years ahead.

Appendix A

The Antarctic Treaty

The Governments of Argentina, Australia, Belgium, Chile, the French Republic, Japan, New Zealand, Norway, the Union of South Africa, the Union of Soviet Socialist Republics, the United Kingdom of Great Britain and Northern Ireland, and the United States of America,

Recognizing that it is in the interest of all mankind that Antarctica shall continue for ever to be used exclusively for peaceful purposes and shall not become the scene or object of international discord;

Acknowledging the substantial contributions to scientific knowledge resulting from international co-operation in scientific investigation in Antarctica;

Convinced that the establishment of a firm foundation for the continuation and development of such co-operation on the basis of freedom of scientific investigation in Antarctica as applied during the International Geophysical Year accords with the interests of science and the progress of all mankind;

Convinced also that a treaty ensuring the use of Antarctica for peaceful purposes only and the continuance of international harmony in Antarctica will further the purposes and principles embodied in the Charter of the United Nations;

Have agreed as follows:

Article I

1. Antarctica shall be used for peaceful purposes only. There shall be prohibited, *inter alia,* any measure of a military nature, such as the establishment of military bases and fortifications, the carrying out of military manoeuvres, as well as the testing of any type of weapon.

2. The present Treaty shall not prevent the use of military personnel or equipment for scientific research or for any other peaceful purpose.

Article II

Freedom of scientific investigation in Antarctica and co-operation toward that end, as applied during the International Geophysical Year, shall continue, subject to the provisions of the present Treaty.

Article III

1. In order to promote international co-operation in scientific investigation in Antarctica, as provided for in Article II of the present Treaty, the Contracting Parties agree that, to the greatest extent feasible and practicable:

(a) information regarding plans for scientific programs in Antarctica shall be exchanged to permit maximum economy of and efficiency of operations;

(b) scientific personnel shall be exchanged in Antarctica between expeditions and stations;

(c) scientific observations and results from Antarctica shall be exchanged and made freely available.

2. In implementing this Article, every encouragement shall be given to the establishment of co-operative working relations with those Specialized Agencies of the United Nations and other international organizations having a scientific or technical interest in Antarctica.

Article IV

1. Nothing contained in the present Treaty shall be interpreted as:

(a) a renunciation by any Contracting Party of previously asserted rights of or claims to territorial sovereignty in Antarctica;

(b) a renunciation or diminution by any Contracting Party of any basis of claim to territorial sovereignty in Antarctica which it may have whether as a result of its activities or those of its nationals in Antarctica, or otherwise;

(c) prejudicing the position of any Contracting Party as regards its recognition or non-recognition of any other State's rights of or claim or basis of claim to territorial sovereignty in Antarctica.

2. No acts or activities taking place while the present Treaty is in force shall constitute a basis for asserting,

supporting or denying a claim to territorial sovereignty in Antarctica or create any rights of sovereignty in Antarctica. No new claim, or enlargement of an existing claim, to territorial sovereignty in Antarctica shall be asserted while the present Treaty is in force.

Article V

1. Any nuclear explosions in Antarctica and the disposal there of radioactive waste material shall be prohibited.

2. In the event of the conclusion of international agreements concerning the use of nuclear energy, including nuclear explosions and the disposal of radioactive waste material, to which all of the Contracting Parties whose representatives are entitled to participate in the meetings provided for under Article IX are parties, the rules established under such agreements shall apply in Antarctica.

Article VI

The provisions of the present Treaty shall apply to the area south of 60° South Latitude, including all ice shelves, but nothing in the present Treaty shall prejudice or in any way affect the rights, or the exercise of the rights, of any State under international law with regard to the high seas within that area.

Article VII

1. In order to promote the objectives and ensure the observance of the provisions of the present treaty, each Contracting Party whose representatives are entitled to participate in the meetings referred to in Article IX of the Treaty shall have the right to designate observers to carry out any inspection provided for by the present Article. Observers shall be nationals of the Contracting Parties which designate them. The names of observers shall be communicated to every other Contracting Party having the right to designate observers, and like notice shall be given of the termination of their appointment.

2. Each observer designated in accordance with the provisions of paragraph 1 of this Article shall have complete freedom of access at any time to any or all areas of Antarctica.

3. All areas of Antarctica, including all stations, installations and equipment within those areas, and all ships and aircraft

at points of discharging or embarking cargoes or personnel in Antarctica, shall be open at all times to inspection by any observers designated in accordance with paragraph 1 of this Article.

4. Aerial observation may be carried out at any time over any or all areas of Antarctica by any of the Contracting Parties having the right to designate observers.

5. Each Contracting Party shall, at the time when the present Treaty enters into force for it, inform the other Contracting Parties, and thereafter shall give them notice in advance, of

(a) all expeditions to and within Antarctica, on the part of its ships or nationals, and all expeditions to Antarctica organized in or proceeding from its territory;

(b) all stations in Antarctica occupied by its nationals; and

(c) any military personnel or equipment intended to be introduced by it into Antarctica subject to the conditions prescribed in paragraph 2 of Article I of the present Treaty.

Article VIII

1. In order to facilitate the exercise of their functions under the present Treaty, and without prejudice to the respective positions of the Contracting Parties relating to jurisdiction over all other persons in Antarctica, observers designated under paragraph 1 of Article VII and scientific personnel exchanged under sub-paragraph 1(b) of Article III of the Treaty, and members of the staffs accompanying any such persons, shall be subject only to the jurisdiction of the Contracting Party of which they are nationals in respect of all acts or omissions occurring while they are in Antarctica for the purpose of exercising their functions.

2. Without prejudice to the provisions of paragraph 1 of this Article, and pending the adoption of measures in pursuance of sub-paragraph 1(e) of Article IX, the Contracting Parties concerned in any case of dispute with regard to the exercise of jurisdiction in Antarctica shall immediately consult together with a view to reaching a mutually acceptable solution.

Article IX

1. Representatives of the Contracting Parties named in the preamble to the present Treaty shall meet at the City of Canberra within two months after the date of entry into force of the

Treaty, and thereafter at suitable intervals and places, for the purpose of exchanging information, consulting together on matters of common interest pertaining to Antarctica, and formulating and considering, and recommending to their Governments, measures in furtherance of the principles and objectives of the Treaty, including measures regarding:

(a) use of Antarctica for peaceful purposes only;

(b) facilitation of scientific research in Antarctica;

(c) facilitation of international scientific co-operation in Antarctica;

(d) facilitation of the exercise of the rights of inspection provided for in Article VII of the Treaty;

(e) questions relating to the exercise of jurisdiction in Antarctica;

(f) preservation and conservation of living resources in Antarctica.

2. Each Contracting Party which has become a party to the present Treaty by accession under Article XIII shall be entitled to appoint representatives to participate in the meetings referred to in paragraph 1 of the present Article, during such times as that Contracting Party demonstrates its interest in Antarctica by conducting substantial research activity there, such as the establishment of a scientific station or the dispatch of a scientific expedition.

3. Reports from the observers referred to in Article VII of the present Treaty shall be transmitted to the representatives of the Contracting Parties participating in the meetings referred to in paragraph 1 of the present Article.

4. The measures referred to in paragraph 1 of this Article shall become effective when approved by all the Contracting Parties whose representatives were entitled to participate in the meetings held to consider those measures.

5. Any or all of the rights established in the present Treaty may be exercised as from the date of entry into force of the Treaty whether or not any measures facilitating the exercise of such rights have been proposed, considered or approved as provided in this Article.

Article X

Each of the Contracting Parties undertakes to exert appropriate efforts, consistent with the Charter of the United Nations, to the end that no one engages in any activity in Antarctica contrary to the principles or purposes of the present Treaty.

Article XI

1. If any dispute arises between two or more of the Contracting Parties concerning the interpretation or application of the present Treaty, those Contracting Parties shall consult among themselves with a view to having the dispute resolved by negotiation, inquiry, mediation, conciliation, arbitration, judicial settlement or other peaceful means of their own choice.

2. Any dispute of this character not so resolved shall, with the consent, in each case, of all parties to the dispute, be referred to the International Court of Justice for settlement; but failure to reach agreement on reference to the International Court shall not absolve parties to the dispute from the responsibility of continuing to seek to resolve it by any of the various peaceful means referred to in paragraph 1 of this Article.

Article XII

1. (a) The present Treaty may be modified or amended at any time by unanimous agreement of the Contracting Parties whose representatives are entitled to participate in the meetings provided for under Article IX. Any such modification or amendment shall enter into force when the depositary Government has received notice from all such Contracting Parties that they have ratified it.

(b) Such modification or amendment shall thereafter enter into force as to any other Contracting Party when notice of ratification by it has been received by the depositary Government. Any such Contracting Party from which no notice of ratification is received within a period of two years from the date of entry into force of the modification or amendment in accordance with the provision of sub-paragraph 1(a) of this Article shall be deemed to have withdrawn from the present Treaty on the date of the expiration of such period.

2. (a) If after the expiration of thirty years from the date of entry into force of the present Treaty, any of the Contracting Parties whose representatives are entitled to participate in the meetings provided for under Article IX so requests by a communication addressed to the depositary Government, a

Conference of all the Contracting Parties shall be held as soon as practicable to review the operation of the Treaty.

(b) Any modification or amendment to the present Treaty which is approved at such a Conference by a majority of the Contracting Parties there represented, including a majority of those whose representatives are entitled to participate in the meetings provided for under Article IX, shall be communicated by the depositary Government to all Contracting Parties immediately after the termination of the Conference and shall enter into force in accordance with the provisions of paragraph 1 of the present Article.

(c) If any such modification or amendment has not entered into force in accordance with the provisions of sub-paragraph 1(a) of this Article within a period of two years after the date of its communication to all the Contracting Parties, any Contracting Party may at any time after the expiration of that period give notice to the depositary Government of its withdrawal from the present Treaty; and such withdrawal shall take effect two years after the receipt of the notice by the depositary Government.

Article XIII

1. The present Treaty shall be subject to ratification by the signatory States. It shall be open for accession by any State which is a Member of the United Nations, or by any other State which may be invited to accede to the Treaty with the consent of all the Contracting Parties whose representatives are entitled to participate in the meetings provided for under Article IX of the Treaty.

2. Ratification of or accession to the present Treaty shall be effected by each State in accordance with its constitutional processes.

3. Instruments of ratification and instruments of accession shall be deposited with the Government of the United States of America, hereby designated as the depositary Government.

4. The depositary Government shall inform all signatory and acceding States of the date of each deposit of an instrument of ratification or accession, and the date of entry into force of the Treaty and of any modification or amendment thereto.

5. Upon the deposit of instruments of ratification by all the signatory States, the present Treaty shall enter into force for

those States and for States which have deposited instruments of accession. Thereafter the Treaty shall enter into force for any acceding State upon the deposit of its instruments of accession.

6. The present Treaty shall be registered by the depositary Government pursuant to Article 102 of the Charter of the United Nations.

Article XIV

The present Treaty, done in the English, French, Russian and Spanish languages, each version being equally authentic, shall be deposited in the archives of the Government of the United States of America, which shall transmit duly certified copies thereof to the Governments of the signatory and acceding States.

In witness whereof, the undersigned Plenipotentiaries, duly authorized, have signed the present Treaty.

Done at Washington this first day of December, one thousand nine hundred and fifty-nine.

Appendix B

Convention for the Conservation
of Antarctic Seals

The Contracting Parties,

Recalling the Agreed Measures for the Conservation of Antarctic Fauna and Flora, adopted under the Antarctic Treaty signed at Washington on 1 December 1959;

Recognizing the general concern about the vulnerability of Antarctic seals to commercial exploitation and the consequent need for effective conservation measures;

Recognizing that the stocks of Antarctic seals are an important living resource in the marine environment which requires an international agreement for its effective conservation;

Recognizing that this resource should not be depleted by overexploitation, and hence that any harvesting should be regulated so as not to exceed the levels of the optimum sustainable yield;

Recognizing that in order to improve scientific knowledge and so place exploitation on a rational basis, every effort should be made both to encourage biological and other research on Antarctic seal populations and to gain information from such research and from the statistics of future sealing operations, so that further suitable regulations may be formulated;

Noting, that the Scientific Committee on Antarctic Research of the International Council of Scientific Unions (SCAR) is willing to carry out the tasks requested of it in this Convention;

Desiring to promote and achieve the objectives of protection, scientific study and rational use of Antarctic seals, and to maintain a satisfactory balance within the ecological system,

Have agreed as follows:

ARTICLE 1
Scope

(1) This Convention applies to the seas south of 60° South Latitude, in respect of which the Contracting Parties affirm the provisions of Article IV of the Antarctic Treaty.

(2) This Convention may be applicable to any or all of the following species:

Southern elephant seal *Mirounga leonina,*

Leopard seal *Hydrurga leptonyx,*

Weddell seal *Leptonychotes weddelli,*

Crabeater seal *Lobodon carcinophagus,*

Ross seal *Ommatophoca rossi,*

Southern fur seals *Arctocephalus* sp.

(3) The Annex to this Convention forms an integral part thereof.

ARTICLE 2
Implementation

(1) The Contracting Parties agree that the species of the seals enumerated in Article 1 shall not be killed or captured within the Convention area by their nationals or vessels under their respective flags except in accordance with the provisions of this Convention.

(2) Each Contracting Party shall adopt for its nationals and for vessels under its flag such laws, regulations and other measures, including a permit system as appropriate, as may be necessary to implement this Convention.

ARTICLE 3
Annexed Measures

(1) This Convention includes an Annex specifying measures which the Contracting Parties hereby adopt. Contracting Parties may from time to time in the future adopt other measures with respect to the conservation, scientific study and rational and humane use of seal resources, prescribing *inter alia:*

(*a*) permissible catch;

(*b*) protected and unprotected species;

(*c*) open and closed seasons;

(*d*) open and closed areas, including the designation of reserves;

(*e*) the designation of special areas where there shall be no disturbance of seals;

(*f*) limits relating to sex, size, or age for each species;

(*g*) restrictions relating to time of day and duration, limitations of effort and methods of sealing;

(*h*) types of specifications of gear and apparatus and appliances which may be used;

(*i*) catch returns and other statistical and biological records;

(*j*) procedures for facilitating the review and assessment of scientific information;

(*k*) other regulatory measures including an effective system of inspection.

(2) The measures adopted under paragraph (1) of this Article shall be based upon the best scientific and technical evidence available.

(3) The Annex may from time to time be amended in accordance with the procedures provided for in Article 9.

ARTICLE 4
Special Permits

(1) Notwithstanding the provisions of this Convention, any Contracting Party may issue permits to kill or capture seals in limited quantities and in conformity with the objectives and principles of this Convention for the following purposes:

(*a*) to provide indispensable food for men or dogs;

(*b*) to provide for scientific research; or

(*c*) to provide specimens for museums, educational or cultural institutions.

(2) Each Contracting Party shall, as soon as possible, inform the other Contracting Parties and SCAR of the purpose and content of all permits issued under paragraph (1) of this Article and subsequently of the numbers of seals killed or captured under these permits.

ARTICLE 5
Exchange of Information and Scientific Advice

(1) Each Contracting Party shall provide to the other Contracting Parties and to SCAR the information specified in the Annex within the period indicated therein.

(2) Each Contracting Party shall also provide to the other Contracting Parties and to SCAR before 31 October each year information on any steps it has taken in accordance with Article 2 of this Convention during the preceding period 1 July to 30 June.

(3) Contracting Parties which have no information to report under the two preceding paragraphs shall indicate this formally before 31 October each year.

(4) SCAR is invited:

(*a*) to assess information received pursuant to this Article; encourage exchange of scientific data and information among the Contracting Parties; recommend programmes for scientific research; recommend statistical and biological data to be collected by sealing expeditions within the Convention area; and suggest amendments to the Annex; and

(*b*) to report on the basis of the statistical, biological and other evidence available when the harvest of any species of seal in the Convention area is having a significantly harmful effect on the total stocks of such species or on the ecological system in any particular locality.

(5) SCAR is invited to notify the Depositary which shall report to the Contracting Parties when SCAR estimates in any sealing season that the permissible catch limits for any species are likely to be exceeded and, in that case, to provide an estimate of the date upon which the permissible catch limits will be reached. Each Contracting Party shall then take appropriate measures to prevent its nationals and vessels under its flag from killing or capturing seals of that species after the estimated date until the Contracting Parties decide otherwise.

(6) SCAR may if necessary seek the technical assistance of the Food and Agriculture Organization of the United Nations in making its assessments.

(7) Notwithstanding the provisions of paragraph (1) of Article 1 the Contracting Parties shall, in accordance with their internal law, report to each other and to SCAR, for consideration, statistics relating to the Antarctic seals listed in paragraph (2) of Article 1 which have been killed or captured by their nationals and vessels under their respective flags in the area of floating sea ice north of 60° South Latitude.

ARTICLE 6
Consultations between Contracting Parties

(1) At any time after commercial sealing has begun a Contracting Party may propose through the Depositary that a meeting of Contracting Parties be convened with a view to:

(a) establishing by a two-thirds majority of the Contracting Parties, including the concurring votes of all States signatory to this Convention present at the meeting, an effective system of control, including inspection, over the implementation of the provisions of this Convention;

(b) establishing a commission to perform such functions under this Convention as the Contracting Parties may deem necessary; or

(c) considering other proposals, including:

    (i) the provision of independent scientific advice;

    (ii) the establishment, by a two-thirds majority, of a scientific advisory committee which may be assigned some or all of the functions requested of SCAR under this Convention, if commercial sealing reaches significant proportions;

    (iii) the carrying out of scientific programmes with the participation of the Contracting Parties; and

    (iv) the provision of further regulatory measures, including moratoria.

(2) If one-third of the Contracting Parties indicate agreement the Depositary shall convene such a meeting, as soon as possible.

(3) A meeting shall be held at the request of any Contracting Party, if SCAR reports that the harvest of any species of Antarctic seal in the area to which this Convention applies is having a significantly harmful effect on the total stocks or the ecological system in any particular locality.

ARTICLE 7
Review of Operations

The Contracting Parties shall meet within five years after the entry into force of this Convention and at least every five years thereafter to review the operation of the Convention.

ARTICLE 8
Amendments to the Convention

(1) This Convention may be amended at any time. The text of any amendment proposed by a Contracting Party shall be submitted to the Depositary, which shall transmit it to all the Contracting Parties.

(2) If one-third of the Contracting Parties request a meeting to discuss the proposed amendment the Depositary shall call such a meeting.

(3) An amendment shall enter into force when the Depositary has received instruments of ratification or acceptance thereof from all the Contracting Parties.

ARTICLE 9
Amendments to the Annex

(1) Any Contracting Party may propose amendments to the Annex to this Convention. The text of any such proposed amendment shall be submitted to the Depositary which shall transmit it to all Contracting Parties.

(2) Each such proposed amendment shall become effective for all Contracting Parties six months after the date appearing on the notification from the Depositary to the Contracting Parties, if within 120 days of the notification date, no objection has been received and two-thirds of the Contracting Parties have notified the Depositary in writing of their approval.

(3) If an objection is received from any Contracting Party within 120 days of the notification date, the matter shall be considered by the Contracting Parties at their next meeting. If unanimity on the matter is not reached at the meeting, the Contracting Parties shall notify the Depositary within 120 days from the date of closure of the meeting of their approval or rejection of the original amendment or of any new amendment proposed by the meeting. If, by the end of this period, two-thirds of the Contracting Parties have approved such amendment, it shall become effective six months from the date of the closure of the meeting for those Contracting Parties which have by then notified their approval.

(4) Any Contracting Party which has objected to a proposed amendment may at any time withdraw that objection, and the proposed amendment shall become effective with respect to

such Party immediately if the amendment is already in effect, or at such time as it becomes effective under the terms of this Article.

(5) The Depositary shall notify each Contracting Party immediately upon receipt of each approval or objection, of each withdrawal of objection, and of the entry into force of any amendment.

(6) Any State which becomes a party to this Convention after an amendment to the Annex has entered into force shall be bound by the Annex as so amended. Any State which becomes a Party to this Convention during the period when a proposed amendment is pending may approve or object to such an amendment within the time limits applicable to other Contracting Parties.

ARTICLE 10
Signature

This Convention shall be open for signature at London from 1 June to 31 December 1972 by States participating in the Conference on the Conservation of Antarctic Seals held at London from 3 to 11 February 1972.

ARTICLE 11
Ratification

This Convention is subject to ratification or acceptance. Instruments of ratification or acceptance shall be deposited with the Government of the United Kingdom of Great Britain and Northern Ireland, hereby designated as the Depositary.

ARTICLE 12
Accession

This Convention shall be open for accession by any State which may be invited to accede to this Convention with the consent of the Contracting Parties.

ARTICLE 13
Entry into Force

(1) This Convention shall enter into force on the thirtieth day following the date of deposit of the seventh instrument of ratification or acceptance.

(2) Thereafter this Convention shall enter into force for each ratifying, accepting or acceding State on the thirtieth day after deposit by such State of its instrument of ratification, acceptance or accession.

ARTICLE 14
Withdrawal

Any Contracting Party may withdraw from this Convention on 30 June of any year by giving notice on or before 1 January of the same year to the Depositary, which upon receipt of such a notice shall at once communicate it to the other Contracting Parties. Any other Contracting Party may, in like manner, within one month of the receipt of a copy of such a notice from the Depositary, give notice of withdrawal, so that the Convention shall cease to be in force on 30 June of the same year with respect to the Contracting Party giving such notice.

ARTICLE 15
Notifications by the Depositary

The Depositary shall notify all signatory and acceding States of the following:

(*a*) signatures of this Convention, the deposit of instruments of ratification, acceptance or accession and notices of withdrawal;

(*b*) the date of entry into force of this Convention and of any amendments to it or its Annex.

ARTICLE 16
Certified Copies and Registration

(1) This Convention, done in the English, French, Russian and Spanish languages, each version being equally authentic, shall be deposited in the archives of the Government of the United Kingdom of Great Britain and Northern Ireland, which shall transmit duly certified copies thereof to all signatory and acceding States.

(2) This Convention shall be registered by the Depositary pursuant to Article 102 of the Charter of the United Nations.

In witness whereof, the undersigned, duly authorized, have signed this Convention.

Done at London, this 1st day of June 1972.

ANNEX

1. Permissible Catch

The Contracting Parties shall in any one year, which shall run from 1 July to 30 June inclusive, restrict the total number of seals of each species killed or captured to the numbers specified below. These numbers are subject to review in the light of scientific assessments:

(*a*) in the case of Crabeater seals *Lobodon carcinophagus,* 175,000;

(*b*) in the case of Leopard seals *Hydruga leptonyx,* 12,000;

(*c*) in the case of Weddell seals *Leptonychotes weddelli,* 5,000.

2. Protected Species

(*a*) It is forbidden to kill or capture Ross seals *Ommatophoca rossi,* Southern elephant seals *Mirounga leonina,* or fur seals of the genus *Arctocephalus.*

(*b*) In order to protect the adult breeding stock during the period with it is most concentrated and vulnerable, it is forbidden to kill or capture any Weddell seal *Leptonychotes weddelli* one year old or older between 1 September and 31 January inclusive.

3. Closed Season and Sealing Season

The period between 1 March and 31 August inclusive is a Closed Season, during which the killing or capturing of seals is forbidden. The period 1 September to the last day in February constitutes a Sealing Season.

4. Sealing Zones

Each of the sealing zones listed in this paragraph shall be closed in numerical sequence to all sealing operations for the seal species listed in paragraph 1 of this Annex for the period 1 September to the last day of February inclusive. Such closures shall begin with the same zone as is closed under paragraph 2 of Annex B to Annex 1 of the Report of the Fifth Antarctic Treaty Consultative Meeting at the moment the Convention enters into force. Upon the expiration of each closed period, the affected zones shall reopen:

Zone 1—between 60° and 120° West Longitude

Zone 2—between 0° and 60° West Longitude, together with that part of the Weddell Sea lying westward of 60° West Longitude

Zone 3—between 0° and 70° East Longitude

Zone 4—between 70° and 130° East Longitude

Zone 5—between 130° East Longitude and 170° West Longitude

Zone 6—between 120° and 170° West Longitude.

5. *Seal Reserves*

It is forbidden to kill or capture seals in the following reserves, which are seal breeding areas or the site of long-term scientific research:

(a) The area around the South Orkney Islands between 60° 20' and 60° 56' South Latitude and 44° 05' and 46° 25' West Longitude.

(b) The area of the southwestern Ross Sea south of 76° South Latitude and west of 170° East Longitude.

(c) The area of Edisto Inlet south and west of a line drawn between Cape Hallett at 72° 19' South Latitude, 170° 18' East Longitude, and Helm Point, at 72° 11' South Latitude, 170° 00' East Longitude.

6. *Exchange of Information*

(a) Contracting Parties shall provide before 31 October each year to other Contracting Parties and to SCAR a summary of statistical information on all seals killed or captured by their nationals and vessels under their respective flags in the Convention area, in respect of the preceding period 1 July to 30 June. This information shall include by zones and months:

(i) The gross and nett tonnage, brake horse-power, number of crew, and number of days' operation of vessels under the flag of the Contracting Party;

(ii) The number of adult individuals and pups of each species taken.

When specially requested, this information shall be provided in respect of each ship, together with its daily position at noon each operating day and the catch on that day.

(b) When an industry has started, reports of the number of seals of each species killed or captured in each zone shall be made to SCAR in the form and at the intervals (not shorter than one week) requested by that body.

(c) Contracting Parties shall provide to SCAR biological information, in particular:

(i) Sex

(ii) Reproductive condition

(iii) Age

SCAR may request additional information or material with the approval of the Contracting Parties.

(*d*) Contracting Parties shall provide to other Contracting Parties and to SCAR at least 30 days in advance of departure from their home ports, information on proposed sealing expeditions.

7. *Sealing Methods*

(*a*) SCAR is invited to report on methods of sealing and to make recommendations with a view to ensuring that the killing or capturing of seals is quick, painless and efficient. Contracting Parties, as appropriate, shall adopt rules for their nationals and vessels under their respective flags engaged in the killing and capturing of seals, giving due consideration to the views of SCAR.

(*b*) In the light of the available and technical data, Contracting Parties agree to take appropriate steps to ensure that their nationals and vessels under their respective flags refrain from killing or capturing seals in the water, except in limited quantities to provide for scientific research in conformity with the objectives and principles of this Convention. Such research shall include studies as to the effectiveness of methods of sealing from the viewpoint of the management and humane and rational utilization of the Antarctic seal resources for conservation purposes. The undertaking and the results of any such scientific research programme shall be communicated to SCAR and the Depositary which shall transmit them to the Contracting Parties.

Appendix C

Convention on the Conservation of Antarctic Marine Living Resources (CCAMLR)

[Preamble]*

The Contracting Parties,

Recognizing the importance of safeguarding the environment and protecting the integrity of the ecosystem of the seas surrounding Antarctica;

Noting the concentration of marine living resources found in Antarctic waters and the increased interest in the possibilities offered by the utilization of these resources as a source of protein;

Conscious of the urgency of ensuring the conservation of Antarctic marine living resources;

Considering that it is essential to increase knowledge of the Antarctic marine ecosystem and its components so as to be able to base decisions on harvesting on sound scientific information;

Believing that the conservation of Antarctic marine living resources calls for international cooperation with due regard for the provisions of the Antarctic Treaty and with the active involvement of all States engaged in research or harvesting activities in Antarctic waters;

Recognizing the prime responsibilities of the Antarctic Treaty Consultative Parties for the protection and preservation of the Antarctic environment and, in particular, their responsibilities under Article IX, paragraph 1(f) of the Antarctic Treaty in respect of the preservation and conservation of living resources in Antarctica;

Note. The text of the Convention does not carry headings to its preamble and articles. Headings, in square brackets, have been inserted for ease of reference.

Recalling the action already taken by the Antarctic Treaty Consultative Parties including in particular the Agreed Measures for the Conservation of Antarctic Fauna and Flora, as well as the provisions of the Convention for the Conservation of Antarctic Seals;

Bearing in mind the concern regarding the conservation of Antarctic marine living resources expressed by the Consultative Parties at the Ninth Consultative Meeting of the Antarctic Treaty and the importance of the provisions of Recommendation IX-2 which led to the establishment of the present Convention;

Believing that it is in the interest of all mankind to preserve the waters surrounding the Antarctic continent for peaceful purposes only and to prevent their becoming the scene or object of international discord;

Recognizing in the light of the foregoing, that it is desirable to establish suitable machinery for recommending, promoting, deciding upon and co-ordinating the measures and scientific studies needed to ensure the conservation of Antarctic marine living organisms;

Have agreed as follows:

ARTICLE I
[Scope and definitions]

1. This Convention applies to the Antarctic marine living resources of the area south of 60° South latitude and to the Antarctic marine living resources of the area between that latitude and the Antarctic Convergence which form part of the Antarctic marine ecosystem.

2. Antarctic marine living resources means the populations of fin fish, molluscs, crustaceans and all other species of living organisms, including birds, found south of the Antarctic Convergence.

3. The Antarctic marine ecosystem means the complex of relationships of Antarctic marine living resources with each other and with their physical environment.

4. The Antarctic Convergence shall be deemed to be a line joining the following points along parallels of latitude and meridians of longitude:

50°S, 0°; 50°S, 30°E; 45°S, 30°E; 45°S, 80°E; 55°S, 80°E;55°S, 150°E; 60°S, 150°E; 60°S, 50°W; 50°S, 50°W; 50°S, 0°.

ARTICLE II
[Objective]

1. The objective of this Convention is the conservation of Antarctic marine living resources.

2. For the purposes of this Convention, the term 'conservation' includes rational use.

3. Any harvesting and associated activities in the area to which this Convention applies shall be conducted in accordance with the provisions of this Convention and with the following principles of conservation:

(a) prevention of decrease in the size of any harvested population to levels below those which ensure its stable recruitment. For this purpose its size should not be allowed to fall below a level close to that which ensures the greatest net annual increment;

(b) maintenance of the ecological relationships between harvested, dependent and related populations of Antarctic marine living resources and the restoration of depleted populations to the levels defined in subparagraph (a) above; and

(c) prevention of changes or minimization of the risk of changes in the marine ecosystem which are not potentially reversible over two or three decades, taking into account the state of available knowledge of the direct and indirect impact of harvesting, the effect of the introduction of alien species, the effects of associated activities on the marine ecosystem and of the effects of environmental changes, with the aim of making possible the sustained conservation of Antarctic marine living resources.

ARTICLE III
[Antarctic Treaty]

The Contracting Parties, whether or not they are Parties to the Antarctic Treaty, agree that they will not engage in any activities in the Antarctic Treaty area contrary to the principles and purposes of that Treaty and that, in their relations with each other, they are bound by the obligations contained in Articles I and V of the Antarctic Treaty.

ARTICLE IV
[Territorial sovereignty and coastal state jurisdiction]

1. With respect to the Antarctic Treaty area, all Contracting Parties, whether not they are Parties to the Antarctic Treaty, are bound by Articles IV and VI of the Antarctic Treaty in their relations with each other.

2. Nothing in this Convention and no acts or activities taking place while the present Convention is in force shall:

    (a) constitute a basis for asserting, supporting or denying a claim to territorial sovereignty in the Antarctic Treaty area or create any rights of sovereignty in the Antarctic Treaty area;

    (b) be interpreted as a renunciation or diminution by any Contracting Party of, or as prejudicing, any right or claim or basis of claim to exercise coastal state jurisdiction under international law within the area to which this Convention applies;

    (c) be interpreted as prejudicing the position of any Contracting Party as regards its recognition or non-recognition of any such right, claim or basis of claim;

    (d) affect the provision of Article IV, paragraph 2, of the Antarctic Treaty that no new claim, or enlargement of an existing claim, to territorial sovereignty in Antarctica shall be asserted while the Antarctic Treaty is in force.

ARTICLE V
[Agreed Measures for the Conservation of Antarctic Fauna and Flora, etc]

1. The Contracting Parties which are not Parties to the Antarctic Treaty acknowledge the special obligations and responsibilities of the Antarctic Treaty Consultative Parties for the protection and preservation of the environment of the Antarctic Treaty area.

2. The Contracting Parties which are not Parties to the Antarctic Treaty agree that, in their activities in the Antarctic Treaty area, they will observe as and when appropriate the Agreed Measures for the Conservation of Antarctic Fauna and Flora and such other measures as have been recommended by the Antarctic Treaty Consultative Parties in fulfillment of their

responsibility for the protection of the Antarctic environment from all forms of harmful human interference.

3. For the purposes of this Convention, "Antarctic Treaty Consultative Parties" means the Contracting Parties to the Antarctic Treaty whose Representatives participate in meetings under Article IX of the Antarctic Treaty.

ARTICLE VI
[Relationship to existing conventions relating to the conservation of whales and seals]

Nothing in this Convention shall derogate from the rights and obligations of Contracting Parties under the International Convention for the Regulation of Whaling and the Convention for the Conservation of Antarctic Seals.

ARTICLE VII
[Commission for the Conservation of Antarctic Marine Living Resources: membership]

1. The Contracting Parties hereby establish and agree to maintain the Commission for the Conservation of Antarctic Marine Living Resources (hereinafter referred to as "the Commission").

2. Membership in the Commission shall be as follows:

(a) each Contracting Party which participated in the meeting at which this Convention was adopted shall be a Member of the Commission;

(b) each State Party which has acceded to this Convention pursuant to Article XXIX shall be entitled to be a Member of the Commission during such time as that acceding party is engaged in research or harvesting activities in relation to the marine living resources to which this Convention applies;

(c) each regional economic integration organization which has acceded to this Convention pursuant to Article XXIX shall be entitled to be a Member of the Commission during such time as its States members are so entitled;

(d) a Contracting Party seeking to participate in the work of the Commission pursuant to subparagraphs (b) and (c) above shall notify the Depositary of the basis upon which it seeks to become a Member of the Commission and of its willingness to accept conservation measures in force. The Depositary shall communicate to each Member of the Commission such notification and accompanying information. Within two months of receipt of such communication from the Depositary, any Member of the Commission may request that a special meeting of the Commission be held to consider the matter. Upon receipt of such request, the Depositary shall call such a meeting. If there is no request for a meeting, the Contracting Party submitting the notification shall be deemed to have satisfied the requirements for Commission Membership.

3. Each Member of the Commission shall be represented by one representative who may be accompanied by alternate representatives and advisers.

ARTICLE VIII
[Commission: legal personality, privileges and immunities]

The Commission shall have legal personality and shall enjoy in the territory of each of the States Parties such legal capacity as may be necessary to perform its function and achieve the purposes of this Convention. The privileges and immunities to be enjoyed by the Commission and its staff in the territory of a State Party shall be determined by agreement between the Commission and the State Party concerned.

ARTICLE IX
[Commission: functions, conservation measures, implementation, objection procedure]

1. The function of the Commission shall be to give effect to the objective and principles set out in Article II of this Convention. To this end, it shall:

   (a) facilitate research into and comprehensive studies of Antarctic marine living resources and of the Antarctic marine ecosystem;

   (b) compile data on the status of and changes in population of Antarctic marine living resources and on factors affecting the distribution, abundance and productivity of harvested species and dependent or related species or populations;

(c) ensure the acquisition of catch and effort statistics on harvested populations;

(d) analyze, disseminate and publish the information referred to in sub-paragraphs (b) and (c) above and the reports of the Scientific Committee;

(e) identify conservation needs and analyze the effectiveness of conservation measures;

(f) formulate, adopt and revise conservation measures on the basis of the best scientific evidence available, subject to the provisions of paragraph 5 of this Article;

(g) implement the system of observation and inspection established under Article XXIV of this Convention;

(h) carry out such other activities as are necessary to fulfil the objective of this Convention.

2. The conservation measures referred to in paragraph 1 (f) above include the following:

(a) the designation of the quantity of any species which may be harvested in the area to which this Convention applies;

(b) the designation of regions and sub-regions based on the distribution of populations of Antarctic marine living resources;

(c) the designation of the quantity which may be harvested from the populations of regions and sub-regions;

(d) the designation of protected species;

(e) the designation of the size, age and, as appropriate, sex of species which may be harvested;

(f) the designation of open and closed seasons for harvesting;

(g) the designation of the opening and closing of areas, regions or sub-regions for purposes of scientific study or conservation, including special areas for protection and scientific study;

(h) regulation of the effort employed and methods of harvesting, including fishing gear, with a view, *inter alia,* to avoiding undue concentration of harvesting in any region or sub-region;

(i) the taking of such other conservation measures as the Commission considers necessary for the fulfillment of the objective of this Convention, including measures concerning the effects of harvesting and associated activities on components of the marine ecosystem other than the harvested populations.

3. The Commission shall publish and maintain a record of all conservation measures in force.

4. In exercising its functions under paragraph 1 above, the Commission shall take full account of the recommendations and advice of the Scientific Committee.

5. The Commission shall take full account of any relevant measures or regulations established or recommended by the Consultative Meetings pursuant to Article IX of the Antarctic Treaty or by existing fisheries commissions responsible for species which may enter the area to which this Convention applies, in order that there shall be no inconsistency between the rights and obligations of a Contracting Party under such regulations or measures and conservation measures which may be adopted by the Commission.

6. Conservation measures adopted by the Commission in accordance with this Convention shall be implemented by Members of the Commission in the following manner;

    (a) the Commission shall notify conservation measures to all Members of the Commission;

    (b) conservation measures shall become binding upon all Members of the Commission 180 days after such notification, except as provided in sub-paragraphs (c) and (d) below;

    (c) if a Member of the Commission, within ninety days following the notification specified in sub-paragraph (a), notifies the Commission that it is unable to accept the conservation measure, in whole or in part, the measure shall not, to the extent stated, be binding upon that Member of the Commission;

    (d) in the event that any Member of the Commission invokes the procedure set forth in subparagraph (c) above, the Commission shall meet at the request of any Member of the Commission to review the conservation measure. At the time of such meeting and within thirty days following the meeting, any Member of the Commission shall have the right to declare that it is no longer able to accept the conservation measure, in which case the Member shall no longer be bound by such measure.

ARTICLE X
[Commission: monitoring function]

1. The Commission shall draw the attention of any State which is not a Party to this Convention to any activity undertaken by its nationals or vessels which, in the opinion of the Commission, affects the implementation of the objective of this Convention.

2. The Commission shall draw the attention of all Contracting Parties to any activity which, in the opinion of the Commission, affects the implementation by a Contracting Party of the objective of this Convention or the compliance by that Contracting Party with its obligations under this Convention.

ARTICLE XI
[Commission: relations with adjacent areas]

The Commission shall seek to co-operate with Contracting Parties which may exercise jurisdiction in marine areas adjacent to the area to which this Convention applies in respect of the conservation of any stock or stocks of associated species which occur both within those areas and the area to which this Convention applies, with a view to harmonizing the conservation measures adopted in respect of such stocks.

ARTICLE XII
[Commission: making of decisions]

1. Decisions of the Commission on matters of substance shall be taken by consensus. The question of whether a matter is one of substance shall be treated as a matter of substance.

2. Decisions on matters other than those referred to in paragraph 1 above shall be taken by a simple majority of the Members of the Commission present and voting.

3. In Commission consideration of any item requiring a decision, it shall be made clear whether a regional economic integration organization will participate in the taking of the decision and, if so, whether any of its member States will also participate. The number of Contracting Parties so participating shall

not exceed the number of member States of the regional economic integration organization which are Members of the Commission.

4.   In the taking of decisions pursuant to this Article, a regional economic integration organization shall have only one vote.

ARTICLE XIII
[Commission: headquarters, meetings, officers, subsidiary bodies]

1.   The headquarters of the Commission shall be established at Hobart, Tasmania, Australia.

2.   The Commission shall hold a regular annual meeting. Other meetings shall also be held at the request of one-third of its members and as otherwise provided in this Convention. The first meeting of the Commission shall be held within three months of the entry into force of this Convention, provided that among the Contracting Parties there are at least two States conducting harvesting activities within the area to which this Convention applies. The first meeting shall, in any event, be held within one year of the entry into force of this Convention. The Depositary shall consult with the signatory States regarding the first Commission meeting, taking into account that a broad representation of such States is necessary for the effective operation of the Commission.

3.   The Depositary shall convene the first meeting of the Commission at the headquarters of the Commission. Thereafter, meetings of the Commission shall be held at its headquarters, unless it decides otherwise.

4.   The Commission shall elect from among its members a Chairman and Vice-Chairman, each of whom shall serve for a term of two years and shall be eligible for re-election for one additional term. The first Chairman shall, however, be elected for an initial term of three years. The Chairman and Vice-Chairman shall not be representatives of the same Contracting Party.

5.   The Commission shall adopt and amend as necessary the rules of procedure for the conduct of its meetings, except with respect to the matters dealt with in Article XII of this Convention.

6.   The Commission may establish such subsidiary bodies as are necessary for the performance of its functions.

ARTICLE XIV
[Scientific Committee: membership, meetings, other experts]

1. The Contracting Parties hereby establish the Scientific Committee for the Conservation of Antarctic Marine Living Resources (hereinafter referred to as 'the Scientific Committee') which shall be a consultative body to the Commission. The Scientific Committee shall normally meet at the headquarters of the Commission unless the Scientific Committee decides otherwise.

2. Each Member of the Commission shall be a member of the Scientific Committee and shall appoint a representative with suitable scientific qualifications who may be accompanied by other experts and advisers.

3. The Scientific Committee may seek the advice of other scientists and experts as may be required on an ad hoc basis.

ARTICLE XV
[Scientific Committee: functions]

1. The Scientific Committee shall provide a forum for consultation and co-operation concerning the collection, study and exchange of information with respect to the marine living resources to which this Convention applies. It shall encourage and promote co-operation in the field of scientific research in order to extend knowledge of the marine living resources of the Antarctic marine ecosystem.

2. The Scientific Committee shall conduct such activities as the Commission may direct in pursuance of the objective of this Convention and shall:

(a) establish criteria and methods to be used for determinations concerning the conservation measures referred to in Article IX of this Convention;

(b) regularly assesses the status and trends of the populations of Antarctic marine living resources;

(c) analyse data concerning the direct and indirect effects of harvesting on the populations of Antarctic marine living resources;

(d) assess the effects of proposed changes in the methods or levels of harvesting and proposed conservation measures;

(e) transmit assessments, analyses, reports and recommendations to the Commission as requested or on its own initiative regarding measures and research to implement the objective of this Convention;

(f) formulate proposals for the conduct of international and national programs of research into Antarctic marine living resources.

3.   In carrying out its functions, the Scientific Committee shall have regard to the work of other relevant technical and scientific organizations and to the scientific activities conducted within the framework of the Antarctic Treaty.

ARTICLE XVI
[Scientific Committee: first meeting, procedure, subsidiary bodies]

1.   The first meeting of the scientific committee shall be held within three months of the first meeting of the Commission. The Scientific Committee shall meet thereafter as often as may be necessary to fulfil its functions.

2.   The Scientific Committee shall adopt and amend as necessary its rules of procedure. The rules and any amendments thereto shall be approved by the Commission. The rules shall include procedures for the presentation of minority reports.

3.   The Scientific Committee may establish, with the approval of the Commission, such subsidiary bodies as are necessary for the performance of its functions.

ARTICLE XVII
[Commission and Scientific Committee: secretariat]

1.   The Commission shall appoint an Executive Secretary to serve the Commission and Scientific Committee according to such procedures and on such terms and conditions as the Commission may determine. His term of office shall be for four years and he shall be eligible for re-appointment.

2.   The Commission shall authorize such staff establishment for the Secretariat as may be necessary and the Executive Secretary shall appoint, direct and supervise such staff according to such rules and procedures and on such terms and conditions as the Commission may determine.

3.   The Executive Secretary and Secretariat shall perform the functions entrusted to them by the Commission.

ARTICLE XVIII
[Languages]

The official languages of the Commission and of the Scientific Committee shall be English, French, Russian and Spanish.

ARTICLE XIX
[Budget and financial obligations]

1.   At each annual meeting, the Commission shall adopt by consensus its budget and the budget of the Scientific Committee.

2.   A draft budget for the Commission and the Scientific Committee and any subsidiary bodies shall be prepared by the Executive Secretary and submitted to the Members of the Commission at least sixty days before the annual meeting of the Commission.

3.   Each Member of the Commission shall contribute to the budget. Until the expiration of five years after the entry into force of this Convention, the contribution of each Member of the Commission shall be equal. Thereafter the contribution shall be determined in accordance with two criteria: the amount harvested and an equal sharing among all Members of the Commission. The Commission shall determine by consensus the proportion in which these two criteria shall apply.

4.   The financial activities of the Commission and Scientific Committee shall be conducted in accordance with financial regulations adopted by the Commission and shall be subject to an annual audit by external auditors selected by the Commission.

5.   Each Member of the Commission shall meet its own expenses arising from attendance at meetings of the Commission and of the Scientific Committee.

6.   A Member of the Commission that fails to pay its contributions for two consecutive years shall not, during the period of its default, have the right to participate in the taking of decisions in the Commission.

ARTICLE XX
[Information: collection and provision]

1.   The Members of the Commission shall, to the greatest extent possible, provide annually to the Commission and to the Scientific Committee such statistical, biological and other data and information as the Commission and Scientific Committee may require in the exercise of their functions.

2.   The Members of the Commission shall provide, in the manner and at such intervals as may be prescribed, information about their harvesting activities, including fishing areas and vessels, so as to enable reliable catch and effort statistics to be compiled.

3.   The Members of the Commission shall provide to the Commission at such intervals as may be prescribed information on steps taken to implement the conservation measures adopted by the Commission.

4.   The Members of the Commission agree that in any of their harvesting activities, advantage shall be taken of opportunities to collect data needed to assess the impact of harvesting.

ARTICLE XXI
[Domestic measures to ensure compliance]

1.   Each Contracting Party shall take appropriate measures within its competence to ensure compliance with the provisions of this Convention and with conservation measures adopted by the Commission to which the Party is bound in accordance with Article IX of this Convention.

2.   Each Contracting Party shall transmit to the Commission information on measures taken pursuant to paragraph 1 above, including the imposition of sanctions for any violation.

ARTICLE XXII
[Activities contrary to objective of Convention]

1.   Each Contracting Party undertakes to exert appropriate efforts, consistent with the Charter of the United Nations, to the end that no one engages in any activity contrary to the objective of this Convention.

2.   Each Contracting Party shall notify the Commission of any such activity which comes to its attention.

ARTICLE XXIII
[Relations with other international organizations]

1.   The Commission and the Scientific Committee shall cooperate with the Antarctic Treaty Consultative Parties on matters falling within the competence of the latter.

2.   The Commission and the Scientific Committee shall cooperate, as appropriate, with the Food and Agriculture Organization of the United Nations and with other Specialised Agencies.

3.   The Commission and the Scientific Committee shall seek to develop co-operative working relationships, as appropriate, with inter-governmental and non-governmental organizations which could contribute to their work, including the

Scientific Committee on Antarctic Research, the Scientific Committee on Oceanic Research and the International Whaling Commission.

4. The Commission may enter into agreements with the organizations referred to in this Article and with other organizations as may be appropriate. The Commission and the Scientific Committee may invite such organizations to send observers to their meetings and to meetings of their subsidiary bodies.

ARTICLE XXIV
[Observation and inspection]

1. In order to promote the objective and ensure observance of the provisions of this Convention, the Contracting Parties agree that a system of observation and inspection shall be established.

2. The system of observation and inspection shall be elaborated by the Commission on the basis of the following principles:

(a) Contracting Parties shall co-operate with each other to ensure the effective implementation of the system of observation and inspection, taking account of the existing international practice. This system shall include, *inter alia,* procedures for boarding and inspection by observers and inspectors designated by the Members of the Commission and procedures for flag state prosecution and sanctions on the basis of evidence resulting from such boarding and inspections. A report of such prosecutions and sanctions imposed shall be included in the information referred to in Article XXI of this Convention;

(b) In order to verify compliance with measures adopted under this Convention, observation and inspection shall be carried out on board vessels engaged in scientific research or harvesting of marine living resources in the area to which this Convention applies, through observers and inspectors designated by the Members of the Commission and operating under terms and conditions to be established by the Commission;

(c) designated observers and inspectors shall remain subject to the jurisdiction of the Contracting Party of which they are nationals. They shall report to the Member of the Commission by which they have been designated which in turn shall report to the Commission.

3.   Pending the establishment of the system of observation and inspection, the Members of the Commission shall seek to establish interim arrangements to designate observers and inspectors and such designated observers and inspectors shall be entitled to carry out inspections in accordance with the principles set out in paragraph 2 above.

ARTICLE XXV
[Dispute settlement]

1.   If any dispute arises between two or more of the Contracting Parties concerning the interpretation or application of this Convention, those Contracting Parties shall consult among themselves with a view to having the dispute resolved by negotiation, inquiry, mediation, conciliation, arbitration, judicial settlement or other peaceful means of their own choice.

2.   Any dispute of this character not so resolved shall, with the consent in each case of all Parties to the dispute, be referred for settlement to the International Court of Justice or to arbitration; but failure to reach agreement on reference to the International Court or to arbitration shall not absolve Parties to the dispute from the responsibility of continuing to seek to resolve it by any of the various peaceful means referred to in paragraph 1 above.

3.   In cases where the dispute is referred to arbitration, the arbitral tribunal shall be constituted as provided in the Annex to this Convention.

ARTICLE XXVI
[Signature]

1.   This Convention shall be open for signature at Canberra from 1 August to 31 December 1980 by the States participating in the Conference on the Conservation of Antarctic Marine Living Resources held at Canberra from 7 to 20 May 1980.

2.   The States which so sign will be the original signatory States of the Convention.

ARTICLE XXVII
[Ratification, acceptance or approval]

1.   This Convention is subject to ratification, acceptance or approval by signatory States.

2. Instruments of ratification, acceptance or approval shall be deposited with the Government of Australia, hereby designated as the Depositary.

ARTICLE XXVIII
[Entry into force]

1. This Convention shall enter into force on the thirtieth day following the date of deposit of the eighth instrument of ratification, acceptance or approval by State referred to in paragraph 1 of Article XXVI of this Convention.

2. With respect to each State or regional economic integration organization which subsequent to the date of entry into force of this Convention deposits an instrument of ratification, acceptance, approval or accession, the Convention shall enter into force on the thirtieth day following such deposit.

ARTICLE XXIX
[Accession]

1. This Convention shall be open for accession by any State interested in research or harvesting activities in relation to the marine living resources to which this Convention applies.

2. This Convention shall be open for accession by regional economic integration organizations constituted by sovereign States which include among their members one or more States Members of the Commission and to which the States members of the organization have transferred, in whole or in part, competences with regard to the matters covered by this Convention. The accession of such regional economic integration organizations shall be the subject of consultations among Members of the Commission.

ARTICLE XXX
[Amendment]

1. This Convention may be amended at any time.

2. If one-third of the Members of the Commission request a meeting to discuss a proposed amendment the Depositary shall call such a meeting.

3. An amendment shall enter into force when the Depositary has received instruments of ratification, acceptance or approval thereof from all the Members of the Commission.

4.   Such amendment shall thereafter enter into force as to any other Contracting Party when notice of ratification, acceptance or approval by it has been received by the Depositary. Any such Contracting Party from which no such notice has been received within a period of one year from the date of entry into force of the amendment in accordance with paragraph 3 above shall be deemed to have withdrawn from this Convention.

ARTICLE XXXI
[Withdrawal]

1.   Any Contracting Party may withdraw from this Convention on 30 June of any year, by giving written notice not later than 1 January of the same year to the Depositary, which, upon receipt of such a notice, shall communicate it forthwith to the other Contracting Parties.

2.   Any other Contracting Party may, within sixty days of the receipt of a copy of such a notice from the Depositary, give written notice of withdrawal to the Depositary in which case the Convention shall cease to be in force on 30 June of the same year with respect to the Contracting Party giving such notice.

3.   Withdrawal from this Convention by any Member of the Commission shall not affect its financial obligations under this Convention.

ARTICLE XXXII
[Functions of depositary]

The Depositary shall notify all Contracting Parties of the following:

(a)   signatures of this Convention and the deposit of instruments of ratification, acceptance, approval or accession;

(b)   the date of entry into force of this Convention and of any amendment thereto.

ARTICLE XXXIII
[Texts]

1.   This Convention, of which the English, French, Russian and Spanish texts are equally authentic, shall be deposited with the Government of Australia which shall transmit duly certified copies thereof to all signatory and acceding Parties.

2.   This Convention shall be registered by the Depositary pursuant to Article 102 of the Charter of the United Nations.

Drawn up at Canberra this twentieth day of May 1980.

IN WITNESS WHEREOF the undersigned, being duly authorized, have signed this Convention.

Annex for an Arbitral Tribunal

The arbitral tribunal referred to in paragraph 3 of Article XXV shall be composed of three arbitrators who shall be appointed as follows:

The Party commencing proceedings shall communicate the name of an arbitrator to the other Party which, in turn, within a period of forty days following such notification, shall communicate the name of the second arbitrator. The Parties shall, within a period of sixty days following the appointment of the second arbitrator, appoint the third arbitrator, who shall not be a national of either Party and shall not be of the same nationality as either of the first two arbitrators. The third arbitrator shall preside over the tribunal.

If the second arbitrator has not been appointed within the prescribed period, or if the Parties have not reached agreement within the prescribed period on the appointment of the third arbitrator, that arbitrator shall be appointed, at the request of either Party, by the Secretary-General of the Permanent Court of Arbitration, from among persons of international standing not having the nationality of a State which is a Party to this Convention.

The arbitral tribunal shall decide where its headquarters will be located and shall adopt its own rules of procedure.

The award of the arbitral tribunal shall be made by a majority of its members, who may not abstain from voting.

Any Contracting Party which is not a Party to the dispute may intervene in the proceedings with the consent of the arbitral tribunal.

The award of the arbitral tribunal shall be final and binding on all Parties to the dispute and on any Party which intervenes in the proceedings and shall be complied with without delay. The arbitral tribunal shall interpret the award at the request of one of the Parties to the dispute or of any intervening Party.

Unless the arbitral tribunal determines otherwise because of the particular circumstances of the case, the expenses of the tribunal, including the remuneration of its members, shall be borne by the Parties to the dispute in equal shares.

Appendix D

Convention on the Regulation of Antarctic Mineral Resource Activities

Preamble

The States Parties to this Convention, hereinafter referred to as the Parties,

Recalling the provisions of the Antarctic Treaty;

Convinced that the Antarctic Treaty system has proved effective in promoting international harmony in furtherance of the purposes and principles of the Charter of the United Nations, in ensuring the absence of any measures of a military nature and the protection of the Antarctic environment and in promoting freedom of scientific research in Antarctica;

Reaffirming that it is in the interest of all mankind that the Antarctic Treaty area shall continue forever to be used exclusively for peaceful purposes and shall not become the scene or object of international discord;

Noting the possibility that exploitable mineral resources may exist in Antarctica;

Bearing in mind the special legal and political status of Antarctica and the special responsibility of the Antarctic Treaty Consultative Parties to ensure that all activities in Antarctica are consistent with the purposes and principles of the Antarctic Treaty;

Bearing in mind also that a regime for Antarctic mineral resources must be consistent with Article IV of the Antarctic Treaty and in accordance therewith be without prejudice and acceptable to those States which assert rights of or claims to territorial sovereignty in Antarctica, and those States which neither recognise nor assert such rights or claims, including those States which assert a basis of claim to territorial sovereignty in Antarctica;

Noting the unique ecological, scientific and wilderness value of Antarctica and the importance of Antarctica to the global environment;

Recognising that Antarctic mineral resource activities could adversely affect the Antarctic environment or dependent or associated ecosystems;

Believing that the protection of the Antarctic environment and dependent and associated ecosystems must be a basic consideration in decisions taken on possible Antarctic mineral resource activities;

Concerned to ensure that Antarctic mineral resource activities, should they occur, are compatible with scientific investigation in Antarctica and other legitimate uses of Antarctica;

Believing that a regime governing Antarctic mineral resource activities will further strengthen the Antarctic Treaty system;

Convinced that participation in Antarctic mineral resource activities should be open to all States which have an interest in such activities and subscribe to a regime governing them and that the special situation of developing country Parties to the regime should be taken into account.

Believing that the effective regulation of Antarctic mineral resource activities is in the interest of the international community as a whole;

HAVE AGREED as follows:

Chapter I: General Provisions
Article 1. Definitions

For the purposes of this Convention:

1 "Antarctic Treaty" means the Antarctic Treaty done at Washington on 1 December 1959.

2 "Antarctic Treaty Consultative Parties" means the Contracting Parties to the Antarctic Treaty entitled to appoint representatives to participate in the meetings referred to in Article IX of that Treaty.

3 "Antarctic Treaty area" means the area to which the provisions of the Antarctic Treaty apply in accordance with Article VI of that Treaty.

4 "Convention for the Conservation of Antarctic Seals" means the Convention done at London on 1 June 1972.

5 "Convention on the Conservation of Antarctic Marine Living Resources" means the Convention done at Canberra on 20 May 1980.

6 "Mineral resources" means all non-living natural non-renewable resources, including fossil fuels, metallic and non-metallic minerals.

7 "Antarctic mineral resource activities" means prospecting, exploration or development, but does not include scientific research activities within the meaning of Article III of the Antarctic Treaty.

8 "Prospecting" means activities, including logistic support, aimed at identifying areas of mineral resource potential for possible exploration and development, including geological, geo-chemical and geophysical investigations and field observations, the use of remote sensing techniques and collection of surface, seafloor and sub-ice samples. Such activities do not include dredging and excavations, except for the purpose of obtaining small-scale samples, or drilling, except shallow drilling into rock and sediment to depths not exceeding 25 metres, or such other depth as the Commission may determine for particular circumstances.

9 "Exploration" means activities, including logistic support, aimed at identifying and evaluating specific mineral resource occurrences or deposits, including exploratory drilling, dredging and other surface or subsurface excavations required to determine the nature and size of mineral resource deposits and the feasibility of their development, but excluding pilot projects or commercial production.

10 "Development" means activities, including logistic support, which take place following exploration and are aimed at or associated with exploitation of specific mineral resource deposits, including pilot projects, processing, storage and transport activities.

11 "Operator" means:

(a) a Party; or

(b) an agency or instrumentality of a Party; or

(c) a juridical person established under the law of a Party; or

(d) a joint venture consisting exclusively of any combination of any of the foregoing,

which is undertaking Antarctic mineral resource activities and for which there is a Sponsoring State.

12 "Sponsoring State" means the Party with which an Operator has a substantial and genuine link, through being:

(a) in the case of a Party, that Party;

(b) in the case of an agency or instrumentality of a Party, that Party;

(c) in the case of a juridical person other than an agency or instrumentality of a Party, the Party:

    (i)   under whose law that juridical person is established and to whose law it is subject, without prejudice to any other law which might be applicable, and

    (ii) in whose territory the management of that juridical person is located, and

    (iii) to whose effective control that juridical person is subject;

(d) in the case of a joint venture not constituting a juridical person:

    (i)   where the managing member of the joint venture is a Party or an agency or instrumentality of a Party, that Party; or

    (ii) in any other case, where in relation to a Party the managing member of the joint venture satisfies the requirements of subparagraph (c) above, that Party.

13 "Managing member of the joint venture" means that member which the participating members in the joint venture have by agreement designated as having responsibility for central management of the joint venture, including the functions of organising and supervising the activities to be undertaken, and controlling the financial resources involved.

14 "Effective control" means the ability of the Sponsoring State to ensure the availability of substantial resources of the Operator for purposes connected with the implementation of this Convention, through the location of such resources in the territory of the Sponsoring State or otherwise.

15 "Damage to the Antarctic environment or dependent or associated ecosystems" means any impact on the living or non-living components of that environment or those ecosystems, including

harm to atmospheric, marine or terrestrial life, beyond that which is negligible or which has been assessed and judged to be acceptable pursuant to this Convention.

16 "Commission" means the Antarctic Mineral Resources Commission established pursuant to Article 18.

17 "Regulatory Committee" means an Antarctic Mineral Resources Regulatory Committee established pursuant to Article 29.

18 "Advisory Committee" means the Scientific, Technical and Environmental Advisory Committee established pursuant to Article 23.

19 "Special Meeting of Parties" means the Meeting referred to in Article 28.

20 "Arbitral Tribunal" means an Arbitral Tribunal constituted as provided for in the Annex, which forms an integral part of this Convention.

Article 2. Objectives and General Principles

1 This Convention is an integral part of the Antarctic Treaty system, comprising the Antarctic Treaty, the measures in effect under that Treaty, and its associated separate legal instruments, the prime purpose of which is to ensure that Antarctica shall continue forever to be used exclusively for peaceful purposes and shall not become the scene or object of international discord. The Parties provide through this Convention, the principles it establishes, the rules it prescribes, the institutions it creates and the decisions adopted pursuant to it, a means for:

(a) assessing the possible impact on the environment of Antarctic mineral resource activities;

(b) determining whether Antarctic mineral resource activities are acceptable;

(c) governing the conduct of such Antarctic mineral resource activities as may be found acceptable; and

(d) ensuring that any Antarctic mineral resource activities are undertaken in strict conformity with this Convention.

2 In implementing this Convention, the Parties shall ensure that Antarctic mineral resource activities, should they occur, take place in a manner consistent with all the components of the Antarctic Treaty system and the obligations flowing therefrom.

3 In relation to Antarctic mineral resource activities, should they occur, the Parties acknowledge the special responsibility of the

Antarctic Treaty Consultative Parties for the protection of the environment and the need to:

(a) protect the Antarctic environment and dependent and associated ecosystems;
(b) respect Antarctica's significance for, and influence on, the global environment;
(c) respect other legitimate uses of Antarctica;
(d) respect Antarctica's scientific value and aesthetic and wilderness qualities;
(e) ensure the safety of operations in Antarctica;
(f) promote opportunities for fair and effective participation of all Parties; and
(g) take into account the interests of the international community as a whole.

Article 3. Prohibition of Antarctic Mineral Resource Activities Outside this Convention

No Antarctic mineral resource activities shall be conducted except in accordance with this Convention and measures in effect pursuant to it and, in the case of exploration or development, with a Management Scheme approved pursuant to Article 48 or 54.

Article 4. Principles Concerning Judgments on Antarctic Mineral Resource Activities

1 Decisions about Antarctic mineral resource activities shall be based upon information adequate to enable informed judgments to be made about their possible impacts and no such activities shall take place unless this information is available for decisions relevant to those activities.

2 No Antarctic mineral resource activity shall take place until it is judged, based upon assessment of its possible impacts on the Antarctic environment and on dependent and on associated ecosystems, that the activity in question would not cause:

(a) significant adverse effects on air and water quality;
(b) significant changes in atmospheric, terrestrial or marine environments;
(c) significant changes in the distribution, abundance or productivity of populations of species of fauna or flora;
(d) further jeopardy to endangered or threatened species or populations of such species; or

(e) degradation of, or substantial risk to, areas of special biological, scientific, historic, aesthetic or wilderness significance.

3 No Antarctic mineral resource activity shall take place until it is judged, based upon assessment of its possible impacts, that the activity in question would not cause significant adverse effects on global or regional climate or weather patterns.

4 No Antarctic mineral resource activity shall take place until it is judged that:

(a) technology and procedures are available to provide for safe operations and compliance with paragraphs 2 and 3 above;

(b) there exists the capacity to monitor key environmental parameters and ecosystem components so as to identify any adverse effects of such activity and to provide for the modification of operating procedures as may be necessary in the light of the results of monitoring or increased knowledge of the Antarctic environment or dependent or associated ecosystems; and

(c) there exists the capacity to respond effectively to accidents, particularly those with potential environmental effects.

5 The judgments referred to in paragraphs 2, 3 and 4 above shall take into account the cumulative impacts of possible Antarctic mineral resource activities both by themselves and in combination with other such activities and other uses of Antarctica.

Article 5. Area of Application

1 This Convention shall, subject to paragraphs 2, 3 and 4 below, apply to the Antarctic Treaty area.

2 Without prejudice to the responsibilities of the Antarctic Treaty Consultative Parties under the Antarctic Treaty and measures pursuant to it, the Parties agree that this Convention shall regulate Antarctic mineral resource activities which take place on the continent of Antarctica and all Antarctic islands, including all ice shelves, south of 60° south latitude and in the seabed and subsoil of adjacent offshore areas up to the deep seabed.

3 For the purposes of this Convention "deep seabed" means the seabed and subsoil beyond the geographic extent of the continental shelf as the term continental shelf is defined in accordance with international law.

4 Nothing in this Article shall be construed as limiting the application of other Articles of this Convention in so far as they

relate to possible impacts outside the area referred to in paragraphs 1 and 2 above, including impacts on dependent or on associated ecosystems.

Article 6. Cooperation and International Participation

In the implementation of this Convention cooperation within its framework shall be promoted and encouragement given to international participation in Antarctic mineral resource activities by interested Parties which are Antarctic Treaty Consultative Parties and by other interested Parties, in particular, developing countries in either category. Such participation may be realised through the Parties themselves and their Operators.

Article 7. Compliance with this Convention

1 Each Party shall take appropriate measures within its competence to ensure compliance with this Convention and any measures in effect pursuant to it.

2 If a Party is prevented by the exercise of jurisdiction by another Party from ensuring compliance in accordance with paragraph 1 above, it shall not, to the extent that it is so prevented, bear responsibility for that failure to ensure compliance.

3 If any jurisdictional dispute related to compliance with this Convention or any measure in effect pursuant to it arises between two or more Parties, the Parties concerned shall immediately consult together with a view to reaching a mutually acceptable solution.

4 Each Party shall notify the Executive Secretary, for circulation to all other Parties, of the measures taken pursuant to paragraph 1 above.

5 Each Party shall exert appropriate efforts, consistent with the Charter of the United Nations, to the end that no one engages in any Antarctic mineral resource activities contrary to the objectives and principles of this Convention.

6 Each Party may, whenever it deems it necessary, draw the attention of the Commission to any activity which in its opinion affects the implementation of the objectives and principles of this Convention.

7 The Commission shall draw the attention of all Parties to any activity which, in the opinion of the Commission, affects the implementation of the objectives and principles of this Convention or the compliance by any Party with its obligations under this Convention and any measures in effect pursuant to it.

8 The Commission shall draw the attention of any State which is not a Party to this Convention to any activity undertaken by that State, its agencies or instrumentalities, natural or juridical persons, ships, aircraft or other means of transportation which, in the opinion of the Commission, affects the implementation of the objectives and principles of this Convention. The Commission shall inform all Parties accordingly.

9 Nothing in this Article shall affect the operation of Article 12(7) of this Convention or Article VIII of the Antarctic Treaty.

Article 8. Response Action and Liability

1 An Operator undertaking any Antarctic mineral resource activity shall take necessary and timely response action, including prevention, containment, clean up and removal measures, if the activity results in or threatens to result in damage to the Antarctic environment or dependent or associated ecosystems. The Operator, through its Sponsoring State, shall notify the Executive Secretary, for circulation to the relevant institutions of this Convention and to all Parties, of action taken pursuant to this paragraph.

2 An Operator shall be strictly liable for:

(a) damage to the Antarctic environment or dependent or associated ecosystems arising from its Antarctic mineral resource activities, including payment in the event that there has been no restoration to the status quo ante;

(b) loss of or impairment to an established use, as referred to in Article 15, or loss of or impairment to an established use of dependent or associated ecosystems, arising directly out of damage described in subparagraph (a) above;

(c) loss of or damage to property of a third party or loss of life or personal injury of a third party arising directly out of damage described in subparagraph (a) above; and

(d) reimbursement of reasonable costs by whomsoever incurred relating to necessary response action, including prevention, containment, clean up and removal measures, and action taken to restore the status quo ante where Antarctic mineral resource activities undertaken by that Operator result in or threaten to result in damage to the Antarctic environment or dependent or associated ecosystems.

3(a) Damage of the kind referred to in paragraph 2 above which would not have occurred or continued if the Sponsoring

State had carried out its obligations under this Convention with respect to its Operator shall, in accordance with international law, entail liability of that Sponsoring State. Such liability shall be limited to that portion of liability not satisfied by the Operator or otherwise.

(b) Nothing in subparagraph (a) above shall affect the application of the rules of international law applicable in the event that damage not referred to in that subparagraph would not have occurred or continued if the Sponsoring State had carried out its obligations under this Convention with respect to its Operator.

4 An Operator shall not be liable pursuant to paragraph 2 above if it proves that the damage has been caused directly by, and to the extent that it has been caused directly by:

(a) an event constituting in the circumstances of Antarctica a natural disaster of an exceptional character which could not reasonably have been foreseen; or

(b) armed conflict, should it occur notwithstanding the Antarctic Treaty, or an act of terrorism directed against the activities of the Operator, against which no reasonable precautionary measures could have been effective.

5 Liability of an Operator for any loss of life, personal injury or loss of or damage to property other than that governed by this Article shall be regulated by applicable law and procedures.

6 If an Operator proves that damage has been caused totally or in part by an intentional or grossly negligent act or omission of the party seeking redress, that Operator may be relieved totally or in part from its obligation to pay compensation in respect of the damage suffered by such party.

7(a) Further rules and procedures in respect of the provisions on liability set out in this Article shall be elaborated through a separate Protocol which shall be adopted by consensus by the members of the Commission and shall enter into force according to the procedure provided for in Article 62 for the entry into force of this Convention.

(b) Such rules and procedures shall be designed to enhance the protection of the Antarctic environment and dependent and associated ecosystems.

(c) Such rules and procedures:

(i)   may contain provisions for appropriate limits on liability, where such limits can be justified;

(ii) without prejudice to Article 57, shall prescribe means and mechanisms such as a claims tribunal or other fora by which claims against Operators pursuant to this Article may be assessed and adjudicated;

(iii) shall ensure that a means is provided to assist with immediate response action, and to satisfy liability under paragraph 2 above in the event, *inter alia,* that an Operator liable is financially incapable of meeting its obligation in full, that it exceeds any relevant limits of liability, that there is a defence to liability or that the loss or damage is of undetermined origin. Unless it is determined during the elaboration of the Protocol that there are other effective means of meeting these objectives, the Protocol shall establish a Fund or Funds and make provision in respect of such Fund or Funds, *inter alia,* for the following:

—financing by Operators or on industry wide bases;

—ensuring the permanent liquidity and mandatory supplementation thereof in the event of insufficiency;

—reimbursement of costs of response action, by whomsoever incurred.

8 Nothing in paragraphs 4, 6 and 7 above or in the Protocol adopted pursuant to paragraph 7 shall affect in any way the provisions of paragraph 1 above.

9 No application for an exploration or development permit shall be made until the Protocol provided for in paragraph 7 above is in force for the Party lodging such application.

10 Each Party, pending the entry into force for it of the Protocol provided for in paragraph 7 above, shall ensure, consistently with Article 7 and in accordance with its legal system, that recourse is available in its national courts for adjudicating liability claims pursuant to paragraphs 2, 4 and 6 above against Operators which are engaged in prospecting. Such recourse shall include the adjudication of claims against any Operator it has sponsored. Each Party shall also ensure, in accordance with its legal system, that the Commission has the right to appear as a party in its national courts to pursue relevant liability claims under paragraph 2(a) above.

11 Nothing in this Article or in the Protocol provided for in paragraph 7 above shall be construed as as to:

(a) preclude the application of existing rules on liability, and the development in accordance with international law of further such rules, which may have application to either States or Operators; or

(b) affect the right of an Operator incurring liability pursuant to this Article to seek redress from another party which caused or contributed to the damage in question.

12 When compensation has been paid other than under this Convention liability under this Convention shall be offset by the amount of such payment.

Article 9. Protection of Legal Positions under the Antarctic Treaty

Nothing in this Convention and no acts or activities taking place while this Convention is in force shall:

(a) constitute a basis for asserting, supporting or denying a claim to territorial sovereignty in the Antarctic Treaty area or create any rights of sovereignty in the Antarctic Treaty area;

(b) be interpreted as a renunciation or diminution by any Party of, or as prejudicing, any right or claim or basis of claim to territorial sovereignty in Antarctica or to exercise coastal state jurisdiction under international law;

(c) be interpreted as prejudicing the position of any Party as regards its recognition or non-recognition of any such right, claim or basis of claim; or

(d) affect the provision of Article IV(2) of the Antarctic Treaty that no new claim, or enlargement of an existing claim, to territorial sovereignty in Antarctica shall be asserted while the Antarctic Treaty is in force.

Article 10. Consistency with the other Components of the Antarctic Treaty System

1 Each Party shall ensure that Antarctic mineral resource activities take place in a manner consistent with the components of the Antarctic Treaty system, including the Antarctic Treaty, the Convention for the Conservation of Antarctic Seals and the Convention on the Conservation of Antarctic Marine Living Resources and the measures in effect pursuant to those instruments.

2 The Commission shall consult and cooperate with the Antarctic Treaty Consultative Parties, the Contracting Parties to the Convention for the Conservation of Antarctic Seals, and the Commission for the Conservation of Antarctic Marine Living Resources with a view to ensuring the achievement of the objectives and principles of this Convention and avoiding any interference with the achievement of the objectives and principles of the Antarctic Treaty, the Convention for the Conservation of Antarctic Seals or the Convention on the Conservation of Antarctic Marine Living Resources, or inconsistency between the measures in effect pursuant to those instruments and measures in effect pursuant to this Convention.

Article 11. Inspection under the Antarctic Treaty

All stations, installations and equipment, in the Antarctic Treaty area, relating to Antarctic mineral resource activities, as well as ships and aircraft supporting such activities at points of discharging or embarking cargoes or personnel at such stations and installations, shall be open at all times to inspection by observers designated under Article VII of the Antarctic Treaty for the purposes of that Treaty.

Article 12. Inspection under this Convention

1 In order to promote the objectives and principles and to ensure the observance of this Convention and measures in effect pursuant to it, all stations, installations and equipment relating to Antarctic mineral resource activities in the area in which these activities are regulated by this Convention, as well as ships and aircraft supporting such activities at points of discharging or embarking cargoes or personnel anywhere in that area shall be open at all times to inspection by:
(a) observers designated by any member of the Commission who shall be nationals of that member; and
(b) observers designated by the Commission or relevant Regulatory Committees.

2 Aerial inspection may be carried out at any time over the area in which Antarctic mineral resource activities are regulated by this Convention.

3 The Commission shall maintain an up-to-date list of observers designated pursuant to paragraph 1(a) and (b) above.

4 Reports from the observers shall be transmitted to the Commission and to any Regulatory Committee having competence in the area where the inspection has been carried out.

5 Observers shall avoid interference with the safe and normal operations of stations, installations and equipment visited and shall respect measures adopted by the Commission to protect confidentiality of data and information.

6 Inspections undertaken pursuant to paragraph 1(a) and (b) above shall be compatible and reinforce each other and shall not impose an undue burden on the operation of stations, installations and equipment visited.

7 In order to facilitate the exercise of their functions under this Convention, and without prejudice to the respective positions of the Parties relating to jurisdiction over all other persons in the area in which Antarctic mineral resource activities are regulated by this Convention, observers designated under this Article shall be subject only to the jurisdiction of the Party of which they are nationals in respect of all acts or omissions occurring while they are in that area for the purpose of exercising their functions.

8 No exploration or development shall take place in an area identified pursuant to Article 41 until effective provision has been made for inspection in that area.

Article 13. Protected Areas

1 Antarctic mineral resource activities shall be prohibited in any area designated as a Specially Protected Area or a Site of Special Scientific Interest under Article IX(1) of the Antarctic Treaty. Such activities shall also be prohibited in any other area designated as a protected area in accordance with Article IX(1) of the Antarctic Treaty, except to the extent that the relevant measure provides otherwise. Pending any designation becoming effective in accordance with Article IX(4) of the Antarctic Treaty, no Antarctic mineral resource activities shall take place in any such area which would prejudice the purpose for which it was designated.

2 The Commission shall also prohibit or restrict Antarctic mineral resource activities in any area which, for historic, ecological, environmental, scientific or other reasons, it has designated as a protected area.

3 In exercising its powers under paragraph 2 above or under Article 41 the Commission shall consider whether to restrict or

prohibit Antarctic mineral resource activities in any area, in addition to those referred to in paragraph 1 above, protected or set aside pursuant to provisions of other components of the Antarctic Treaty system, to ensure the purposes for which they are designated.

4 In relation to any area in which Antarctic mineral resource activities are prohibited or restricted in accordance with paragraph 1, 2 or 3 above, the Commission shall consider whether, for the purposes of Article 4(2)(e), it would be prudent, additionally, to prohibit or restrict Antarctic mineral resource activities in adjacent areas for the purpose of creating a buffer zone.

5 The Commission shall give effect to Article 10(2) in acting pursuant to paragraphs 2, 3 and 4 above.

6 The Commission shall, where appropriate, bring any decisions it takes pursuant to this Article to the attention of the Antarctic Treaty Consultative Parties, the Contracting Parties to the Convention for the Conservation of Antarctic Seals, the Commission for the Conservation of Antarctic Marine Living Resources and the Scientific Committee on Antarctic Research.

Article 14. Non-Discrimination

In the implementation of this Convention there shall be no discrimination against any Party or its Operators.

Article 15. Respect for Other Uses of Antarctica

1 Decisions about Antarctic mineral resource activities shall take into account the need to respect other established uses of Antarctica, including:

(a) the operation of stations and their associated installations, support facilities and equipment in Antarctica;

(b) scientific investigation in Antarctica and cooperation therein;

(c) the conservation, including rational use, of Antarctic marine living resources;

(d) tourism;

(e) the preservation of historic monuments; and

(f) navigation and aviation,

that are consistent with the Antarctic Treaty system.

2 Antarctic mineral resource activities shall be conducted so as to respect any uses of Antarctica as referred to in paragraph 1 above.

Article 16. Availability and Confidentiality of Data and Information

Data and information obtained from Antarctic mineral resource activities shall, to the greatest extent practicable and feasible, be made freely available, provided that:

(a) as regards data and information of commercial value deriving from prospecting, they may be retained by the Operator in accordance with Article 37;

(b) as regards data and information deriving from exploration or development, the Commission shall adopt measures relating, as appropriate, to their release and to ensure the confidentiality of data and information of commercial value.

Article 17. Notifications and Provisional Exercise of Functions of the Executive Secretary

1 Where in this Convention there is a reference to the provision of information, a notification or a report to any institution provided for in this Convention and that institution has not been established, the information, notification or report shall be provided to the Executive Secretary who shall circulate it as required.

2 Where in this Convention a function is assigned to the Executive Secretary and no Executive Secretary has been appointed under Article 33, that function shall be performed by the Depositary.

Chapter II: Institutions

Article 18. Commission

1 There is hereby established the Antarctic Mineral Resources Commission.

2 Membership of the Commission shall be as follows:

(a) each Party which was an Antarctic Treaty Consultative Party on the date when this Convention was opened for signature; and

(b) each other Party during such time as it is actively engaged in substantial scientific, technical or environmental research in the area to which this Convention applies directly relevant to decisions about Antarctic mineral resource activities, particularly the assessments and judgments called for in Article 4; and

(c) each other Party sponsoring Antarctic mineral resource exploration or development during such time as the relevant Management Scheme is in force.

3 A Party seeking to participate in the work of the Commission pursuant to subparagraph (b) or (c) above shall notify the Depositary of the basis upon which it seeks to become a member of the Commission. In the case of a Party which is not an Antarctic Treaty Consultative Party, such notification shall include a declaration of intent to abide by recommendations pursuant to Article IX(1) of the Antarctic Treaty. The Depositary shall communicate to each member of the Commission such notification and accompanying information.

4 The Commission shall consider the notification at its next meeting. In the event that a Party referred to in paragraph 2(b) above submitting a notification pursuant to paragraph 3 above is an Antarctic Treaty Consultative Party, it shall be deemed to have satisfied the requirements for Commission membership unless more than one-third of the members of the Commission object at the meeting at which such notification is considered. Any other Party submitting a notification shall be deemed to have satisfied the requirements for Commission membership if no member of the Commission objects at the meeting at which such notification is considered.

5 Each member of the Commission shall be represented by one representative who may be accompanied by alternate representatives and advisers.

6 Observer status in the Commission shall be open to any Party and to any Contracting Party to the Antarctic Treaty which is not a Party to this Convention.

Article 19. Commission Meetings

1(a) The first meeting of the Commission, held for the purpose of taking organisational, financial and other decisions necessary for the effective functioning of this Convention and its institutions, shall be convened within six months of the entry into force of this Convention.

(b) After the Commission has held the meeting or meetings necessary to take the decisions referred to in subparagraph (a) above, the Commission shall not hold further meetings except in accordance with paragraph 2 or 3 below.

2 Meetings of the Commission shall be held within two months of:

(a) receipt of a notification pursuant to Article 39;

(b) a request by at least six members of the Commission; or

(c) a request by a member of a Regulatory Committee in accordance with Article 49(1).

3 The Commission may establish a regular schedule of meetings if it determines that it is necessary for the effective functioning of this Convention.

4 Unless the Commission decides otherwise, its meetings shall be convened by the Executive Secretary.

Article 20. Commission Procedure

1 The Commission shall elect from among its members a Chairman and two Vice-Chairmen, each of whom shall be a representative of a different Party.

2(a) Until such time as the Commission has established a regular schedule of meetings in accordance with Article 19(3), the Chairman and Vice-Chairmen shall be elected to serve for a period of two years, provided that if no meeting is held during that period they shall continue to serve until the conclusion of the first meeting held thereafter.

 (b) When a regular schedule of meetings has been established, the Chairman and Vice-Chairmen shall be elected to serve for a period of two years.

3 The Commission shall adopt its rules of procedure. Such rules may include provisions concerning the number of terms of office which the Chairman and Vice-Chairmen may serve and for the rotation of such offices.

4 The Commission may establish such subsidiary bodies as are necessary for the performance of its functions.

5 The Commission may decide to establish a permanent headquarters which shall be in New Zealand.

6 The Commission shall have legal personality and shall enjoy in the territory of each Party such legal capacity as may be necessary to perform its functions and achieve the objectives of this Convention.

7 The privileges and immunities to be enjoyed by the Commission, the Secretariat and representatives attending meetings in the territory of a Party shall be determined by agreement between the Commission and the Party concerned.

Article 21. Functions of the Commission

1 The functions of the Commission shall be:

(a) to facilitate and promote the collection and exchange of scientific, technical and other information and research projects necessary to predict, detect and assess the possible environmental impact of Antarctic mineral resource activities, including the monitoring of key environmental parameters and ecosystem components;

(b) to designate areas in which Antarctic mineral resource activities shall be prohibited or restricted in accordance with Article 13, and to perform the related functions assigned to it in that Article;

(c) to adopt measures for the protection of the Antarctic environment and dependent and associated ecosystems and for the promotion of safe and effective exploration and development techniques and, as it may deem appropriate, to make available a handbook of such measures;

(d) to determine, in accordance with Article 41, whether or not to identify an area for possible exploration and development, and to perform the related functions assigned to it in Article 42;

(e) to adopt measures relating to prospecting applicable to all relevant Operators:
  (i) to determine for particular circumstances maximum drilling depths in accordance with Article 1(8);
  (ii) to restrict or prohibit prospecting consistently with Articles 13, 37 and 38;

(f) to ensure the effective application of Articles 12(4), 37(7) and (8), 38(2) and 39(2), which require the submission to the Commission of information, notifications and reports;

(g) to give advance public notice of matters upon which it is requesting the advice of the Advisory Committee;

(h) to adopt measures relating to the availability and confidentiality of data and information, including measures pursuant to Article 16;

(i) to elaborate the principle of non-discrimination set forth in Article 14;

(j) to adopt measures with respect to maximum block sizes;

(k) to perform the functions assigned to it in Article 29;

(l) to review action by Regulatory Committees in accordance with Article 49;

(m) to adopt measures in accordance with Articles 6 and 41(1)(d) related to the promotion of cooperation and to participation in Antarctic mineral resource activities;

(n) to adopt general measures pursuant to Article 51(6);

(o) to take decisions on budgetary matters and adopt financial regulations in accordance with Article 35;

(p) to adopt measures regarding fees payable in connection with notifications submitted pursuant to Articles 37 and 39 and applications lodged pursuant to Articles 44 and 53, the purpose of which fees shall be to cover the administrative costs of handling such notifications and applications;

(q) to adopt measures regarding levies payable by Operators engaged in exploration and development, the principal purpose of which levies shall be to cover the costs of the institutions of this Convention;

(r) to determine in accordance with Article 35(7) the disposition of revenues, if any, accruing to the Commission which are surplus to the requirements for financing the budget pursuant to Article 35;

(s) to perform the functions assigned to it in Article 7(7) and (8);

(t) to perform the functions relating to inspection assigned to it in Article 12;

(u) to consider monitoring reports received pursuant to Article 52;

(v) to perform the functions relating to dispute settlement assigned to it in Article 59;

(w) to perform the functions relating to consultation and cooperation assigned to it in Articles 10(2) and 34;

(x) to keep under review the conduct of Antarctic mineral resource activities with a view to safeguarding the protection of the Antarctic environment in the interest of all mankind; and

(y) to perform such other functions as are provided for elsewhere in this Convention.

2 In performing its functions the Commission shall seek and take full account of the views of the Advisory Committee provided in accordance with Article 26.

3 Each measure adopted by the Commission shall specify the date on which it comes into effect.

4 The Commission shall, subject to Article 16 and measures in effect pursuant to it and paragraph 1(h) above, ensure that a publicly available record of its meetings and decisions and of information, notifications and reports submitted to it is maintained.

Article 22. Decision Making in the Commission

1 The Commission shall take decisions on matters of substance by a three-quarters majority of the members present and voting. When a question arises as to whether a matter is one of substance or not, that matter shall be treated as one of substance unless otherwise decided by a three-quarters majority of the members present and voting.

2 Notwithstanding paragraph 1 above, consensus shall be required for the following:

(a) the adoption of the budget and decisions on budgetary and related matters pursuant to Article 21(1)(p), (q) and (r) and Article 35(1), (2), (3), (4) and (5);

(b) decisions taken pursuant to Article 21(1)(i);

(c) decisions taken pursuant to Article 41(2).

3 Decisions on matters of procedure shall be taken by a simple majority of the members present and voting.

4 Nothing in this Article shall be interpreted as preventing the Commission, in taking decisions on matters of substance, from endeavouring to reach a consensus.

5 For the purposes of this Article, consensus means the absence of a formal objection. If, with respect to any decision covered by paragraph 2(c) above, the Chairman of the Commission determines that there would be such an objection he shall consult the members of the Commission. If, as a result of these consultations, the Chairman determines that an objection would remain, he shall convene those members most directly interested for the purpose of seeking to reconcile the differences and producing a generally acceptable proposal.

Article 23. Advisory Committee

1 There is hereby established the Scientific, Technical and Environmental Advisory Committee.

2 Membership of the Advisory Committee shall be open to all Parties.

3 Each member of the Advisory Committee shall be represented by one representative with suitable scientific, technical or

environmental competence who may be accompanied by alternate representatives and by experts and advisers.

4 Observer status in the Advisory Committee shall be open to any Contracting Party to the Antarctic Treaty or to the Convention on the Conservation of Antarctic Marine Living Resources which is not a Party to this Convention.

Article 24. Advisory Committee Meetings

1 Unless the Commission decides otherwise, the Advisory Committee shall be convened for its first meeting within six months of the first meeting of the Commission. It shall meet thereafter as necessary to fulfil its functions on the basis of a schedule established by the Commission.

2 Meetings of the Advisory Committee, in addition to those scheduled pursuant to paragraph 1 above, shall be convened at the request of at least six members of the Commission or pursuant to Article 40(1).

3 Unless the Commission decides otherwise, the meetings of the Advisory Committee shall be convened by the Executive Secretary.

Article 25. Advisory Committee Procedure

1 The Advisory Committee shall elect from among its members a Chairman and two Vice-Chairmen, each of whom shall be a representative of a different Party.

2(a) Until such time as the Commission has established a schedule of meetings in accordance with Article 24(1), the Chairman and Vice-Chairmen shall be elected to serve for a period of two years, provided that if no meeting is held during that period they shall continue to serve until the conclusion of the first meeting held thereafter.

(b) When a schedule of meetings has been established, the Chairman and Vice-Chairmen shall be elected to serve for a period of two years.

3 The Advisory Committee shall give advance public notice of its meetings and of matters to be considered at each meeting so as to permit the receipt and consideration of views on such matters from international organisations having an interest in them. For this purpose the Advisory Committee may, subject to review by the Commission, establish procedures for the transmission of relevant information to these organisations.

4 The Advisory Committee shall, by a two-thirds majority of the members present and voting, adopt its rules of procedure. Such rules may include provisions concerning the number of terms of office which the Chairman and Vice-Chairmen may serve and for the rotation of such offices. The rules of procedure and any amendments thereto shall be subject to approval by the Commission.

5 The Advisory Committee may establish such subcommittees, subject to budgetary approval, as may be necessary for the performance of its functions.

Article 26. Functions of the Advisory Committee

1 The Advisory Committee shall advise the Commission and Regulatory Committees, as required by this Convention, or as requested by them, on the scientific, technical and environmental aspects of Antarctic mineral resource activities. It shall provide a forum for consultation and cooperation concerning the collection, exchange and evaluation of information related to the scientific, technical and environmental aspects of Antarctic mineral resource activities.

2 It shall provide advice to:

(a) the Commission relating to its functions under Articles 21(1)(a) to (f), (u) and (x) and 35(7)(a) (in matters relating to scientific research) as well as on the implementation if Article 4; and

(b) Regulatory Committees with respect to:
   (i)   the implementation of Article 4;
   (ii) scientific, technical and environmental aspects of Articles 43(3) and (5), 45, 47, 51, 52 and 54;
   (iii) data to be collected and reported in accordance with Articles 47 and 52; and
   (iv) the scientific, technical and environmental implications of reports and reported data provided in accordance with Articles 47 and 52.

3 It shall provide advice to the Commission and to Regulatory Committees on:

(a) criteria in respect of the judgments required under Article 4(2) and (3) for the purposes of Article 4(1);

(b) types of data and information required to carry out its functions, and how they should be collected, reported and archived;

(c) scientific research which would contribute to the base of data and information required in subparagraph (b) above;

(d) effective procedures and systems for data and information analysis, evaluation, presentation and dissemination to facilitate the judgments referred to in Article 4; and

(e) possibilities for scientific, technical and environmental cooperation amongst interested Parties which are developing countries and other Parties.

4 The Advisory Committee, in providing advice on decisions to be taken in accordance with Articles 41, 43, 45 and 54 shall, in each case, undertake a comprehensive environmental and technical assessment of the proposed actions. Such assessments shall be based on all information, and any amplifications thereof, available to the Advisory Committee, including the information provided pursuant to Articles 39(2)(e), 44(2)(b)(iii) and 53(2)(b). The assessments of the Advisory Committee shall, in each case, address the nature and scope of the decisions to be taken and shall include consideration, as appropriate, of, inter alia:

(a) the adequacy of existing information to enable informed judgments to be made;

(b) the nature, extent, duration and intensity of likely direct environmental impacts resulting from the proposed activity;

(c) possible indirect impacts;

(d) means and alternatives by which such direct or indirect impacts might be reduced, including environmental consequences of the alternative of not proceeding;

(e) cumulative impacts of the proposed activity in the light of existing or planned activities;

(f) capacity to respond effectively to accidents with potential environmental effects;

(g) the environmental significance of unavoidable impacts; and

(h) the probabilities of accidents and their environmental consequences.

5 In preparing its advice the Advisory Committee may seek information and advice from other scientists and experts or scientific organisations as may be required on an ad hoc basis.

6 The Advisory Committee shall, with a view to promoting international participation in Antarctic mineral resource activities as provided for in Article 6, provide advice concerning the availability to interested developing country Parties and other Parties,

of the information referred to in paragraph 3 above, of training programmes related to scientific, technical and environmental matters bearing on Antarctic mineral resource activities, and of opportunities for cooperation among Parties in these programmes.

Article 27. Reporting by the Advisory Committee

The Advisory Committee shall present a report on each of its meetings to the Commission and to any relevant Regulatory Committee. The report shall cover all matters considered at the meeting and shall reflect the conclusions reached and all the views expressed by members of the Advisory Committee. The report shall be circulated by the Executive Secretary to all Parties, and to observers attending the meeting, and shall thereupon be made publicly available.

Article 28. Special Meeting of Parties

1 A Special Meeting of Parties shall, as required, be convened in accordance with Article 40(2) and shall have the functions, in relation to the identification of an area for possible exploration and development, specified in Article 40(3).

2 Membership of a Special Meeting of Parties shall be open to all Parties, each of which shall be represented by one representative who may be accompanied by alternate representatives and advisers.

3 Observers status at a Special Meeting of Parties shall be open to any Contracting Party to the Antarctic Treaty which is not a Party to this Convention.

4 Each Special Meeting of Parties shall elect from among its members a Chairman and Vice-Chairmen, each of whom shall serve for the duration of that meeting. The Chairman and Vice-Chairmen shall not be representatives of the same Party.

5 The Special Meeting of Parties shall, by a two-thirds majority of the members present and voting, adopt its rules of procedure. Until such time as this has been done the Special Meeting of Parties shall apply provisional rules of procedure drawn up by the Commission.

6 Unless the Commission decides otherwise, a Special Meeting of Parties shall be convened by the Executive Secretary and shall be held at the same venue as the meeting of the Commission convened to consider the identification of an area for possible exploration and development.

Article 29. Regulatory Committees

1 An Antarctic Mineral Resources Regulatory Committee shall be established for each area identified by the Commission pursuant to Article 41.

2 Subject to paragraph 6 below, each Regulatory Committee shall consist of 10 members. Membership shall be determined by the Commission in accordance with this Article and, taking into account Article 9, shall include:

(a) the member, if any, or if there are more than one, those members of the Commission identified by reference to Article 9(b) which assert rights or claims in the identified area;

(b) the two members of the Commission also identified by reference to Article 9(b) which assert a basis of claim in Antarctica;

(c) other members of the Commission determined in accordance with this Article so that the Regulatory Committee shall, subject to paragraph 6 below, consist, in total, of 10 members:

　(i) four members identified by reference to Article 9(b) which assert rights or claims, including the member or members, if any, referred to in subparagraph (a) above and

　(ii) six members which do not assert rights or claims as described in Article 9(b), including the two members referred to in subparagraph (b) above.

3 Upon the identification of an area in accordance with Article 41(2), the Chairman of the Commission shall, as soon as possible and in any event within 90 days, make a recommendation to the Commission concerning the membership of the Regulatory Committee. To this end the Chairman shall consult, as appropriate, with the Chairman of the Advisory Committee and all members of the Commission. Such recommendation shall comply with the requirements of paragraphs 2 and 4 of this Article and shall ensure:

(a) the inclusion of members of the Commission which, whether through prospecting, scientific research or otherwise, have contributed substantial scientific, technical or environmental information relevant to the identification of the area by the Commission pursuant to Article 41;

(b) adequate and equitable representation of developing country members of the Commission, having regard to the overall balance between developed and developing country members of the Commission, including at least three developing country members of the Commission;

(c) that account is taken of the value of a rotation of membership of Regulatory Committees as a further means of ensuring equitable representation of members of the Commission.

4(a) When there are one or more members of the Regulatory Committee referred to in paragraph 2(a) above, the Chairman of the Commission shall make the recommendation in respect of paragraph 2(c)(i) above upon the nomination, if any, of such member or members which shall take into account paragraph 3 above, in particular subparagraph (b) of that paragraph.

  (b) In making the recommendation in respect of paragraph 2(c)(ii) above, the Chairman of the Commission shall give full weight to the views (which shall take into account paragraph 3 above) which may be presented on behalf of those members of the Commission which do not assert rights of or claims to territorial sovereignty in Antarctica and, with reference to the requirements of paragraph 3(b) above, to the views which may be presented on behalf of the developing countries among them.

5 The recommendation of the Chairman of the Commission shall be deemed to have been approved by the Commission if it does not decide otherwise at the same meeting as the recommendation is submitted. In taking any decision in accordance with this Article the Commission shall ensure that the requirements of paragraphs 2 and 3 above are complied with and that the nomination, if any, referred to in paragraph 4(a) above is given effect.

6(a) If a member of the Commission which has sponsored prospecting in the identified area and submitted the notification pursuant to Article 39 upon which the Commission based its identification of the area pursuant to Article 41, is not a member of the Regulatory Committee by virtue of paragraphs 2 and 3 above, that member of the Commission shall be a member of the Regulatory Committee until such time as an application for an exploration permit is lodged pursuant to Article 44.

  (b) If a Party lodging an application for an exploration permit pursuant to Article 44 is not a member of the Regulatory

Committee by virtue of paragraphs 2 and 3 above, that Party shall be a member of the Regulatory Committee for its consideration of that application. Should such application result in approval of a Management Scheme pursuant to Article 48, the Party in question shall remain a member of the Regulatory Committee during such time as that Management Scheme is in force with the right to take part in decisions on matters affecting that Management Scheme.

7 Nothing in this Article shall be interpreted as affecting Article IV of the Antarctic Treaty.

Article 30. Regulatory Committee Procedure

1 The first meeting of each Regulatory Committee shall be convened by the Executive Secretary in accordance with Article 43(1). Each Regulatory Committee shall meet thereafter when and where necessary to fulfil its functions.

2 Each member of a Regulatory Committee shall be represented by one representative who may be accompanied by alternate representatives and advisers.

3 Each Regulatory Committee shall elect from among its members a Chairman and Vice-Chairman. The Chairman and Vice-Chairman shall not be representatives of the same Party.

4 Any Party may attend meetings of a Regulatory Committee as an observer.

5 Each Regulatory Committee shall adopt its rules of procedure. Such rules may include provisions concerning the period and number of terms of office which the Chairman and Vice-Chairman may serve and for the rotation of such offices.

Article 31. Functions of Regulatory Committees

1 The functions of each Regulatory Committee shall be:

(a) to undertake the preparatory work provided for in Article 43;

(b) to consider applications for exploration and development permits in accordance with Articles 45, 46 and 54;

(c) to approve Management Schemes and issue exploration and development permits in accordance with Articles 47, 48 and 54;

(d) to monitor exploration and development activities in accordance with Article 52;

(e) to perform the functions assigned to it in Article 51;

(f) to perform the functions relating to inspection assigned to it in Article 12;

(g) to perform the functions relating to dispute settlement assigned to it in Article 47(r); and

(h) to perform such other functions as are provided for elsewhere in this Convention.

2 In performing its functions each Regulatory Committee shall seek and take full account of the views of the Advisory Committee provided in accordance with Article 26.

3 Each Regulatory Committee shall, subject to Article 16 and measures in effect pursuant to it and Article 21(1)(h), ensure that a publicly available record of its decisions, and of Management Schemes in force, is maintained.

Article 32. Decision Making in Regulatory Committees

1 Decisions by a Regulatory Committee pursuant to Articles 48 and 54(5) shall be taken by a two-thirds majority of the members present and voting, which majority shall include a simple majority of those members present and voting referred to in Article 29(2)(c)(i) and also a simple majority of those members present and voting referred to in Article 29(2)(c)(ii).

2 Decisions by a Regulatory Committee pursuant to Article 43(3) and (5) shall be taken by a two-thirds majority of the members present and voting, which majority shall include at least half of those members present and voting referred to in Article 29(2)(c)(i) and also at least half of those members present and voting referred to in Article 29(2)(c)(ii).

3 Decisions on all other matters of substance shall be taken by a two-thirds majority of the members present and voting. When a question arises as to whether a matter is one of substance or not, that matter shall be treated as one of substance unless otherwise decided by a two-thirds majority of the members present and voting.

4 Decisions on matters of procedure shall be taken by a simple majority of the members present and voting.

5 Nothing in this Article shall be interpreted as preventing a Regulatory Committee, in taking decisions on matters of substance, from endeavouring to reach a consensus.

Article 33. Secretariat

1 The Commission may establish a Secretariat to serve the Commission, Regulatory Committees, the Advisory Committee, the Special Meeting of Parties and any subsidiary bodies established.

2 The Commission may appoint an Executive Secretary, who shall be the head of the Secretariat, according to such procedures and on such terms and conditions as the Commission may determine. The Executive Secretary shall serve for a four year term and may be reappointed.

3 The Commission may, with due regard to the need for efficiency and economy, authorise such staff establishment for the Secretariat as may be necessary. The Executive Secretary shall appoint, direct and supervise the staff according to such rules and procedures and on such terms and conditions as the Commission may determine.

4 The Secretariat shall perform the functions specified in this Convention and, subject to the approved budget, the tasks entrusted to it by the Commission, Regulatory Committees, the Advisory Committee and the Special Meeting of Parties.

Article 34. Cooperation with International Organisations

1 The Commission and, as appropriate, the Advisory Committee shall cooperate with the Antarctic Treaty Consultative Parties, the Contracting Parties to the Convention for the Conservation of Antarctic Seals, the Commission for the Conservation of Antarctic Marine Living Resources, and the Scientific Committee on Antarctic Research.

2 The Commission shall cooperate with the United Nations, its relevant Specialised Agencies, and, as appropriate, any international organisation which may have competence in respect of mineral resources in areas adjacent to those covered by this Convention.

3 The Commission shall also, as appropriate, cooperate with the International Union for the Conservation of Nature and Natural Resources, and with other relevant international organisations, including non-governmental organisations, having a scientific, technical or environmental interest in Antarctica.

4 The Commission may, as appropriate, accord observer status in the Commission and in the Advisory Committee to such relevant international organisations, including non-governmental organisations, as might assist in the work of the institution in question. Observer status at a Special Meeting of Parties shall be open to such organisations as have been accorded observer status in the Commission or the Advisory Committee.

5 The Commission may enter into agreements with the organisations referred to in this Article.

Article 35. Financial Provisions

1 The Commission shall adopt a budget, on an annual or other appropriate basis, for:

(a) its activities and the activities of Regulatory Committees, the Advisory Committee, the Special Meeting of Parties, any subsidiary bodies established and the Secretariat; and

(b) the progressive reimbursement of any contributions paid under paragraph 5 and 6 below whenever revenues under paragraph 4 below exceed expenditure.

2 The first draft budget shall be submitted by the Depositary at least 90 days before the first meeting of the Commission. At that meeting the Commission shall adopt its first budget and decide upon arrangements for the preparation of subsequent budgets.

3 The Commission shall adopt financial regulations.

4 Subject to paragraph 5 below, the budget shall be financed, *inter alia*, by:

(a) fees prescribed pursuant to Articles 21(1)(p) and 43(2)(b);

(b) levies on Operators, subject to any measures adopted by the Commission in accordance with Article 21(1)(q), pursuant to Article 47(k)(i); and

(c) such other financial payments by Operators pursuant to Article 47(k)(ii) as may be required to be paid to the institutions of this Convention.

5 If the budget is not fully financed by revenues in accordance with paragraph 4 above, and subject to reimbursement in accordance with paragraph 1(b) above, the budget shall, to the extent of any shortfall and subject to paragraph 6 below, be financed by contributions from the members of the Commission. To this end, the Commission shall adopt as soon as possible a method of equitable sharing of contributions to the budget. The budget shall, in the meantime, to the extent of any shortfall, be financed by equal contributions from each member of the Commission.

6 In adopting the method of contributions referred to in paragraph 5 above the Commission shall consider the extent to which members of and observers at institutions of this Convention may be called upon to contribute to the costs of those institutions.

7 The Commission, in determining the disposition of revenues accruing to it, which are surplus to the requirements for financing the budget pursuant to this Article, shall:

(a) promote scientific research in Antarctica, particularly that related to the Antarctic environment and Antarctic resources, and a wide spread of participation in such research by all Parties, in particular developing country Parties;

(b) ensure that the interests of the members of Regulatory Committees having the most direct interest in the matter in relation to the areas in question are respected in any disposition of that surplus.

8 The finances of the Commission, Regulatory Committees, the Advisory Committee, the Special Meeting of Parties, any subsidiary bodies established and the Secretariat shall accord with the financial regulations adopted by the Commission and shall be subject to an annual audit by external auditors selected by the Commission.

9 Each member of the Commission, Regulatory Committees, the Advisory Committtee, the Special Meeting of Parties and any subsidiary bodies established, as well as any observer at a meeting of any of the institutions of this Convention, shall meet its own expenses arising from attendance at meetings.

10 A member of the Commission that fails to pay its contribution for two consecutive years shall not, during the period of its continuing subsequent default, have the right to participate in the taking of decisions in any of the institutions of this Convention. If it continues to be in default for a further two consecutive years, the Commission shall decide what further action should be taken, which may include loss by that member of the right to participate in meetings of the institutions of this Convention. Such member shall resume the full enjoyment of its rights upon payment of the outstanding contributions.

11 Nothing in this Article shall be construed as prejudicing the position of any member of a Regulatory Committee on the outcome of consideration by the Regulatory Committee of terms and conditions in a Management Scheme pursuant to Article 47(k)(ii).

Article 36. Official and Working Languages

The official and working languages of the Commission, Regulatory Committees, the Advisory Committee, the Special Meeting of Parties and any meeting convened under Article 64 shall be English, French, Russian and Spanish.

Chapter III. Prospecting

Article 37. Prospecting

1   Prospecting shall not confer upon any Operator any right to Antarctic mineral resources.

2   Prospecting shall at all times be conducted in compliance with this Convention and with measures in effect pursuant to this Convention, but shall not require authorisation by the institutions of this Convention.

3(a) The Sponsoring State shall ensure that its Operators undertaking prospecting maintain the necessary financial and technical means to comply with Article 8(1), and, to the extent that any such Operator fails to take response action as required in Article 8(1), shall ensure that this is undertaken.

  (b) The Sponsoring State shall also ensure that its Operators undertaking prospecting maintain financial capacity, commensurate with the nature and level of the activity undertaken and the risks involved, to comply with Article 8(2).

4 In cases where more than one Operator is engaged in prospecting in the same general area, the Sponsoring State or States shall ensure that those Operators conduct their activities with due regard to each others' rights.

5 Where an Operator wishes to conduct prospecting in an area identified under Article 41 in which another Operator has been authorised to undertake exploration or development, the Sponsoring State shall ensure that such prospecting is carried out subject to the rights of any authorised Operator and any requirements to protect its rights specified by the relevant Regulatory Committee.

6 Each Operator shall ensure upon cessation of prospecting the removal of all installations and equipment and site rehabilitation. On the request of the Sponsoring State, the Commission may waive the obligation to remove installations and equipment.

7 The Sponsoring State shall notify the Commission at least nine months in advance of the commencement of planned prospecting. The notification shall be accompanied by such fees as may be established by the Commission in accordance with Article 21(1)(p) and shall:

(a) identify, by reference to coordinates of latitude and longitude or identifiable geographic features, the general area in which the prospecting is to take place;

(b) broadly identify the mineral resource or resources which are to be the subject of the prospecting;

(c) describe the prospecting, including the methods to be used, and the general programme of work to be undertaken and its expected duration;

(d) provide an assessment of the possible environmental and other impacts of the prospecting, taking into account possible cumulative impacts as referred to in Article 4(5).

(e) describe the measures, including monitoring programmes, to be adopted to avoid harmful environmental consequences or undue interference with other established uses of Antarctica, and outline the measures to be put into effect in the event of any accident and contingency plans for evacuation in an emergency;

(f) provide details on the Operator and certify that it:
   (i) has a substantial and genuine link with the Sponsoring State as defined in Article 1(12); and
   (ii) is financially and technically qualified to carry out the proposed prospecting in accordance with this Convention; and

(g) provide such further information as may be required by measures adopted by the Commission.

8 The Sponsoring State shall subsequently provide to the Commission:

(a) notification of any changes to the information referred to in paragraph 7 above;

(b) notification of the cessation of prospecting, including removal of any installations and equipment as well as site rehabilitation; and

(c) a general annual report on the prospecting undertaken by the Operator.

9 Notifications and reports submitted pursuant to this Article shall be circulated by the Executive Secretary without delay to all Parties and observers attending Commission meetings.

10 Paragraphs 7, 8 and 9 above shall not be interpreted as requiring the disclosure of data and information of commercial value.

11 The Sponsoring State shall ensure that basic data and information of commercial value generated by prospecting are maintained in archives and may at any time release part of or all such

data and information, on conditions which it shall establish, for scientific or environmental purposes.

12 The Sponsoring State shall ensure that basic data and information, other than interpretative data, generated by prospecting are made readily available when such data and information are not, or are no longer, of commercial value and, in any event, no later than 10 years after the year the data and information were collected, unless it certifies to the Commission that the data and information continue to have commercial value. It shall review at regular intervals whether such data and information may be released and shall report the results of such reviews to the Commission.

13 The Commission may adopt measures consistent with this Article relating to the release of data and information of commercial value including requirements for certifications, the frequency of reviews and maximum time limits for extensions of the protection of such data and information.

Article 38. Consideration of Prospecting
by the Commission

1 If a member of the Commission considers that a notification submitted in accordance with Article 37(7) or (8), or ongoing prospecting, causes concern as to consistency with this Convention or measures in effect pursuant thereto, that member may request the Sponsoring State to provide a clarification. If that member considers that an adequate response is not forthcoming from the Sponsoring State within a reasonable time, the member may request that the Commission be convened in accordance with Article 19(2)(b) to consider the question and take appropriate action.

2 If measures applicable to all relevant Operators are adopted by the Commission following a request made in accordance with paragraph 1 above, Sponsoring States that have submitted notifications in accordance with Article 37(7) or (8), and Sponsoring States whose Operators are conducting prospecting, shall ensure that the plans and activities of their Operators are modified to the extent necessary to conform with those measures within such time limit as the Commission may prescribe, and shall notify the Commission accordingly.

Chapter IV: Exploration

Article 39. Requests for Identification of an Area for Possible Exploration and Development

1 Any Party may submit to the Executive Secretary a notification requesting that the Commission identify an area for possible exploration and development of a particular mineral resource or resources.

2 Any such notification shall be accompanied by such fees as may be established by the Commission in accordance with Article 21(1)(p) and shall contain:

(a) a precise delineation, including coordinates, of the area proposed for identification;

(b) specification of the resource or resources for which the area would be identified and any relevant data and information, excluding data and information of commercial value, concerning that resource or those resources, including a geological description of the proposed area;

(c) a detailed description of the physical and environmental characteristics of the proposed area;

(d) a description of the likely scale of exploration and development for the resource or resources involved in the proposed area and of the methods which could be employed in such exploration and development;

(e) a detailed assessment of the environmental and other impacts of possible exploration and development for the resource or resources involved, taking into account Articles 15 and 26(4); and

(f) such other information as may be required pursuant to measures adopted by the Commission.

3 A notification under paragraph 1 above shall be referred promptly by the Executive Secretary to all Parties and shall be circulated to observers attending the meeting of the Commission to be convened pursuant to Article 19(2)(a).

Article 40. Action by the Advisory Committee and Special Meeting of Parties

1 The Advisory Committee shall meet as soon as possible after the meeting of the Commission convened pursuant to Article 19(2)(a) has commenced. The Advisory Committee shall provide advice to the Commission on the notification submitted pursuant

to Article 39(1). The Commission may prescribe a time limit for the provision of such advice.

2 A Special Meeting of Parties shall meet as soon as possible after circulation of the report of the Advisory Committee and in any event not later than two months after that report has been circulated.

3 The Special Meeting of Parties shall consider whether identification of an area by the Commission in accordance with the request contained in the notification would be consistent with this Convention, and shall report thereon to the Commission as soon as possible and in any event not later than 21 days from the commencement of the meeting.

4 The report of the Special Meeting of Parties to the Commission shall reflect the conclusions reached and all the views expressed by Parties participating in the meeting.

Article 41. Action by the Commission

1 The Commission shall, as soon as possible after receipt of the report of the Special Meeting of Parties, consider whether or not it will identify an area as requested. Taking full account of the views and giving special weight to the conclusions of the Special Meeting of Parties, and taking full account of the views and the conclusions of the Advisory Committee, the Commission shall determine whether such identification would be consistent with this Convention. For this purpose:

(a) the Commission shall ensure that an area to be identified shall be such that, taking into account all factors relevant to such identification, including the physical, geological, environmental and other characteristics of such area, it forms a coherent unit for the purposes of resource management. The Commission shall thus consider whether an area to be identified should include all or part of that which was requested in the notification and, subject to the necessary assessments having been made, adjacent areas not covered by that notification;

(b) the Commission shall consider whether there are, within an area requested or to be identified, any areas in which exploration and development are or should be prohibited or restricted in accordance with Article 13;

(c) the Commission shall specify the mineral resource or resources for which the area would be identified;

(d) the Commission shall give effect to Article 6, by elaborating opportunities for joint ventures or different forms of participation, up to a defined level, including procedures for offering such participation, in possible exploration and development, within the area, by interested Parties which are Antarctic Treaty Consultative Parties and by other interested Parties, in particular, developing countries in either category;

(e) the Commission shall prescribe any additional associated conditions necessary to ensure that an area to be identified is consistent with other provisions of this Convention and may prescribe general guidelines relating to the operational requirements for exploration and development in an area to be identified including measures establishing maximum block sizes and advice concerning related support activities; and

(f) the Commission shall give effect to the requirement in Article 59 to establish additional procedures for the settlement of disputes.

2 After it has completed its consideration in accordance with paragraph 1 above, the Commission shall identify an area for possible exploration and development if there is a consensus of Commission members that such identification is consistent with this Convention.

Article 42. Revision in the Scope of an Identified Area

1 If, after an area has been identified in accordance with Article 41, a Party requests identification of an area, all or part of which is contained within the boundaries of the area already identified but in respect of a mineral resource or resources different from any resource in respect of which the area has already been identified, the request shall be dealt with in accordance with Articles 39, 40 and 41. Should the Commission identify an area in respect of such different mineral resource or resources, it shall have regard, in addition to the requirements of Article 41(1)(a), to the desirability of specifying the boundaries of the area in such a way that it can be assigned to the Regulatory Committee with competence for the area already identified.

2 In the light of increased knowledge bearing on the effective management of the area, and after seeking the views of the Advisory Committee and the relevant Regulatory Committee,

the Commission may amend the boundaries of any area it has identified. In making any such amendment the Commission shall ensure that authorised exploration and development in the area are not adversely affected. Unless there are compelling reasons for doing so, the Commission shall not amend the boundaries of an area it has identified in such a way as to involve a change in the composition of the relevant Regulatory Committee.

Article 43. Preparatory Work by Regulatory Committees

1 As soon as possible after the identification of an area pursuant to Article 41, the relevant Regulatory Committee established in accordance with Article 29 shall be convened.

2 The Regulatory Committee shall:

(a) subject to any measures adopted by the Commission pursuant to Article 21(1)(j) relating to maximum block sizes, divide its area of competence into blocks in respect of which applications for exploration and development may be submitted and make provision for a limit in appropriate circumstances on the number of blocks to be accorded to any Party;

(b) subject to any measures adopted by the Commission pursuant to Article 21(1)(p), establish fees to be paid with any application for an exploration or development permit lodged pursuant to Article 44 or 53;

(c) establish periods within which applications for exploration and development may be lodged, all applications received within each such period being considered as simultaneous;

(d) establish procedures for the handling of applications; and

(e) determine a method of resolving competing applications which are not resolved in accordance with Article 45(4)(a), which method shall, provided that all other requirements of this Convention are satisfied and consistently with measures adopted pursuant to Article 41(1)(d), include priority for the application with the broadest participation among interested Parties which are Antarctic Treaty Consultative Parties, in particular, developing countries in either category.

3 The Regulatory Committee shall adopt guidelines which are consistent with, and which taken together with, the provisions of this Convention and measures of general applicability adopted by the Commission, as well as associated conditions and general guidelines adopted by the Commission when identifying the

area, shall, by addressing the relevant items in Article 47, identify the general requirements for exploration and development in its area of competence.

4 Upon adoption of guidelines under paragraph 3 above the Executive Secretary shall, without delay, inform all members of the Commission of the decisions taken by the Regulatory Committee pursuant to paragraphs 2 and 3 above and shall make them publicly available together with relevant measures, associated conditions and general guidelines adopted by the Commission.

5 The Regulatory Committee may from time to time revise guidelines adopted under paragraph 3 above, taking into account any views of the Commission.

6 In performing its functions under paragraphs 3 and 5 above, the Regulatory Committee shall seek and take full account of the views of the Advisory Committee provided in accordance with Article 26.

Article 44. Application for an Exploration Permit

1 Following completion of the work undertaken pursuant to Article 43, any Party, on behalf of an Operator for which it is the Sponsoring State, may lodge with the Regulatory Committee an application for an exploration permit within the periods established by the Regulatory Committee pursuant to Article 43(2)(c).

2 An application shall be accompanied by the fees established by the Regulatory Committee in accordance with Article 43(2)(b) and shall contain:

(a) a detailed description of the Operator, including its managerial structure, financial composition and resources and technical expertise, and, in the case of an Operator being a joint venture, the inclusion of a detailed description of the degree to which Parties are involved in the Operator through, inter alia, juridical persons with which Parties have substantial and genuine links, so that each component of the joint venture can be easily attributed to a Party or Parties for the purposes of identifying the level of Antarctic mineral resource activities thereof, which description of substantial and genuine links shall include a description of equity sharing;

(b) a detailed description of the proposed exploration activities and a description in as much detail as possible of proposed development activities, including:

    (i)   an identification of the mineral resource or resources and the block to which the application applies;

    (ii) a detailed explanation of how the proposed activities conform with the general requirements referred to in Article 43(3);

    (iii) a detailed assessment of the environmental and other impacts of the proposed activities, taking into account Articles 15 and 26(4); and

    (iv) a description of the capacity to respond effectively to accidents, especially those with potential environmental effects;

(c) a certification by the Sponsoring State of the capacity of the Operator to comply with the general requirements referred to in Article 43(3);

(d) a certification by the Sponsoring State of the technical competence and financial capacity of the Operator and that the Operator has a substantial and genuine link with it as defined in Article 1(12);

(e) a description of the manner in which the application complies with any measures adopted by the Commission pursuant to Article 41(1)(d); and

(f) such further information as may be required by the Regulatory Committee or in measures adopted by the Commission.

Article 45. Examination of Applications

1 The Regulatory Committee shall meet as soon as possible after an application has been lodged pursuant to Article 44, for the purpose of elaborating a Management Scheme. In performing this function it shall:

(a) determine whether the application contains sufficient or adequate information pursuant to Article 44(2). To this end, it may at any time seek further information from the Sponsoring State consistent with Article 44(2);

(b) consider the exploration and development activities proposed in the application, and such elaborations, revisions or adaptations as necessary:

    (i) to ensure their consistency with this Convention as well as measures in effect pursuant thereto and the general requirements referred to in Article 43(3); and

    (ii) to prescribe the specific terms and conditions of a Management Scheme in accordance with Article 47.

2 At any time during the process of consideration described above, the Regulatory Committee may decline the application if it considers that the activities proposed therein cannot be elaborated, revised or adapted to ensure consistency with this Convention as well as measures in effect pursuant thereto and the general requirements referred to in Article 43(3).

3 In performing its functions under this Article, the Regulatory Committee shall seek and take full account of the views of the Advisory Committee. To that end the Regulatory Committee shall refer to the Advisory Committee all parts of the application which are necessary for it to provide advice pursuant to Article 26, together with any other relevant information.

4 If two or more applications meeting the requirements of Article 44(2) are lodged in respect of the same block:

(a) the competing applicants shall be invited by the Regulatory Committee to resolve the competition amongst themselves, by means of their own choice within a prescribed period;

(b) if the competition is not resolved pursuant to subparagraph (a) above it shall be resolved by the Regulatory Committee in accordance with the method determined by it pursuant to Article 43(2)(e).

Article 46. Management Scheme

In performing its functions under Article 45, including the preparation of a Management Scheme, and under Article 54, the Regulatory Committee shall have recourse to the Sponsoring State and the member or members, if any, referred to in Article 29(2)(a) and, as may be required, one or two additional members of the Regulatory Committee.

Article 47. Scope of the Management Scheme

The Management Scheme shall prescribe the specific terms and conditions for exploration and development of the mineral resource or resources concerned within the relevant block. Such terms and conditions shall be consistent with the general requirements referred to in Article 43(3), and shall cover, inter alia:

(a) duration of exploration and development permits;

(b) measures and procedures for the protection of the Antarctic environment and dependent and associated ecosystems, including methods, activities and undertakings by the Operator to minimise environmental risks and damage;

(c) provision for necessary and timely response action, including prevention, containment and clean up and removal measures, for restoration to the status quo ante, and for contingency plans, resources and equipment to enable such action to be taken;

(d) procedures for the implementation of different stages of exploration and development;

(e) performance requirements;

(f) technical and safety specifications, including standards and procedures to ensure safe operations;

(g) monitoring and inspection;

(h) liability;

(i) procedures for the development of mineral deposits which extend outside the area covered by a permit;

(j) resource conservation requirements;

(k) financial obligations of the Operator including:

  (i) levies in accordance with measures adopted pursuant to Article 21(1)(q);

  (ii) payments in the nature of and similar to taxes, royalties or payments in kind;

(l) financial guarantees and insurance;

(m) assignment and relinquishment;

(n) suspension and modification of the Management Scheme, or cancellation of the Management Scheme, exploration or development permit, and the imposition of monetary penalties, in accordance with Article 51;

(o) procedures for agreed modifications;

(p) enforcement of the Management Scheme;

(q) applicable law to the extent necessary;

(r) effective additional procedures for the settlement of disputes;

(s) provisions to avoid and to resolve conflict with other legitimate uses of Antarctica;

(t) data and information collection, reporting and notification requirements;

(u) confidentiality; and

(v) removal of installations and equipment, as well as site rehabilitation.

Article 48. Approval of the Management Scheme

A Management Scheme prepared in accordance with Articles 45, 46 and 47 shall be subject to approval pursuant to Article 32.

Such approval shall constitute authorisation for the issue without delay of an exploration permit by the Regulatory Committee. The exploration permit shall accord exclusive rights to the Operator to explore and, subject to Articles 53 and 54, to develop the mineral resource or resources which are the subject of the Management Scheme exclusively in accordance with the terms and conditions of the Management Scheme.

Article 49. Review

1 Any member of the Commission, or any member of a Regulatory Committee, may within one month of a decision by that Regulatory Committee to approve a Management Scheme or issue a development permit, request that the Commission be convened in accordance with Article 19(2)(b) or (c), as the case may be, to review the decision of the Regulatory Committee for consistency with the decision taken by the Commission to identify the area pursuant to Article 41 and any measures in effect relevant to that decision.

2 The Commission shall complete its consideration within three months of a request made pursuant to paragraph 1 above. In performing its functions the Commission shall not assume the functions of the Regulatory Committee, nor shall it substitute its discretion for that of the Regulatory Committee.

3 Should the Commission determine that a decision to approve a Management Scheme or issue a development permit is inconsistent with the decision taken by the Commission to identify the area pursuant to Article 41 and any measures in effect relevant to that decision, it may request that Regulatory Committee to reconsider its decision.

Article 50. Rights of Authorised Operators

1 No Management Scheme shall be suspended or modified and no Management Scheme, exploration or development permit shall be cancelled without the consent of the Sponsoring State except pursuant to Article 51, or Article 54 or the Management Scheme itself.

2 Each Operator authorised to conduct activities pursuant to a Management Scheme shall exercise its rights with due regard to the rights of other Operators undertaking exploration or development in the same identified area.

Article 51. Suspension, Modification or Cancellation of the Management Scheme and Monetary Penalties

1 If a Regulatory Committee determines that exploration or development authorised pursuant to a Management Scheme has resulted or is about to result in impacts on the Antarctic environment or dependent or associated ecosystems beyond those judged acceptable pursuant to this Convention, it shall suspend the relevant activities and as soon as possible modify the Management Scheme so as to avoid such impacts. If such impacts cannot be avoided by the modification of the Management Scheme, the Regulatory Committee shall suspend it, or cancel it and the exploration or development permit.

2 In performing its functions under paragraph 1 above a Regulatory Committee shall, unless emergency action is required, seek and take into account the views of the Advisory Committee.

3 If a Regulatory Committee determines that an Operator has failed to comply with this Convention or with measures in effect pursuant to it or a Management Scheme applicable to that Operator, the Regulatory Committee may do all or any of the following:

(a) modify the Management Scheme;

(b) suspend the Management Scheme;

(c) cancel the Management Scheme and the exploration or development permit; and

(d) impose a monetary penalty.

4 Sanctions determined pursuant to paragraph 3(a) to (d) above shall be proportionate to the seriousness of the failure to comply.

5 A Regulatory Committee shall cancel a Management Scheme and the exploration or development permit if an Operator ceases to have a substantial and genuine link with the Sponsoring State as defined in Article 1(12).

6 The Commission shall adopt general measures, which may include mitigation, relating to action by Regulatory Committees pursuant to paragraphs 1 and 3 above and, as appropriate, to the consequences of such action. No application pursuant to Article 44 may be lodged until such measures have come into effect.

Article 52. Monitoring in relation to Management Schemes

1 Each Regulatory Committee shall monitor the compliance of Operators with Management Schemes within its area of competence.

2 Each Regulatory Committee, taking into account the advice of the Advisory Committee, shall monitor and assess the effects on the Antarctic environment and on dependent and on associated ecosystems of Antarctic mineral resource activities within its area of competence, particularly by reference to key environmental parameters and ecosystem components.

3 Each Regulatory Committee shall, as appropriate, inform the Commission and the Advisory Committee in a timely fashion of monitoring under this Article.

Chapter 5. Development

Article 53. Application for a Development Permit

1 At any time during the period in which an approved Management Scheme and exploration permit are in force for an Operator, the Sponsoring State may, on behalf of that Operator, lodge with the Regulatory Committee an application for a development permit.

2 An application shall be accompanied by the fees established by the Regulatory Committee in accordance with Article 43(2)(b) and shall contain:

(a) an updated description of the planned development identifying any modifications proposed to the approved Management Scheme and any additional measures to be taken, consequent upon such modifications, to ensure consistency with this Convention, including any measures in effect pursuant thereto and the general requirements referred to in Article 43(3);

(b) a detailed assessment of the environmental and other impacts of the planned development, taking into account Articles 15 and 26(4);

(c) a recertification by the Sponsoring State of the technical competence and financial capacity of the Operator and that the Operator has a substantial and genuine link with it as defined in Article 1(12);

(d) a recertification by the Sponsoring State of the capacity of the Operator to comply with the general requirements referred to in Article 43(3);

(e) updated information in relation to all other matters specified in Article 44(2); and

(f) such further information as may be required by the Regulatory Committee or in measures adopted by the Commission.

Article 54. Examination of Applications and Issue of Development Permits

1 The Regulatory Committee shall meet as soon as possible after an application has been lodged pursuant to Article 53.

2 The Regulatory Committee shall determine whether the application contains sufficient or adequate information pursuant to Article 53(2). In performing this function it may at any time seek further information from the Sponsoring State consistent with Article 53(2).

3 The Regulatory Committee shall consider whether:

(a) the application reveals modifications to the planned development previously envisaged;

(b) the planned development would cause previously unforeseen impacts on the Antarctic environment or dependent or associated ecosystems, either as a result of any modifications referred to in subparagraph (a) above or in the light of increased knowledge.

4 The Regulatory Committee shall consider any modifications to the Management Scheme necessary in the light of paragraph 3 above to ensure that the development activities proposed would be undertaken consistently with this Convention as well as measures in effect pursuant thereto and the general requirements referred to in Article 43(3). However, the financial obligations specified in the approved Management Scheme may not be revised without the consent of the Sponsoring State, unless provided for in the Management Scheme itself.

5 If the Regulatory Committee in accordance with Article 32 approves modifications under paragraph 4 above, or if it does not consider that such modifications are necessary, the Regulatory Committee shall issue without delay a development permit.

6 In performing its functions under this Article, the Regulatory Committee shall seek and take full account of the views of the Advisory Committee. To that end the Regulatory Committee shall refer to the Advisory Committee all parts of the application which are necessary for it to provide advice pursuant to Article 26, together with any other relevant information.

Chapter 6. Disputes Settlement

Article 55. Disputes Between Two or More Parties

Articles 56, 57 and 58 apply to disputes between two or more Parties.

Article 56. Choice of Procedure

1 Each Party, when signing, ratifying, accepting, approving or acceding to this Convention, or at any time thereafter, may choose, by written declaration, one or both of the following means for the settlement of disputes concerning the interpretation or application of this Convention:
(a) the International Court of Justice;
(b) the Arbitral Tribunal.

2 A declaration made under paragraph 1 above shall not affect the operation of Article 57(1), (3), (4) and (5).

3 A Party that has not made a declaration under paragraph 1 above or in respect of which a declaration is no longer in force shall be deemed to have accepted the competence of the Arbitral Tribunal.

4 If the parties to a dispute have accepted the same means for the settlement of a dispute, the dispute may be submitted only to that procedure, unless the parties otherwise agree.

5 If the parties to a dispute have not accepted the same means for the settlement of a dispute, or if they have both accepted both means, the dispute may be submitted only to the Arbitral Tribunal, unless the parties otherwise agree.

6 A declaration made under paragraph 1 above shall remain in force until it expires in accordance with its terms or until 3 months after written notice of revocation has been deposited with the Depositary.

7 A new declaration, a notice of revocation or the expiry of a declaration shall not in any way affect proceedings pending before the International Court of Justice or the Arbitral Tribunal, unless the parties to the dispute otherwise agree.

8 Declarations and notices referred to in this Article shall be deposited with the Depositary who shall transmit copies thereof to all Parties.

Article 57. Procedure for Dispute Settlement

1 If a dispute arises concerning the interpretation or application of this Convention, the parties to the dispute shall, at the request of any one of them, consult among themselves as soon as possible with a view to having the dispute resolved by negotiation, enquiry, mediation, conciliation, arbitration, judicial settlement or other peaceful means of their choice.

2 If the parties to a dispute concerning the interpretation or application of this Convention have not agreed on a means for

resolving it within 12 months of the request for consultation pursuant to paragraph 1 above, the dispute shall be referred, at the request of any party to the dispute, for settlement in accordance with the procedure determined by the operation of Article 56(4) and (5).

3 If a dispute concerning the interpretation or application of this Convention relates to a measure in effect pursuant to this Convention or a Management Scheme and the parties to such a dispute:

(a) have not agreed on a means for resolving the dispute within 6 months of the request for consultation pursuant to paragraph 1 above, the dispute shall be referred, at the request of any party to the dispute, for discussion in the institution which adopted the instrument in question;

(b) have not agreed on a means for resolving the dispute within 12 months of the request for consultation pursuant to paragraph 1 above, the dispute shall be referred for settlement, at the request of any party to the dispute, to the Arbitral Tribunal.

4 The Arbitral Tribunal shall not be competent to decide or otherwise rule upon any matter within the scope of Article 9. In addition, nothing in this Convention shall be interpreted as conferring competence or jurisdiction on the International Court of Justice or any other tribunal established for the purpose of settling disputes between Parties to decide or otherwise rule upon any matter within the scope of Article 9.

5 The Arbitral Tribunal shall not be competent with regard to the exercise by an institution of its discretionary powers in accordance with this Convention; in no case shall the Arbitral Tribunal substitute its discretion for that of an institution. In addition, nothing in this Convention shall be interpreted as conferring competence or jurisdiction on the International Court of Justice or any other tribunal established for the purpose of settling disputes between Parties with regard to the exercise by an institution of its discretionary powers or to substitute its discretion for that of an institution.

Article 58. Exclusion of Categories of Disputes

1 Any Party, when signing, ratifying, accepting, approving or acceding to this Convention, or at any time thereafter, may, by written declaration, exclude the operation of Article 57(2) or (3)

without its consent with respect to a category or categories of disputes specified in the declaration. Such declaration may not cover disputes concerning the interpretation or application of:

(a) any provision of this Convention or of any measure in effect pursuant to it relating to the protection of the Antarctic environment or dependent or associated ecosystems;

(b) Article 7(1);

(c) Article 8;

(d) Article 12;

(e) Article 14;

(f) Article 15; or

(g) Article 37.

2 Nothing in paragraph 1 above or in any declaration made under it shall affect the operation of Article 57(1), (4) and (5).

3 A declaration made under paragraph 1 above shall remain in force until it expires in accordance with its terms or until 3 months after written notice of revocation has been deposited with the Depositary.

4 A new declaration, a notice of revocation or the expiry of a declaration shall not in any way affect proceedings pending before the International Court of Justice or the Arbitral Tribunal, unless the parties to the dispute otherwise agree.

5 Declarations and notices referred to in this Article shall be deposited with the Depositary who shall transmit copies thereof to all Parties.

6 A Party which, by declaration made under paragraph 1 above, has excluded a specific category or categories of disputes from the operation of Article 57(2) or (3) without its consent shall not be entitled to submit any dispute falling within that category or those categories for settlement pursuant to Article 57(2) or (3), as the case may be, without the consent of the other party or parties to the dispute.

Article 59. Additional Dispute Settlement Procedures

1 The Commission, in conjunction with its responsibilities pursuant to Article 41(1), shall establish additional procedures for third-party settlement, by the Arbitral Tribunal or through other similar procedures, of disputes which may arise if it is alleged that a violation of this Convention has occurred by virtue of:

(a) a decision to decline a Management Scheme;

(b) a decision to decline the issue of a development permit; or

(c) a decision to suspend, modify or cancel a Management Scheme or to impose monetary penalties.

2 Such procedures shall:

(a) permit, as appropriate, Parties and Operators under their sponsorship, but not both in respect of any particular dispute, to initiate proceedings against a Regulatory Committee;

(b) require disputes to which they relate to be referred in the first instance to the relevant Regulatory Committee for consideration;

(c) incorporate the rules in Article 57(4) and (5).

Chapter VII. Final Clauses

Article 60. Signature

This Convention shall be open for signature at Wellington from 25 November 1988 to 25 November 1989 by States which participated in the final session of the Fourth Special Antarctic Treaty Consultative Meeting.

Article 61. Ratification, Acceptance, Approval or Accession

1 This Convention is subject to ratification, acceptance or approval by Signatory States.

2 After 25 November 1989 this Convention shall be open for accession by any State which is a Contracting Party to the Antarctic Treaty.

3 Instruments of ratification, acceptance, approval or accession shall be deposited with the Government of New Zealand, hereby designated as the Depositary.

Article 62. Entry Into Force

1 This Convention shall enter into force on the thirtieth day following the date of deposit of instruments of ratification, acceptance, approval or accession by 16 Antarctic Treaty Consultative Parties which participated as such in the final session of the Fourth Special Antarctic Treaty Consultative Meeting, provided that number includes all the States necessary in order to establish all of the institutions of the Convention in respect of every area of Antarctica, including 5 developing countries and 11 developed countries.

2 For each State which, subsequent to the date of entry into force of this Convention, deposits an instrument of ratification, acceptance, approval or accession, the Convention shall enter into force on the thirtieth day following such deposit.

Article 63. Reservations, Declarations and Statements

1 Reservations to this Convention shall not be permitted. This does not preclude a State, when signing, ratifying, accepting, approving or acceding to this Convention, from making declarations or statements, however phrased or named, with a view, *inter alia,* to the harmonisation of its laws and regulations with this Convention, provided that such declarations or statements do not purport to exclude or to modify the legal effect of this Convention in its application to that State.

2 The provisions of this Article are without prejudice to the right to make written declarations in accordance with Article 58.

Article 64. Amendment

1 This Convention shall not be subject to amendment until after the expiry of 10 years from the date of its entry into force. Thereafter, any Party may, by written communication addressed to the Depositary, propose a specific amendment to this Convention and request the convening of a meeting to consider such proposed amendment.

2 The Depositary shall circulate such communication to all Parties. If within 12 months of the date of circulation of the communication at least one-third of the Parties reply favourably to the request, the Depositary shall convene the meeting.

3 The adoption of an amendment considered at such a meeting shall require the affirmative votes of two-thirds of the Parties present and voting, including the concurrent votes of the members of the Commission attending the meeting.

4 The adoption of any amendment relating to the Special Meeting of Parties or to the Advisory Committee shall require the affirmative votes of three-quarters of the Parties present and voting, including the concurrent votes of the members of the Commission attending the meeting.

5 An amendment shall enter into force for those Parties having deposited instruments of ratification, acceptance or approval thereof 30 days after the Depositary has received such instruments of ratification, acceptance or approval from all the members of the Commission.

6 Such amendment shall thereafter enter into force for any other Party 30 days after the Depositary has received its instrument of ratification, acceptance or approval thereof.

7 An amendment that has entered into force pursuant to this Article shall be without prejudice to the provisions of any Management Scheme approved before the date on which the amendment entered into force.

Article 65. Withdrawal

1 Any Party may withdraw from this Convention by giving to the Depositary notice in writing of its intention to withdraw. Withdrawal shall take effect two years after the date of receipt of such notice by the Depositary.

2 Any Party which ceases to be a Contracting Party to the Antarctic Treaty shall be deemed to have withdrawn from this Convention on the date that it ceases to be a Contracting Party to the Antarctic Treaty.

3 Where an amendment has entered into force pursuant to Article 64(5), any Party from which no instrument of ratification, acceptance or approval of the amendment has been received by the Depositary within a period of two years from the date of the entry into force of the amendment shall be deemed to have withdrawn from this Convention on the date of the expiration of a further two year period.

4 Subject to paragraphs 5 and 6 below, the rights and obligations of any Operators pursuant to this Convention shall cease at the time its Sponsoring State withdraws or is deemed to have withdrawn from this Convention.

5 Such Sponsoring State shall ensure that the obligations of its Operators have been discharged no later than the date on which its withdrawal takes effect.

6 Withdrawal from this Convention by any Party shall not affect its financial or other obligations under this Convention pending on the date withdrawal takes effect. Any dispute settlement procedure in which that Party is involved and which has been commenced prior to that date shall continue to its conclusion unless agreed otherwise by the parties to the dispute.

Article 66. Notifications by the Depositary

The Depositary shall notify all Contracting Parties to the Antarctic Treaty of the following:

(a) signatures of this Convention and the deposit of instruments of ratification, acceptance, approval or accession;
(b) the deposit of instruments of ratification, acceptance or approval of any amendment adopted pursuant to Article 64;
(c) the date of entry into force of this Convention and of any amendment thereto;
(d) the deposit of declarations and notices pursuant to Articles 56 and 58;
(e) notifications pursuant to Article 18; and
(f) the withdrawal of a Party pursuant to Article 65.

Article 67. Authentic Texts, Certified Copies and Registration with the United Nations

1 This Convention of which the Chinese, English, French, Russian and Spanish texts are equally authentic shall be deposited with the Government of New Zealand which shall transmit duly certified copies thereof to all Signatory and Acceding States.

2 The Depositary shall also transmit duly certified copies to all Signatory and Acceding States of the text of this Convention in any additional language of a Signatory or Acceding State which submits such text to the Depositary.

3 This Convention shall be registered by the Depositary pursuant to Article 102 of the Charter of the United Nations.

Done at Wellington this second day of June 1988.
In witness whereof, the undersigned, duly authorised, have signed this Convention.

ANNEX FOR AN ARBITRAL TRIBUNAL

Article 1

The Arbitral Tribunal shall be constituted and shall function in accordance with this Convention, including this Annex.

Article 2

1 Each Party shall be entitled to designate up to three Arbitrators, at least one of whom shall be designated within three months of the entry into force of this Convention for that Party. Each Arbitrator shall be experienced in Antarctic affairs, with knowledge of international law and enjoying the highest reputation for fairness, competence and integrity. The names of the

persons so designated shall constitute the list of Arbitrators. Each Party shall at all times maintain the name of at least one Arbitrator on the list.

2 Subject to paragraph 3 below, an Arbitrator designated by a Party shall remain on the list for a period of five years and shall be eligible for redesignation by that Party for additional five year periods.

3 An Arbitrator may by notice given to the Party which designated that person withdraw his name from the list. If an Arbitrator dies or gives notice of withdrawal of his name from the list or if a Party for any reason withdraws from the list the name of an Arbitrator designated by it, the Party which designated the Arbitrator in question shall notify the Executive Secretary promptly. An Arbitrator whose name is withdrawn from the list shall continue to serve on any Arbitral Tribunal to which that Arbitrator has been appointed until the completion of proceedings before the Arbitral Tribunal.

4 The Executive Secretary shall ensure that an up-to-date list is maintained of the Arbitrators designated pursuant to this Article.

Article 3

1 The Arbitral Tribunal shall be composed of three Arbitrators who shall be appointed as follows:

(a) The party to the dispute commencing the proceedings shall appoint one Arbitrator, who may be its national, from the list referred to in Article 2 of this Annex. This appointment shall be included in the notification referred to in Article 4 of this Annex.

(b) Within 40 days of the receipt of that notification, the other party to the dispute shall appoint the second Arbitrator, who may be its national, from the list referred to in Article 2 of this Annex.

(c) Within 60 days of the appointment of the second Arbitrator, the parties to the dispute shall appoint by agreement the third Arbitrator from the list referred to in Article 2 of this Annex. The third Arbitrator shall not be either a national of, or a person designated by, a party to the dispute, or of the same nationality as either of the first two Arbitrators. The third Arbitrator shall be the Chairman of the Arbitral Tribunal.

(d) If the second Arbitrator has not been appointed within the prescribed period, or if the parties to the dispute have not

reached agreement within the prescribed period on the appointment of the third Arbitrator, the Arbitrator or Arbitrators shall be
appointed, at the request of any party to the dispute and within
30 days of the receipt of such request, by the President of the
International Court of Justice from the list referred to in Article 2
of this Annex and subject to the conditions prescribed in sub-
paragraphs (b) and (c) above. In performing the functions
accorded him in this subparagraph, the President of the Court
shall consult the parties to the dispute and the Chairman of the
Commission.

(e) If the President of the International Court of Justice is unable
to perform the functions accorded him in subparagraph (d) above
or is a national of a party to the dispute, the functions shall be
performed by the Vice-President of the Court, except that if the
Vice-President is unable to perform the functions or is a national
of a party to the dispute the functions shall be performed by the
next most senior member of the Court who is available and is
not a national of a party to the dispute.

2 Any vacancy shall be filled in the manner prescribed for the
initial appointment.

3 In disputes involving more than two Parties, those Parties having the same interest shall appoint one Arbitrator by agreement
within the period specified in paragraph 1(b) above.

Article 4

The party to the dispute commencing proceeding shall so notify
the other party or parties to the dispute and the Executive Secretary in writing. Such notification shall include a statement of the
claim and the grounds on which it is based. The notification
shall be transmitted by the Executive Secretary to all Parties.

Article 5

1 Unless the parties to the dispute agree otherwise, arbitration
shall take place at the headquarters of the Commission, where
the records of the Arbitral Tribunal shall be kept. The Arbitral
Tribunal shall adopt its own rules of procedure. Such rules shall
ensure that each party to the dispute has a full opportunity to be
heard and to present its case and shall also ensure that the proceedings are conducted expeditiously.

2 The Arbitral Tribunal may hear and decide counter-claims
arising out of the dispute.

Article 6

1 The Arbitral Tribunal, where it considers that prima facie it has jurisdiction under this Convention, may:

(a) at the request of any party to a dispute, indicate such provisional measures as it considers necessary to preserve the respective rights of the parties to the dispute;

(b) prescribe any provisional measures which it considers appropriate under the circumstances to prevent serious harm to the Antarctic environment or dependent or associated ecosystems.

2 The parties to a dispute shall comply promptly with any provisional measures prescribed under paragraph 1(b) above pending an award under Article 9 of this Annex.

3 Notwithstanding Article 57(1), (2) and (3) of this Convention, a party to any dispute that may arise falling within the categories specified in Article 58(1)(a) to (g) of this Convention may at any time, by notification to the other party or parties to the dispute and to the Executive Secretary in accordance with Article 4 of this Annex, request that the Arbitral Tribunal be constituted as a matter of exceptional urgency to indicate or prescribe emergency provisional measures in accordance with this Article. In such case, the Arbitral Tribunal shall be constituted as soon as possible in accordance with Article 3 of this Annex, except that the time periods in Article 3(1)(b), (c) and (d) shall be reduced to 14 days in each case. The Arbitral Tribunal shall decide upon the request for emergency provisional measures within two months of the appointment of its Chairman.

4 Following a decision by the Arbitral Tribunal upon a request for emergency provisional measures in accordance with paragraph 3 above, settlement of the dispute shall proceed in accordance with Articles 56 and 57 of this Convention.

Article 7

Any Party which believes it has a legal interest, whether general or individual, which may be substantially affected by the award of an Arbitral Tribunal, may, unless the Arbitral Tribunal decides otherwise, intervene in the proceedings.

Article 8

The parties to the dispute shall facilitate the work of the Arbitral Tribunal and, in particular, in accordance with their law and using all means at their disposal, shall provide it with all relevant documents and information, and enable it, when necessary, to call witnesses or experts and receive their evidence.

Article 9
If one of the parties to the dispute does not appear before the Arbitral Tribunal or fails to defend its case, any other party to the dispute may request the Arbitral Tribunal to continue the proceedings and make its award.

Article 10
1 The Arbitral Tribunal shall decide, on the basis of this Convention and other rules of law not incompatible with it, such disputes as are submitted to it.
2 The Arbitral Tribunal may decide, *ex aequo et bono*, a dispute submitted to it, if the parties to the dispute so agree.

Article 11
1 Before making its award, the Arbitral Tribunal shall satisfy itself that it has competence in respect of the dispute and that the claim or counterclaim is well founded in fact and law.
2 The award shall be accompanied by a statement of reasons for the decision and shall be communicated to the Executive Secretary who shall transmit it to all Parties.
3 The award shall be final and binding on the parties to the dispute and on any Party which intervened in the proceedings and shall be complied with without delay. The Arbitral Tribunal shall interpret the award at the request of a party to the dispute or of any intervening Party.
4 The award shall have no binding force except in respect of that particular case.
5 Unless the Arbitral Tribunal decides otherwise, the expenses of the Arbitral Tribunal, including the remuneration of the Arbitrators, shall be borne by the parties to the dispute in equal shares.

Article 12
All decisions of the Arbitral Tribunal, including those referred to in Articles 5, 6 and 11 of this Annex, shall be made by a majority of the Arbitrators who may not abstain from voting.

Notes

Chapter 1

1. Argentina and Chile reject the notion that Antarctica was *terra nullius* (nobody's land) prior to its discovery for reasons discussed below. Philip W. Quigg, *A Pole Apart: The Emerging Issue of Antarctica* (New York: McGraw-Hill Book Company, 1983), p. 114.
2. Peter J. Beck, *The International Politics of Antarctica* (New York: St. Martin's Press, 1986), p. 122.
3. C. Hartley Grattan, *The Southwest Pacific to 1900: A Modern History* (Ann Arbor: The University of Michigan Press, 1963), pp. 223-7.
4. Peter J. Beck, "British Antarctic Policy in the Early 20th Century," *Polar Record*, Vol. 21, No. 134, 1983, pp. 476-7.
5. Ibid., p. 480; and Report of the Committee Appointed by the Imperial Conference 1926 to Consider British Policy in the Antarctic, 19 November 1926, in W. M. Bush, ed., *Antarctica and International Law: A Collection of Interstate and National Documents* (London: Oceana Publications, Inc., 1982), ii, 100ff (hereinafter cited as *AIL*).
6. Order in Council ... Providing for the Government of the Ross Dependency, 30 July 1923, in *AIL*, iii, pp. 44-45.
7. Order in Council Placing Certain Territory in the Antarctic Seas under the Authority of the Commonwealth of Australia, 7 February 1933, and the Australian Antarctic Acceptance Act, 13 June 1933, in *AIL*, ii, pp. 142-3, 146-7.
8. French Note to United Kingdom, 16 April 1912; and Decree Attaching French Antarctic Territories to the Government General of Madagascar, 21 November 1924, in *AIL*, ii, pp. 481-2, 494.

9. Quigg, *A Pole Apart*, p. 112; and Deborah Shapley, *The Seventh Continent: Antarctica in the Resource Age* (Washington, DC: Resources for the Future, Inc., 1985), p. 73.

10. Decree Defining the Limits of Adelie Land, 1 April 1938, in *AIL*, ii, pp. 505-6.

11. Royal proclamations of 23 January 1928, 1 May 1931, and 14 January 1939, in *AIL*, iii, pp. 115-6. 134-5. Also, "Norway in the Antarctic," *News of Norway*, Vol. 41, No. 7, 18 May 1984, pp. 39-40.

12. Decree No. 1,747, 6 November 1940, in *AIL*, ii, pp. 310-11.

13. Speech by Chilean Minister for Foreign Affairs, 21 January 1947, in *AIL*, ii, pp. 334ff.

14. Ibid.

15. Ibid.; and Luis H. Mericq, *Antarctica: Chile's Claim* (Washington, DC: National Defense University Press, 1987), pp. 89-97.

16. Argentine Foreign Minister to Chilean Ambassador, Buenos Aires, 12 November 1940, and Argentine Foreign Minister to British Ambassador, Buenos Aires, 15 February 1947, in *AIL*, i, pp. 608, 634.

17. Ibid.

18. Ibid.

19. International legal scholars have analyzed the basis and validity of each nation's claim in exhaustive detail. See especially F. M. Auburn, *Antarctic Law and Politics* (Bloomington: Indiana University Press, 1982), chapters ii and iii; Beck, *The International Politics of Antarctica*, chapter vi; and Quigg, *A Pole Apart*, chapter iv.

20. British Ambassador, Buenos Aires, to Argentine Foreign Minister, 17 December 1947; British Ambassador, Santiago, to Chilean Foreign Minister, 17 December 1947; Argentine Ministry of Foreign Affairs and Public Worship to the British Embassy, Buenos Aires, 4 May 1955, in *AIL*, i, p. 644; ii, pp. 7, 372.

21. Argentine Foreign Minister to British Ambassador, Buenos Aires, 28 January 1948; Chilean Foreign Minister to British Ambassador, Santiago, 31 January 1948, in *AIL*, i, 649, ii, p. 377.

22. Argentine Ambassador, The Hague, to the Registrar of the International Court of Justice, 1 August 1955, in *AIL*, ii, p. 10.

23. British Embassy, Paris, to French Foreign Ministry, 25 October 1938, and French Foreign Ministry to British Embassy, Paris, 25 October 1938, in *AIL*, ii, pp. 508-9.

24. Notes to the Antarctic Treaty in *AIL*, i, p. 58.

25. Auburn, *Antarctic Law and Politics*, pp. 56-7; Joint Declaration of Argentina and Chile Concerning the South American Antarctic, 12 July 1947, and 4 March 1948, in *AIL*, i, pp. 639-40, 661.

26. Kenneth J. Bertrand, *Americans in Antarctica, 1775-1948* (New York: American Geographical Society, 1971), p. 16; and Beck, *The International Politics of Antarctica*, p. 32.

27. Ibid, pp. 33-4. Tripartite Naval Declarations between Argentina, Chile, and the United Kingdom, 18 Jan 1949, in *AIL*, i, p. 674.

28. British Counsellor, Buenos Aires, to Argentine Foreign Minister, 3 February 1952, and Argentine Foreign Minister to British Ambassador, Buenos Aires, 27 February 1952, in *AIL*, i, pp. 690-2. Also, Beck, *The International Politics of Antarctica*, p. 35.

29. British Ambassador, Buenos Aires, to Argentine Acting Foreign Minister, 16 February 1953, in *AIL*, i, pp. 695-6.

30. Argentine Foreign Minister to British Ambassador, Buenos Aires, 27 February 1952, in *AIL*, i, p. 692.

31. Paper Prepared by the Policy Planning Staff, US Department of State, PPS-31, 9 June 1948, in US Department of State, *Foreign Relations of the United States*, 1948 (Washington, DC: US Government Printing Office, 1975), Vol. 1, Pt. 2, p. 981 (hereinafter cited as *FRUS*). The National Security Council subsequently circulated PPS-31 as NSC-21.

32. A detailed account of American participation in Antarctic exploration is provided in Bertrand, *Americans in Antarctica*. On the *Belgica* expedition, see *Belgica: Le Premier Hivernage dans l'Antarctique, 1897-1899* (Antwerp: Musee National de Marine, 1988).

33. Secretary of State to the Norwegian Minister, 2 April 1924, in *FRUS*, 1924, ii, p. 519.

34. British Ambassador to the Secretary of State, 29 January 1934, and Secretary of State to the British Ambassador, 14 November 1934, in *FRUS*, i, pp. 1010-3.

35. US Ambassador, Paris, to French Minister for Foreign Affairs, 26 May 1939, in *AIL*, ii, pp. 513-4.

36. Department of State Policy and Information Statement, 27 January 1947, in *FRUS*, 1947, i, p. 1049.

37. Ibid, p. 1049.

38. Department of State Policy Statement, 1 July 1951, in *FRUS*, 1951, i, p. 1729.

39. British Ambassador to the Secretary of State, 29 January 1934, in *FRUS*, 1934, i, pp. 1010-1; Shapley, *The Seventh Continent*, p. 43-6.

40. Department of State Policy and Information Statement, 27 January 1947, in *FRUS*, 1947, i, p. 1047.

41. Roosevelt to Byrd, 25 November 1939, reproduced in Bertrand, *Americans in Antarctica*, pp. 472-4.

42. Paper Prepared by the Department of State, undated [c. August 1948], in *FRUS*, 1948, i, p. 1001.

43. Department of State Policy and Information Statement, 27 January 1947, and Secretary of State to the Embassy in the United Kingdom, 30 January 1947, in *FRUS*, 1947, i, pp. 1050, 1056.

44. Memorandum of Conversation with the Chilean Ambassador, 26 March 1948, in *FRUS*, 1948, i, p. 970.

45. Secretary of State to the Embassy in the United Kingdom, 8 September 1947, in *FRUS*, 1947, i, p. 1051.

46. PPS-31, 9 June 1948, in *FRUS*, 1948, i, p. 981.

47. Ibid, p. 985. Ambassador in the United Kingdom to the Secretary of State, 9 July 1948; Draft Agreement Prepared by the Department of State, undated [c. July 1948]; Ambassador in Chile to the Secretary of State, 19 July 1948; Ambassador in Buenos Aires to the Secretary of State, 21 July 1948, in *FRUS*, 1948, i, pp. 993, 995, 998.

48. NSC 5424, 28 June 1954, in *FRUS*, 1952-1954, i, p. 1754.

49. Secretary of Defense to the Secretary of State, 12 April 1948, in *FRUS*, 1948, i, pp. 971-3.

50. Acting Secretary of State to the British Ambassador, 13 April 1948, in *FRUS*, 1948, i, p. 974.

51. PPS-31, 9 June 1948, in *FRUS*, 1948, i, p. 979.

52. Lisle A. Rose, *Assault on Eternity: Richard E. Byrd and the Exploration of Antarctica, 1946-47* (Annapolis, Md.: Naval Institute Press, 1980), pp. 41, 47, 252; and Bertrand, *Americans in Antarctica*, pp. 484-8, 534-5.

53. Secretary of Defense to the Secretary of State, 12 April 1948, in *FRUS*, 1948, i, p. 973.

54. *FRUS*, 1949, i, p. 794n. For a non-Soviet account of Bellingshausen's voyage, see Grattan, *The Southwest Pacific to 1900*, pp. 227-30.

55. Embassy of the Soviet Union to the Department of State, 9 June 1950, in *FRUS*, 1950, i, pp. 911-3.

56. PPS-31, 9 June 1948, in *FRUS*, 1948, i, p. 980; Department of State Policy Statement, 1 July 1951, in *FRUS*, 1951, i, p. 1729.

57. NSC 5424, 28 June 1954, in *FRUS*, 1954, p. 1743ff.

58. Memorandum of Discussion of the 206th Meeting of the National Security Council (NSC), 15 July 1954, in *FRUS*, 1954, i, pp. 1758-9.

59. NSC 5424/1, 16 July 1954, in *FRUS*, 1954, i, p. 1761.

60. Auburn, *Antarctic Law and Politics*, p. 93.

61. Walter Sullivan, *Assault on the Unknown: The International Geophysical Year* (New York: McGraw-Hill Book Company, Inc., 1961), pp. 20-27; US Congress, House, Committee on Interstate and Foreign Commerce, *International Geophysical Year, The Arctic, Antarctica*, Report No. 1348, 85th Cong., 2d Sess. (Washington, DC: US Government Printing Office, 1958), pp. 10-12.

62. See documents on the First International Geophysical Year Antarctic Conference, Paris, 6 and 10 July 1955, in *AIL*, i, pp. 500-2; US Congress, House, Committee on Foreign Affairs, *The Political Legacy of the International Geophysical Year*, Committee Print (Washington, DC: US Government Printing Office, 1973), p. 56.

63. Sullivan, *Assault on the Unknown*, p. 294.

64. Beck, *The International Politics of Antarctica*, p. 48; Shapley, *The Seventh Continent*, p. 84.

65. US Congress, House, Committee on Interstate and Foreign Commerce, *International Geophysical Year, The Arctic, Antarctica*, pp. 16-17.

66. Ibid., pp. 126-8.

67. Shapley, *The Seventh Continent*, pp. 63-64.

68. US Congress, House, Committee on Interstate and Foreign Commerce, *International Geophysical Year, The Arctic, Antarctica*, p. 18; and Sullivan, *Assault on the Unknown*, pp. 291, 325-31.

69. Quigg, *A Pole Apart*, p. 142; Shapley, *The Seventh Continent*, p. 90; and Beck, *The International Politics of Antarctica*, pp. 50-51.

70. US Congress, House, Committee on Interstate and Foreign Commerce, *International Geophysical Year, The Arctic, Antarctica*, pp. 44-45.

71. Ibid., p. 18; and Shapley, *The Seventh Continent*, p. 84.

72. Auburn, *Antarctic Law and Politics*, p. 90.

73. Indian Explanatory Memoranda, 16 October 1956 and 15 July 1958, in *AIL*, i, pp. 505-6, 509-10.

74. Text of US Note of 2 May 1958, in US Congress, Senate, Committee on Foreign Relations, *The Antarctic Treaty*, 86th Cong., 2d sess. (Washington, DC: US Government Printing Office, 1960), pp. 13-15.

75. Statement by the President Concerning Antarctica, 3 May 1958, in US President, *The Public Papers of the President of the United States, Dwight D. Eisenhower, 1958* (Washington, DC: US Government Printing Office, 1959), p. 367. (*Public Papers of the President* hereinafter cited as *PPP*.)

76. Text of United States Note of 2 May 1958.

77. Ibid.

78. Ibid.

79. Quigg, *A Pole Apart*, pp. 143-5.

80. Ibid., pp. 145-6; and Peter J. Beck, "Preparatory Meetings for the Antarctic Treaty, 1958-59," *Polar Record*, Vol. 22, No. 141, September 1985, pp. 653-63.

81. Ibid.

82. Statement by Sir Harold Caccia, 1 December 1959, in US Department of State, *Conference on Antarctica* (Washington, DC: US Government Printing Office, 1960), p. 54.

Chapter 2

1. John Heap, ed., *Handbook of the Antarctic Treaty System*, 6th ed. (Cambridge, England: Polar Publications, April 1989), p. xii (hereinafter cited as *ATS Handbook*). For a discussion of the objections some scholars make to the use of the term "system" in this context, see Beck, *The International Politics of Antarctica*, pp. 149-50.

2. Article XII(1), The Antarctic Treaty, in *AIL*, i, p. 46ff.

3. J. Peter A. Bernhardt, "Sovereignty in Antarctica," reprinted in US Congress, Senate, Committee on Foreign Relations,

U.S. Antarctic Policy, Hearings, 94th Cong., 1st sess. (Washington, DC: US Government Printing Office, 1975), pp. 91-2.

4. Beck, *The International Politics of Antarctica*, p. 166.

5. Article XII(2), The Antarctic Treaty.

6. Article VI, The Antarctic Treaty; and Report by the Secretary of State to the President on the Antarctic Treaty and the Final Act of the Conference, 4 February 1960, in US Department of State, *The Conference on Antarctica*, p. 72.

7. Notes to Article VI, The Antarctic Treaty in *AIL*, i, p. 66.

8. US Congress, Senate, Committee on Foreign Relations, *The Antarctic Treaty*, p. 66.

9. George A. Knox, "The Living Resources of the Southern Ocean," in Francisco Orrega Vicuna, ed., *Antarctic Resources Policy: Scientific, Legal and Political Issues* (Cambridge, England: Cambridge University Press, 1983), pp. 23-4; and Quigg, *A Pole Apart*, p. 37.

10. Beck, "Preparatory Meetings for the Antarctic Treaty," pp. 658-9.

11. Articles I and V, The Antarctic Treaty.

12. Auburn, *Antarctic Law and Politics*, p. 138.

13. Article I(2), The Antarctic Treaty.

14. US Department of the Navy, Naval Support Force Antarctica, *Operation Deep Freeze 87 End of Season Report*, 11 May 1987, on file in the Division of Polar Programs, National Science Foundation, Washington, DC.

15. Beck, *International Politics of Antarctica*, pp. 71-72; and Jack Child, "South American Geopolitics and Antarctica: Confrontation or Cooperation?" in Phillip Kelly and Jack Child, eds., *Geopolitics of the Southern Cone and Antarctica* (Boulder, Colo.: Lynne Rienner Publishers, 1988), p. 198.

16. Article VII, The Antarctic Treaty.

17. Beck, *International Politics of Antarctica*, pp. 74-79, 105-6.

18. US Department of State, *1985 United States Antarctic Observer Team Report*, no date, pp. 2-4, on file in the Division of Polar Programs, National Science Foundation, Washington, DC; and US Arms Control and Disarmament Agency, *Report of the United States Antarctic Inspection, 1989*, dated October 1989.

19. Article IV, The Antarctic Treaty.

20. Auburn, *Antarctic Law and Politics*, p. 110.

21. R. Tucker Scully, "The Antarctic System: Overview and Analysis," and commentary by William R. Mansfield in Lewis M. Alexander and Lynne Carter Hanson, eds., *Antarctic Politics and Marine Resources: Critical Choices for the 1980s* (Kingston: University of Rhode Island, 1984), pp. 4-5, 23-24; and Gillian Triggs, "The Antarctic Treaty Regime: A Workable Compromise or a 'Purgatory of Ambiguity'?", *Case Western Reserve Journal of International Law*, Vol. 17, No. 2, Spring 1985, pp. 199-201.

22. Article III, The Antarctic Treaty.

23. Notes to Article IX, The Antarctic Treaty, in *AIL*, i, pp. 82-83.

24. Article IX, The Antarctic Treaty.

25. Article XIII, The Antarctic Treaty.

26. Article IX(2), The Antarctic Treaty.

27. Ibid.; US National Science Foundation, *United States Antarctic Research Program Information*, No. 4, 11 December 1986; and "*L'Antarctique: Le Retour du Grand Sud*," *Le Vif/ L'Express* (Brussels), 19 May 1989, p. 47.

28. Notes to Article VIII, The Antarctic Treaty, in *AIL*, i, pp. 76-77.

29. Article VIII, The Antarctic Treaty.

30. Auburn, *Antarctic Law and Politics*, chapter vi; Quigg, *A Pole Apart*, pp. 150-2.

31. Article XI, The Antarctic Treaty.

32. Article X, The Antarctic Treaty.

33. Auburn, *Antarctic Law and Politics*, p. 113.

34. Shapley, *The Seventh Continent*, pp. 91, 100.

35. Article IX, The Antarctic Treaty.

36. Recommendation I-XIV, in *AIL*, i, p. 128. The approved recommendations of the consultative meetings are designated by two numbers: The first is the meeting number, always written as a Roman numeral; the second is the recommendation number for that meeting. For the first three meetings, Roman numerals were used for the second number; thereafter, Arabic numerals are used.

37. Rule 2, Rules of Procedure, in *AIL*, i, p. 116.

38. Secretary of State to American Embassy, Paris, 25 October 1989, Subject: 15th Antarctic Treaty Consultative Meeting (ATCM XV), 9-21 October, Paris, France (unclassified message provided at the author's request).

39. Rule 7, Rules of Procedure, in *AIL*, i, p. 116.

40. Report of the VIIth ATCM, in *AIL*, i, p. 268.

41. Beck, *International Politics of Antarctica*, p. 172.

42. Auburn, *Antarctic Law and Politics*, p. 159.

43. Report of the IXth ATCM, in *AIL*, i, p. 342.

44. Report of the XIIIth ATCM, in *ATS Handbook*, p. 1409.

45. Secretary of State to American Embassy, Brasilia, 23 October 1987, Subject: 14th Antarctic Treaty Consultative Meeting (ATCM XIV), 5-16 October, Rio de Janeiro, Brazil.

46. Recommendation XIII-15, in *ATS Handbook*, p. 1406.

47. Rules 25-28, Revised Rules of Procedure, September 1983, in *ATS Handbook*, Annex D.

48. Secretary of State to American Embassy, Brasilia, 23 October 1987; and Secretary of State to American Embassy, Paris, 25 October 1989.

49. Article IX, The Antarctic Treaty.

50. Rule 23, Rules of Procedure, in *AIL*, i, p. 117.

51. Jeffrey D. Myhre, *The Antarctic Treaty System: Politics, Law, and Diplomacy* (Boulder, Colo.: Westview Press, 1986), p. 42.

52. Beck, *International Politics of Antarctica*, p. 133.

53. Auburn, *Antarctic Law and Politics*, pp. 161-2.

54. Secretary of State to American Embassy, Brasilia, 23 October 1987.

55. Sullivan, *Assault on the Unknown*, pp. 412-3.

56. SCAR Constitution, in *AIL*, i, p. 5ff.

57. Recommendations I-I and I-IV, in *AIL*, i, pp. 121-2.

58. Myhre, *The Antarctic Treaty System*, p. 83.

59. Recommendation IV-24 and subsequent note, in *AIL*, i, pp. 192-3.

60. Final Report of the First Special Antarctic Treaty Consultative Meeting, 29 July 1977, in *AIL*, i, p. 331.

61. *ATS Handbook*, pp. 3205, 3308.

62. Recommendation XIV-5, on file in the Division of Polar Programs, National Science Foundation, Washington, DC.

63. Recommendation VI-4, in *AIL*, i, p. 236.

64. Knox, "The Living Resources of the Southern Ocean," pp. 27, 32-3, 49.

65. Recommendation I-VIII, in *AIL*, i, p. 124.

66. Recommendation III-VIII, in *AIL*, i, p. 146ff.

67. *ATS Handbook*, p. 2418. At the 15th consultative meeting in Paris, one Specially Protected Area (Cape Shirreff) was redesignated as a Site of Special Scientific Interest.

68. US National Science Foundation, *Antarctic Journal of the United States*, Vol. 25, No. 1, March 1990, p. 18.

69. Quigg, *A Pole Apart*, p. 159.

70. Recommendation VI-4, in *AIL*, i, p. 236.

71. Recommendation VIII-11, in *AIL*, i, p. 324ff.

72. Secretary of State to American Embassy, Brasilia, 23 October 1987; Secretary of State to American Embassy, Paris, 25 October 1989; Lee Kimball, *Report on Antarctica* (New York: World Resources Institute, November 1989), pp. 1-3, 12-16; and Australia Department of Foreign Affairs and Trade, Fact Sheet on Australia, "Australia and the Antarctic Environment," April 1990.

73. Knox, "The Living Resources of the Southern Ocean," p. 37.

74. T. Oritsland, "Sealing and Seal Research in the South-west Atlantic Pack Ice, September-October 1964" in M.W. Holdgate, *Antarctic Ecology* (London: Academic Press, 1970), p. 367; and Beck, *International Politics of Antarctica*, p. 220.

75. Recommendation III-VIII, in *AIL*, i, p. 146ff.

76. British Statement on the Relationship of the Proposed Convention for the Conservation of Antarctic Seals with the Antarctic Treaty Regime, 3 February 1972, in *AIL*, i, p. 247.

77. Recommendation III-11, in *AIL*, i, p. 144.

78. Recommendation IV-21, in *AIL*, i, pp. 190-1.

79. Report of the VIth ATCM, in *AIL*, i, p. 227.

80. Convention on the Conservation of Antarctic Seals, with notes, in *AIL*, i, p. 248ff.

81. Ibid.

82. Ibid.

83. Lee Kimball, *Report on Antarctica* (Washington, DC: International Institute for Environment and Development, December 1987), p. 27; and Barbara Mitchell, "Undermining Antarctica," *Technology Review*, Vol. 91, No. 2, February/March 1988, p. 53.

84. Knox, "The Living Resources of the Southern Ocean," p. 21.

85. Barbara Mitchell and Jon Tinker, *Antarctica and Its Resources* (London: Earthscan, 1979), pp. 38ff; Shapley, *The Seventh Continent*, p. 122; and Peter J. Beck, "A New Polar Factor in International Relations," *World Today*, Vol. 45, No. 4, April 1989, p. 66.

86. Knox, "The Living Resources of the Southern Ocean," p. 36.

87. Ibid., pp. 48ff.

88. Recommendation VIII-10, in *AIL*, i, pp. 323-4.

89. Takesi Nagata, "The Implementation of the Convention on the Conservation of Antarctic Marine Living Resources: Needs and Problems," in Vicuña, ed., *Antarctic Resources Policy*, pp. 128-9; and "Australia's Participation in SIBEX-1 Cancelled," *Australian Foreign Affairs Record*, Vol. 55, No. 2, February 1984, pp. 98-99.

90. Recommendation IX-2, in *AIL*, i, pp. 348-51.

91. *ATS Handbook*, p. 3201.

92. Beck, *International Politics of Antarctica*, pp. 225-6; and Quigg, *A Pole Apart*, pp. 189-191.

93. Articles III and V, Convention on the Conservation of Antarctic Marine Living Resources, in *AIL*, i, p. 398ff.

94. *ATS Handbook*, p. 3218; also, Kimball, *Report on Antarctica* (December 1987), p. 15.

95. Article I, Convention on the Conservation of Antarctic Marine Living Resources.

96. Final Act of the Canberra Conference, in *AIL*, i, pp. 391-4.

97. Article IV, Convention on the Conservation of Antarctic Marine Living Resources. (See also notes to Article IV.2(b) in *AIL*, pp. 405-6.)

98. Articles VII-XVII, Ibid.

99. Shapley, *The Seventh Continent*, p. 151.

100. US National Science Foundation, *Antarctic Journal of the United States*, Vol. 25, No. 1, March 1990, p. 19.

101. Mitchell, "Undermining Antarctica," p. 53.

102. Kimball, *Report on Antarctica* (December 1987), p. 17.

103. John D. Negroponte, "The Success of the Antarctic Treaty," *Department of State Bulletin*, Vol. 87, No. 2123, June 1987, p. 29.

104. *ATS Handbook*, p. xii.

105. Mitchell, "Undermining Antarctica," p. 52.

106. Statement of James Barnes, 24 September 1984, in US Congress, Senate, Committee on Commerce, Science and Transportation, *Antarctica*, Hearings, 98th Cong., 2nd sess.

(Washington, DC: US Government Printing Office, 1984), p. 62.

107. Kimball, *Report on Antarctica* (December 1987), pp. 16, 18.

Chapter 3

1. Yves-Joseph de Kerguelen-Tremarec quoted in Quigg, *A Pole Apart*, p. 7.

2. Statement of Dr. Laurence Gould, 14 June 1960, in US Congress, Senate, Committee on Foreign Relations, *The Antarctic Treaty*, p. 75.

3. The countries include Argentina, Australia, Chile, and France. See *AIL*, ii, pp. 71, 204, 448, and 586-9.

4. N. A. Wright and P. L. Williams, eds., *Mineral Resources of Antarctica*, Geological Survey Circular 705 (Washington, DC: US Government Printing Office, 1974), pp. 1, 6; James H. Zumberge, "Mineral Resources and Geopolitics in Antarctica," *American Scientist*, Vol. 67, No. 1, January-February 1979, p. 72; and Stephan A. Zorn, "Antarctic Minerals: A Common Heritage Approach," *Resources Policy*, Vol. 10, No. 1, March 1984, p. 3.

5. John C. Behrendt, "Are There Petroleum Resources in Antarctica?" in John C. Behrendt, ed., *Petroleum and Mineral Resources of Antarctica*, Geological Survey Circular 909 (Washington, DC: US Government Printing Office, 1983), p. 4.

6. Ibid., p. 9.

7. Ibid., pp. 17-18.

8. Barbara Mitchell, "Undermining Antarctica," p. 54.

9. Peter D. Rowley, Paul L. Williams, and Douglas E. Pride, "Mineral Occurrences in Antarctica," in Behrendt, ed., *Petroleum and Mineral Resources of Antarctica*, pp. 29ff.

10. Letter to the Editor from Charles D. Masters, US Geological Survey, 12 March 1975, reprinted in US, Congress, Senate, Committee on Foreign Relations, *U.S. Antarctic Policy*, p. 34.

11. Quoted in Zumberge, "Mineral Resources and Geopolitics in Antarctica," p. 74.

12. Ibid., p. 72.

13. Rowley, et al., "Mineral Occurrences in Antarctica," p. 26.

14. Zumberge, "Mineral Resources and Geopolitics in Antarctica," pp. 72, 74.

15. Mitchell and Tinker, *Antarctica and Its Resources*, p. 30. For a description of technology and procedures that might be used in Antarctic oil operations, see also K. R. Croasdale, ''Arctic Offshore Technology and Its Relevance to the Antarctic,'' in Polar Research Board, National Research Council, *Antarctic Treaty System: An Assessment* (Washington, DC: National Academy Press, 1986), pp. 245ff, and US Congress, Office of Technology Assessment, *Polar Prospects: A Minerals Treaty for Antarctica*, OTA-O-428 (Washington, DC: US Government Printing Office, September 1989), pp. 165-8.

16. Rowley, et al., ''Mineral Occurrences in Antarctica,'' p. 26.

17. Behrendt, ''Are There Petroleum Resources in Antarctica?'' p.3; and US Congress, Office of Technology Assessment, *Polar Prospects*, p. 4.

18. Statement of Dixy Lee Ray, 15 May 1975, in US Congress, Senate, Committee on Foreign Relations, *U.S. Antarctic Policy*, pp. 5-6.

19. Testimony of R. Tucker Scully, 1 May 1979, in US Congress, House of Representatives, Committee on Science and Technology, *U.S. Antarctic Policy*, p. 38.

20. Ibid., p. 33.

21. Recommendation VIII-14, reproduced in *ATS Handbook*, p. 3303.

22. Ibid.

23. Report of the Group of Experts on Mineral Exploration and Exploitation, September 1977, in *ATS Handbook*, pp. 3335ff; and Report of the Group of Ecological, Technical, and Other Related Experts on Mineral Exploration and Exploitation in Antarctica, June 1979, in ibid., pp. 3349ff.

24. Recommendation XI-1.

25. *ATS Handbook*, p. 3301; and Christopher D. Beeby, ''The Antarctic Treaty System as a Resource Management Mechanism,'' in Polar Research Board, *Antarctic Treaty System: An Assessment*, p. 274.

26. Testimony of R. Tucker Scully, 1 May 1979, in US Congress, House of Representatives, Committee on Science and Technology, *U.S. Antarctic Policy*, p. 34.

27. A more extensive elaboration of this point is provided in William E. Westermeyer, *The Politics of Mineral Resource Development in Antarctica: Alternative Regimes for the Future* (Boulder, Colo.: Westview Press, 1984), p. 34.

28. Report of the Group of Experts on Mineral Exploration and Exploitation, September 1977, in *ATS Handbook*, pp. 3335ff; and Mitchell and Tinker, *Antarctica and Its Resources*, pp. 31, 34.

29. Ibid., pp. 36-37.

30. Quoted in *International Herald Tribune*, 9 January 1989, p. 2.

31. Statement of James N. Barnes, 24 September 1984, in US Congress, Senate, Committee on Commerce, Science, and Transportation, *Antarctica*, p. 68; and Kimball, *Report on Antarctica* (November 1989), p. 1.

32. Recommendation XI-1.

33. After 1983, the consultative parties permitted representatives from the other Antarctic Treaty nations to attend negotiating sessions as observers. Thirteen acceding states took part in the final session. See, Final Report of the Fourth Special Antarctic Consultative Meeting on Antarctic Mineral Resources, AMR/SCM/88/79, Antarctic Treaty Special Consultative Meeting on Antarctic Mineral Resources, Wellington, New Zealand, 2 June 1988.

34. Articles 60 and 62, Convention on the Regulation of Antarctic Mineral Resource Activities, Antarctic Treaty Special Consultative Meeting on Antarctic Mineral Resources, Wellington, New Zealand, 2 June 1988, in *ATS Handbook,* pp. 3311ff.

35. Final Act of the Fourth Special Antarctic Consultative Meeting on Antarctic Mineral Resources, Wellington, New Zealand, 2 June 1988, in *ATS Handbook,* pp. 3309-10.

36. Article 1, Convention on the Regulation of Antarctic Mineral Resource Activities.

37. Final Act of the Fourth Special Antarctic Consultative Meeting on Antarctic Mineral Resources. The 1989 consultative meeting did in fact address this issue, recommending that no commercial exploitation of Antarctic ice take place prior to further study by the consultative parties. Kimball, *Report on Antarctica* (November 1989), p. 6.

38. Article 1, Convention on the Regulation of Antarctic Mineral Resource Activities.

39. Ibid., Article 18.

40. Ibid., Articles 20 and 33.

41. Ibid., Articles 23-28.

42. Ibid., Article 29.

43. Ibid., Articles 31 and 43.

44. Ibid., Article 47.

45. Lee A. Kimball, *Antarctic Minerals Convention* (Washington, DC: International Institute for Environment and Development-North America, July 1988), pp. 2-3; Beck, "A New Polar Factor in International Relations," p. 67; and Australia Department of Foreign Affairs and Trade, Fact Sheet on Australia, "Australia and the Antarctic Environment," April 1990.

46. Article 8, Convention on the Regulation of Antarctic Mineral Resource Activities.

47. For more detailed analyses of the new minerals convention, especially the various "accommodations" its negotiators had to make in achieving consensus, see Kimball, *Antarctic Minerals Convention*; R. Tucker Scully and Lee A. Kimball, "Antarctica: Is There Life After Minerals?" in *Marine Policy*, Vol. 13, No. 2, April 1989, pp. 87ff; and US Congress, Office of Technology Assessment, *Polar Prospects*, chap. iii.

48. Article 41, Convention on the Regulation of Antarctic Mineral Resource Activities.

49. Ibid., Article 35.

50. Ibid., Article 9.

51. Ibid., Article 5.

52. Final Act of the Fourth Special Antarctic Consultative Meeting on Antarctic Mineral Resources.

53. Article 12, Convention on the Regulation of Antarctic Mineral Resource Activities.

54. Ibid., Article 32.

55. Ibid., Article 22.

56. Paper Presented by the Policy Planning Staff, PPS-31, 9 June 1948, in *FRUS*, 1948, i, p. 981.

57. Quigg, *A Pole Apart*, p. 165.

58. Indian Explanatory Memorandum, 16 October 1956 and 15 July 1958, in *AIL*, i, pp. 505-6, 509-10.

59. Beck, *The International Politics of Antarctica*, p. 272.

60. Quigg, *A Pole Apart*, p. 167.

61. Beck, *The International Politics of Antarctica*, p. 276.

62. Ibid., p. 274.

63. Rosen, Steven J. and Walter S. Jones, *The Logic of International Relations*, 2nd. ed. (Cambridge, Mass.: Winthrop Publishers, Inc., 1977), pp. 355-6.

64. Many discussions of the "common heritage" principle have been held, particularly as it relates (or does not relate) to

Antarctica. See, for example, S. Z. Qasim and H. P. Rajan, "The Antarctic Treaty System from the Perspective of a New Member," in Polar Research Board, *Antarctic Treaty System: An Assessment*, pp. 368-9.

65. M. J. Peterson, "Antarctic Implications of the New Law of the Sea," *Ocean Development and International Law*, Vol. 16, No. 2, 1986, pp. 162-3.

66. Quoted in Beck, *The International Politics of Antarctica*, p. 279.

67. Quoted in ibid., p. 280.

68. Ibid., p. 281.

69. UN General Assembly, 37th Session, A/57/PV. 10, 1 October 1982.

70. Final Communique, Meeting of Ministers and Heads of Delegations of the Non-Aligned Countries to the 38th Session of the UN General Assembly, in UN General Assembly, 38th Session, A/38/495, 12 October 1983; and UN General Assembly, 38th Session, A/38/646, 12 December 1983.

71. UN General Assembly, 39th Session, Question of Antarctica, Report of the Secretary-General, A/39/583/Part I, 31 October 1984; and UN General Assembly, 38th Session, A/38/PV. 20, 6 October 1983 and A/38/PV. 31, 15 October 1983.

72. See, for example, Letter from the Permanent Representative of Australia to the UN to the Secretary General, in UN General Assembly, 38th Session, A/38/439 Rev. 1, 10 October 1983; and UN General Assembly, 39th Session, Question of Antarctica, Report of the Secretary-General, A/39/583/Part I, 31 October 1984.

73. Richard A. Woolcott, "The Interaction between the Antarctic Treaty System and the United Nations System," in Polar Research Board, *Antarctic Treaty System: An Assessment*, p. 390.

74. UN General Assembly, 38th Session, A/38/PV. 17, 4 October 1983.

75. UN General Assembly, 38th Session, A/C.1/38/L.80, 28 November 1983, and A/38/PV.97, 25 December 1983.

76. UN General Assembly, 39th Session, A/C.1/39/L.83, 30 November 1984.

77. "First Committee Reviews Question of Antarctica for Third Time," *UN Chronicle*, Vol. 23, No. 2, February 1986, p. 66; also Peter J. Beck, "Antarctica at the United Nations, 1985: The End

of Consensus?'' *Polar Record*, Vol. 23, No. 143, 1986, pp. 159-66.

78. UN General Assembly, 41st Session, A/RES/41/88A-C; and ''U.N. Members Seek Role in Antarctic Treaty,'' *The Washington Post*, 19 November 1987, p. A51.

79. Kimball, *Antarctic Minerals Convention*, pp. 19-20.

80. See, for example, commentary by Christopher C. Joyner, in Alexander and Hanson, eds., *Antarctic Politics and Marine Resources*, p. 33; and US Congress, Office of Technology Assessment, *Polar Prospects*, p. 53.

81. ''The Value of the Antarctic Treaty System,'' *Australian Foreign Affairs Record*, Vol. 55, No. 9, September 1984, p. 907.

82. John D. Negroponte, ''The Success of the Antarctic Treaty,'' p. 30.

83. Ibid.

84. Beck, *The International Politics of Antarctica*, p. 299.

85. Christopher C. Joyner, ''Security Issues and the Law of the Sea: The Southern Ocean,'' *Ocean Development and International Law*, Vol. 15, No. 2, 1985, p. 185.

86. Evan Luard, ''Who Owns the Antarctic?'' *Foreign Affairs*, Vol. 62, No. 5, Summer 1984.

87. Jack Child, *Geopolitics and Conflict in South America: Quarrels Among Neighbors* (New York: Praeger, 1985), pp. 140, 142; and Jack Child, *Antarctica and South American Geopolitics: Frozen Lebensraum*, (New York: Praeger, 1988), chapters iv and v.

88. Ibid.; and Beck, *The International Politics of Antarctica*, p. 129.

89. Mericq, *Antarctica: Chile's Claim*, p. 102.

90. Michael Parfit, ''The Last Continent,'' *Smithsonian*, Vol. 15, No. 8, November 1984, p. 50.

91. Anthony Bergin, ''Recent Developments in Australia's Antarctic Policy,'' *Marine Policy*, Vol. 9, No. 3, July 1985, p. 181.

92. ''Antarctica Under Threat?'' *Australian Foreign Affairs Record*, Vol. 56, No. 9, September 1985, p. 840.

93. Bill Hayden, ''Keeping Tension Out of the Last Continent,'' *Australian Foreign Affairs Record*, Vol. 56, No. 1, January 1985, p. 26.

94. Bergin, "Recent Developments in Australia's Antarctic Policy," p. 187; and "Australia's Participation in SIBEX-1 Cancelled."

95. *The Australian Bicentennial Survey*, January 1988, p. 17.

96. Beck, *The International Politics of Antarctica*, p. 132.

97. Peter J. Beck, "Britain's Antarctic Dimension," *International Affairs*, Vol. 59, No. 3, Summer 1983, pp. 431-2.

98. Ibid.

99. US Congress, Senate, Committee on Commerce, Science, and Transportation, *Antarctica*, pp. 61-2; Mitchell, "Undermining Antarctica," p. 52; Beck, "A New Polar Factor in International Relations," p. 66; and "*L'Antarctique: Le Retour de Grand Sud*," p. 48.

100. Beck, *The International Politics of Antarctica*, p. 132.

101. "Norway in the Antarctic," p. 41.

102. *Stars and Stripes*, 30 November 1989, p. 8.

103. Lawson W. Brigham, "The Soviet Antarctic Program," *Oceanus*, Vol. 31, No. 2, Summer 1988, pp. 89-92; and Shapley, *The Seventh Continent*, p. 202.

104. Child, *Geopolitics and Conflict in South America*, pp. 37, 134-5; Orlando Bonturi, *Brazil and the Vital South Atlantic* (Washington, DC: National Defense University Press, 1988), pp. 15, 43-47; Jefferson Simoes, "Brazilian Antarctic Research Programme," *Polar Record*, Vol. 22, September 1984, pp. 325-6; and Shapley, *The Seventh Continent*, p. 224.

105. Secretary of State to American Embassy, Paris, 25 October 1989.

106. Shapley, *The Seventh Continent*, p. 241.

107. Child, *Geopolitics and Conflict in South America*, p. 131.

Chapter 4

1. Statement by the President Concerning Antarctica, 3 May 1958, in *PPP*, 1958, p. 367.

2. Statement by Dixy Lee Ray, Assistant Secretary of State, 15 May 1975, in US Congress, Senate, Committee on Foreign Relations, *U.S. Antarctic Policy*, p. 5; and statement by R. Tucker Scully, 24 September 1984, in US Congress, Senate, Committee on Commerce, Science, and Transportation, *Antarctica*, p. 2.

3. Major public documents or statements by the presidents on Antarctica include "Statement by the President upon Entry into Force of the Antarctic Treaty," 23 June 1961, in *PPP*, 1961, p. 472 (Kennedy); "Remarks Following a Meeting with Members of the Antarctic Policy Group," 20 May 1965, in *PPP*, 1965, p. 564 (Johnson); White House Press Release, 13 October 1970, reproduced in US Congress, Senate, Committee on Foreign Relations, *U.S. Antarctic Policy*, p. 30 (Nixon); and Presidential Memorandum No. 6646, 5 February 1982, reproduced in US Congress, House of Representatives, Committee on Science and Technology, *Pacific Basin Study Mission*, Report (Washington, DC: US Government Printing Office, 1983), pp. 74-75 (Reagan).

4. For example, Lyndon Johnson in Message to the Congress, 17 February 1967, in *PPP*, 1967, p. 207.

5. Remarks Following a Meeting with the Antarctic Policy Group, 20 May 1965, in *PPP*, 1965, p. 564.

6. White House Press Release, 13 October 1970, reproduced in US Congress, Senate, Committee on Foreign Relations, *U.S. Antarctic Policy*, p. 30.

7. Statement by Dixy Lee Ray, 15 May 1975, pp. 5-6.

8. For example, Statement by R. Tucker Scully, 24 September 1984. See also US Congress, Office of Technology Assessment, *Polar Prospects*, pp. 47ff.

9. Statement by R. Tucker Scully, 24 September 1984.

10. US Office of Management and Budget, "The U.S. Antarctic Program," A Report Submitted by the Office of Management and Budget to the Committees on Appropriation of the US Senate and House of Representatives, May 1983, on file in the Division of Polar Programs, National Science Foundation, Washington, DC.

11. Statement by R. Tucker Scully, 24 September 1984.

12. *ATS Handbook*, p. 2201.

13. *Fortune*, Vol. 118, No. 5, 29 August 1988, pp. 10-11; *International Herald Tribune*, 30 December 1988. p. 9; and Michael Parfit, "The Growth of Antarctic Tourism," *The Washington Post*, 24 January 1988, p. E-4.

14. Ibid.

15. *ATS Handbook*, pp. 2201-8.

16. Statement by R. Tucker Scully, 24 September 1984.

17. US Department of State, Bureau of Public Affairs, *Antarctic Treaty*, October 1987.

18. Presidential Memorandum No. 6646, 5 February 1982.

19. Charles O. Jones summarizes the academic literature on policy networks in *The United States Congress: People, Place, and Policy* (Homewood, Ill.: The Dorsey Press, 1982), pp. 358-65.

20. Note to Statement by the President in Response to a Progress Report by the Antarctic Policy Group, 1 May 1965, in *PPP*, 1965, p. 469.

21. OMB Circular A-51 (revised), 4 August 1971, reproduced in US Congress, Senate Committee on Foreign Relations, *U.S. Antarctic Policy*, pp. 27-28.

22. Ibid.

23. Ibid.

24. Secretary of State to American Embassy, Paris, 25 October 1989.

25. OMB Circular A-51 (revised), 4 August 1971; US Congress, Senate, Committee on Commerce, Science, and Transportation, *National Science Foundation Authorization*, Hearings, 98th Cong., 1st sess. (Washington, DC: US Government Printing Office, 1983), p. 32; and US National Science Foundation, Division of Polar Program, *Facts about the United States Antarctic Program*, July 1986, p. 6.

26. OMB Circular A-51 (revised), 4 August 1971.

27. US National Science Foundation, Division of Polar Programs, *Facts about the United States Antarctic Program*, p. 6.

28. US Congress, Senate, Committee on Commerce, Science, and Transportation, *National Science Foundation Authorization*, p. 32.

29. Statement by John Byrne, Administrator, National Oceanic and Atmospheric Administration (NOAA), 24 September 1984, in US Congress, Senate, Committee on Commerce, Science, and Transportation, *Antarctica*, pp. 41-44; Statement by Susan Soloman, NOAA, 9 March 1987, in US Congress, House of Representatives, Committee on Energy and Commerce, *Ozone Layer Depletion*, Hearings, 100th Cong., 1st. sess. (Washington, DC: US Government Printing Office, 1987), p. 36; and US Congress, Office of Technology Assessment, *Polar Prospects*, p. 27.

30. Statement of Dr. Robert J. Hofman, Marine Mammal Commission, 24 September 1984, in US Congress, Senate,

Committee on Commerce, Science, and Transportation, *Antarctica*, pp. 14-17.

31. John C. Behrendt, ed., *Petroleum and Mineral Resources of Antarctica*, p. 1.

32. Secretary of State to American Embassy, Paris, 25 October 1989.

33. US Office of Management and Budget, *The United States Budget in Brief, Fiscal Year 1988* (Washington, DC: US Government Printing Office, 1989), p. 89.

34. Walter J. Oleszek, *Congressional Procedures and the Policy Process*, 2nd. ed. (Washington, DC: CQ Press, 1984), p. 44.

35. Ibid., p. 45.

36. US Congress, Senate, Committee on Labor and Human Resources, *Authorizing Appropriations for the National Science Foundation, Fiscal Year 1985*, Report No. 98-495, 98th Cong., 2nd sess. (Washington, DC: US Government Printing Office, 1984), p. 9.

37. US Congress, Senate, Committee on Commerce, Science, and Transportation, *National Science Foundation Authorization*, Hearings, 97th Cong., 1st sess. (Washington, DC: US Government Printing Office, 1981), pp. 1-2.

38. For example, US Congress, House of Representatives, Committee on Science, Space, and Technology, *National Science Foundation Act for Fiscal Year 1987*, Report No. 99-619, 99th Cong., 2nd sess. (Washington, DC: US Government Printing Office, 1986), p. 15; and US Congress, House of Representatives, Committee on Appropriations, *Department of Housing and Urban Development-Independent Agencies Appropriations Bill, 1988*, Report No. 100-189, 100th Cong., 1st sess. (Washington, DC: US Government Printing Office, 1987), p. 45.

39. US Office of Management and Budget, *Budget of the United States Government, Fiscal Year 1989, Appendix* (Washington, DC: US Government Printing Office, 1988), I-Z66.

40. US Congress, Senate, Committee on Appropriations, *Department of Housing and Urban Development-Independent Agencies*, Report No. 97-549, 97th Cong., 1st sess. (Washington, DC: US Government Printing Office, 1982), pp. 676-8.

41. US Congress, House of Representatives, Committee of Conference, *Making Appropriations for the Department of Housing and Urban Development, and for Sundry Independent Agencies, Boards, Commissions, Corporations, and Offices*, Report No.

97-891, 97th Cong., 2nd sess. (Washington, DC: US Government Printing Office, 1982), p. 13; and US Office of Management and Budget, "The U.S. Antarctic Program," p. 28.

42. US Congress, Senate, Committee on Labor and Human Resources, *Authorizing Appropriations for the National Science Foundation, Fiscal Year 1986*, Report No. 99-131, 99th Cong., 1st sess. (Washington, DC: US Government Printing Office, 1985), p.10.

43. US Congress, Senate, Committee on Labor and Human Resources, *National Science Foundation Authorization Act of 1987*, Report No. 100-148, 100th Cong., 1st sess. (Washington, DC: US Government Printing Office, 1987), pp. 15-16.

44. US Congress, House of Representatives, Committee on Science, Space, and Technology, *National Science Foundation Authorization Act for Fiscal Year 1988*, Report No. 100-110, 100th Cong., 1st sess. (Washington, DC: US Government Printing Office, 1987), p. 16.

45. See, for example, US Congress, House of Representatives, Committee on Science, Space, and Technology, *U.S. Antarctic Program*, Hearings, 96th Cong., 1st sess. (Washington, DC: US Government Printing Office, 1979), p. 104.

46. Ibid., p. 109.

47. US Congress, Senate, Committee on Commerce, Science, and Transportation, *Antarctica*, p. 76.

48. Lee Kimball, "The Role of Non-Governmental Organizations in Antarctic Affairs," in Christopher C. Joyner and Sudhir K. Chopra, eds., *The Antarctic Legal Regime* (Dordrecht: Martinus Nijhoff Publishers, 1988). As noted in the text, Ms. Kimball has served as an adviser to the US Government on Antarctic issues.

49. Ibid., p. 62n.

50. Statement of James Barnes in US Congress, Senate, Committee on Commerce, Science, and Transportation, *Antarctica*, pp. 64-67.

51. For example, *U.S. Research in Antarctica in 2000 AD and Beyond: A Preliminary Assessment*, Polar Research Board Report (Washington, DC: National Academy Press, 1986).

52. US National Science Foundation, *The Role of the National Science Foundation in Polar Regions*, A Report to the National Science Board, 19 June 1987.

53. Such as in US Congress, Senate, Committee on Commerce, Science, and Transportation, *Antarctica*, pp. 44ff.

54. US Congress, Senate, Committee on Labor and Human Resources, *Authorizing Appropriations for the National Science Foundation for Fiscal Year 1987*, Report No. 99-325, 99th Cong., 2nd sess. (Washington, DC: US Government Printing Office, 1986), p. 3.

55. For various criticisms of the National Science Foundation's management of the US Antarctic program, see US Congress, Senate, Committee on Commerce, Science, and Transportation, *Antarctica*, pp. 76ff; Quigg, *A Pole Apart*, pp. 70-74, 216-7; Shapley, *The Seventh Continent*, pp. 183ff; and US Congress, Office of Technology Assessment, *Polar Prospects*, pp. 26-27.

Chapter 5

1. Presidential Memorandum No. 6646, 1 February 1982.

2. Ibid.

3. For example, Quigg, *A Pole Apart*, p. 217; and Shapley, *The Seventh Continent*, pp. 172, 196.

4. American activities during the International Geophysical Year are described in Chapter 1.

5. US Office of Management and Budget, "The U.S. Antarctic Program," pp. 8-9; and US Congress, House of Representatives, Committee on Appropriations, *Department of Housing and Urban Development—Independent Agencies Appropriations for 1988*, Hearings, 100th Cong., 1st sess. (Washington, DC: US Government Printing Office, 1987), p. 346.

6. US Office of Management and Budget, *Budget of the United States Government, Fiscal Year 1990, Appendix*, p. I-Z72.

7. The discussion on the importance of scientific research in the Antarctic is derived from the statement by A. N. Fowler, National Science Foundation, 24 September 1984, US Congress, Senate, Committee on Commerce, Science, and Transportation, *Antarctica*, pp. 23-34; US National Science Foundation, *The Role of the National Science Foundation in Polar Regions*, A Report to the National Science Board, 19 June 1987, pp. 15ff; and Gunter Weller, et al., "Laboratory Antarctica: Research Contributions to Global Problems," *Science*, Vol. 238, 4 December 1987, pp. 1361-8.

8. Ibid.

9. Ibid.

10. Ibid.

11. US Office of Management and Budget, "The U.S. Antarctic Program," p. 5.

12. For example, NASA has used a research version of the U-2 reconnaissance aircraft to collect ozone data in the Antarctic. See Ellen Ruppel Shell, "Solo Flights into the Ozone Hole Reveal Its Causes," *Smithsonian*, Vol. 18, No. 11, February 1988, pp. 142-8.

13. US National Science Foundation, *The United States Antarctic Program* 1990, p. 20; US Congress, Senate, Committee on Commerce, Science, and Transportation, *NSF Authorization*, Hearings (Washington, DC: US Government Printing Office, 1986), p. 48.

14. Shapley, *The Seventh Continent*, p. 175.

15. *Long Range Development Plan, Volume II, McMurdo Station, Antarctica*, prepared by Holmes and Narver, Inc., c. 1979, on file in the Division of Polar Programs, National Science Foundation, Washington, DC.

16. US Congress, House of Representatives, Committee on Appropriations, *Department of Housing and Urban Development—Independent Agencies Appropriations for 1988*, p. 352.

17. US National Science Foundation, *The United States Antarctic Program*, p. 21.

18. Ibid.

19. US Department of the Navy, Naval Support Force Antarctica, *Operation DEEP FREEZE 89/90 End of Season Report*, p. IV-4.

20. US Office of Management and Budget, "The U.S. Antarctic Program," p. 20.

21. See also Shapley, *The Seventh Continent*, pp. 201-2.

22. US National Science Foundation, *The United States Antarctic Program*, p. 22.

23. US Department of the Navy, Naval Support Force Antarctica, *Operation DEEP FREEZE 89/90 End of Season Report*, p. IV-4; "On the Ice-Resupplying Antarctica," *The MAC Flyer*, Vol. 24, No. 9, September 1982, pp. 7-9; and Colonel James Abbee, "Operation DEEP FREEZE," *The Air Reservist*, Vol. 37, No. 2, Spring 1985, pp. 20-23.

24. US National Science Foundation, *The United States Antarctic Program*, p. 23; and US Department of the Navy, Naval Support Force Antarctica, *Operation DEEP FREEZE 89/90 End of Season Report*, p. III-14.

25. US Congress, House of Representatives, Committee on Appropriations, *Department of Housing and Urban Development-Independent Agencies Appropriations for 1988*, pp. 81-2, 352.

26. *The Washington Post*, 10 December 1987, p. A51.

27. US National Science Foundation, *The United States Antarctic Program*, p. 23.

28. See the exchange of notes between the United States and New Zealand in US Department of State, *United States Treaties and Other International Agreements*, Vol. 9, 1958, pp. 1502-9, and Vol. 11, pt. 2, 1960, pp. 2205-7.

29. US Department of the Navy, Naval Support Force Antarctica, *Operation DEEP FREEZE 89/90 End of Season Report*, Chapter IV.

30. Dr. Dora Alves gives the background to the US-New Zealand dispute on port calls in *Anti-Nuclear Attitudes in New Zealand and Australia* (Washington, DC: National Defense University Press, 1985).

31. US Congress, House of Representatives, Committee on Interstate and Foreign Commerce, *International Geophysical Year in the Arctic, Antarctic*, pp. 35, 45.

32. *Long Range Development Plan, Volume III, Marble Point, Antarctica*, prepared by Holmes and Narver, Inc., c. 1979, on file in the Division of Polar Programs, National Science Foundation, Washington, DC.

33. US National Science Foundation, *The Role of the National Science Foundation in Polar Regions*, p. 46.

34. Statements of Admiral James S. Gracey, US Coast Guard, and Dr. Edward P. Todd, National Science Foundation, in US Congress, Senate, Committee on Commerce, Science, and Technology, *Coast Guard Polar Icebreaking Operations*, Hearings, 98th Cong., 2nd sess. (Washington, DC: US Government Printing Office, 1984), pp. 11, 29.

35. Ibid., pp. 3, 27.

36. Ibid., p. 27.

37. US National Science Foundation, *The United States Antarctic Program*, p. 19.

38. US National Science Foundation, *The Role of the National Science Foundation in Polar Regions*, p. 52.

39. US Congress, House of Representatives, Committee on Appropriations, *Department of Housing and Urban Development-Independent Agencies Appropriations for 1988*, p. 80.

40. Ibid., p. 81.

41. US Congress, House of Representatives, Committee on Science, Space, and Technology, *National Science Foundation Authorization Act for Fiscal Year 1988*, p. 16.

42. US Congress, House of Representatives, Committee on Appropriations, *Department of Housing and Urban Development-Independent Agencies Appropriations for 1988*, pp. 348-9, 352.

43. Ibid.

44. US Department of the Navy, Naval Support Force Antarctica, *Operation DEEP FREEZE 89/90 End of Season Report*, p. IV-6; Captain Mark Henderson, US Army, "Assignment Antarctica," *Translog*, Vol. 15, No. 4, April 1984, pp. 10-12.

45. For example, Shapley, *The Seventh Continent*, p. 176.

46. US Congress, House of Representatives, Committee on Appropriations, *Department of Housing and Urban Development-Independent Agencies Appropriations for 1988*, p. 349.

47. US National Science Foundation, *The Role of the National Science Foundation in Polar Regions*, p. 52.

Selected Bibliography

Books

Alexander, Lewis M. and Lynne Carter Hanson, eds. *Antarctic Politics and Marine Resources: Critical Choices for the 1980s.* Kingston: University of Rhode Island, 1984.

Alves, Dora. *Anti-Nuclear Attitudes in New Zealand and Australia.* Washington, DC: National Defense University Press, 1985.

Auburn, F.M. *Antarctic Law and Politics.* Bloomington: Indiana University Press, 1982.

Beck, Peter J. *The International Politics of Antarctica.* New York: St. Martin's Press, 1986.

Belgica: Le Premier Hivernage dans l'Antarctique, 1897-1899. Antwerp: Musee National de Marine, 1988.

Bertrand, Kenneth J. *Americans in Antarctia, 1775-1948.* New York: American Geographical Society, 1971.

Bonturi, Orlando. *Brazil and the Vital South Atlantic.* Washington, DC: National Defense University Press, 1988.

Child, Jack. *Antarctica and South American Geopolitics: Frozen Lebensraum.* New York: Praeger, 1988.

_____. *Geopolitics and Conflict in South America: Quarrels Among Neighbors.* New York: Praeger, 1985.

Grattan, C. Hartley. *The Southwest Pacific to 1900: A Modern History.* Ann Arbor: The University of Michigan Press, 1963.

Holdgate, M.W. *Antarctic Ecology.* London: Academic Press, 1970.

Joyner, Christopher C. and Sudhir K. Chopra, eds. *The Antarctic Legal Regime*. Dordrecht, the Netherlands: Martinus Hijoff Publishers, 1988.

Kelly, Phillip and Jack Child, eds. *Geopolitics of the Southern Cone and Antarctica*. Boulder, Colo.: Lynne Reinner Publishers, 1988.

Mericq, Luis H. *Antarctica: Chile's Claim*. Washington, DC: National Defense University Press, 1987.

Mitchell, Barbara and Jon Tinker. *Antarctica and Its Resources*. London: Earthscan, 1979.

Myhre, Jeffrey D. *The Antarctic Treaty System: Politics, Law, and Diplomacy*. Boulder, Colo.: Westview Press, 1986.

Quigg, Philip W. *A Pole Apart: The Emerging Issue of Antarctica*. New York: McGraw-Hill Book Company, 1983.

Rose, Lisle A. *Assault on Eternity: Richard E. Byrd and the Exploration of Antarctica, 1946-47*. Annapolis, Md.: Naval Institute Press, 1980.

Shapley, Deborah. *The Seventh Continent: Antarctica in the Resource Age*. Washington, DC: Resources for the Future, Inc., 1985.

Sullivan, Walter. *Assault on the Unknown: The International Geophysical Year*. New York: McGraw-Hill Book Company, Inc., 1961.

Vicuña, Francisco Orrega, ed. *Antarctic Resources Policy: Scientific, Legal, and Political Issues*. Cambridge, England: Cambridge University Press, 1983.

Westermeyer, William E. *The Politics of Mineral Resource Development in Antarctica: Alternative Regimes for the Future*. Boulder, Colo.: Westview Press, 1984.

US Government Documents

Arms Control and Disarmament Agency
Report of the United States Antarctic Inspection, 1989, October 1989.

Central Intelligence Agency
Polar Regions Atlas, May 1978.

US Congress, House

Committee of Conference. *Making Appropriations for the Department of Housing and Urban Development, and for Sundry Independent Agencies, Boards, Commissions, Corporations, and Offices.* Report No. 97-891. 97th Congress, 2nd Session. Washington, DC: US Government Printing Office, 1982.

Committee on Appropriations. *Department of Housing and Urban Development-Independent Agencies Appropriations Bill, 1988.* Report No. 100-189, 100th Congress, 1st Session. Washington, DC: US Government Printing Office, 1987.

_____. *Department of Housing and Urban Development-Independent Agencies Appropriations for 1988.* Hearings, 100th Congress, 1st Session. Washington, DC: US Government Printing Office, 1987.

Committee on Energy and Commerce. *Ozone Layer Depletion.* Hearings. 100th Congress, 1st Session. Washington, DC: US Government Printing Office, 1987.

Committee on Foreign Affairs. *The Political Legacy of the International Geophysical Year.* Committee Print. Washington, DC: US Government Printing Office, 1973.

Committee on Interstate and Foreign Commerce. *International Geophysical Year, The Arctic, Antarctica.* Report No. 1348. 85th Congress, 2nd Session. Washington, DC: US Government Printing Office, 1958.

Committee on Science, Space, and Technology. *National Science Foundation Act for Fiscal Year 1987.* Report No. 99-619. 99th Congress, 2nd Session. Washington, DC: US Government Printing Office, 1986.

_____. *National Science Foundation Authorization Act for Fiscal Year 1988.* Report No. 100-110, 100th Congress, 1st Session. Washington, DC: US Government Printing Office, 1987.

_____. *Pacific Basin Study Mission.* Washington, DC: US Government Printing Office, 1983.

_____. *US Antarctic Program.* Hearings. 96th Congress, 1st Session. Washington, DC: US Government Printing Office, 1979.

US Congress, Office of Technology Assessment

Polar Prospects: A Minerals Treaty for Antarctica. OTA-0-428. Washington, DC: US Government Printing Office, September 1989.

US Congress, Senate

Committee on Appropriations. *Department of Housing and Urban Development-Independent Agencies.* Report No. 97-549. 97th Congress, 1st Session. Washington, DC: US Government Printing Office, 1982.

Committee on Commerce, Science, and Technology. *Coast Guard Polar Icebreaking Operations.* Hearings. 98th Congress, 2nd Session. Washington, DC: US Government Printing Office, 1984.

Committee on Commerce, Science, and Transportation. *Antarctica.* Hearings. 98th Congress, 2nd Session. Washington, DC: US Government Printing Office. 1984.

_____. *National Science Foundation Authorization.* Hearings. 97th Congress, 1st Session. Washington, DC: US Government Printing Office, 1981.

_____. *National Science Foundation Authorization.* Hearings. 98th Congress, 1st Session. Washington, DC: US Government Printing Office, 1983.

_____. *NSF Authorization.* Hearings. Washington, DC: US Government Printing Office, 1986.

Committee on Foreign Relations. *The Antarctic Treaty.* Hearings. 86th Congress, 2nd Session. Washington, DC: US Government Printing Office, 1960.

_____. *US Antarctic Policy.* Hearings. 94th Congress, 1st Session. Washington, DC: US Government Printing Office, 1975.

Committee on Labor and Human Resources. *Authorizing Appropriations for the National Science Foundation, Fiscal Year 1985.* Report No. 98-495. 98th Congress, 2nd Session. Washington, DC: US Government Printing Office, 1984.

_____. *Authorizing Appropriations for the National Science Foundation, Fiscal Year 1986.* Report No. 99-131. 99th Congress, 1st Session. Washington, DC: US Government Printing Office, 1985.

_____. *Authorizing Appropriations for the National Science Foundation, Fiscal Year 1987*. Report No. 99-325. 99th Congress, 2nd Session. Washington, DC: US Government Printing Office, 1986.

_____. *National Science Foundation Authorization Act of 1987*. Report No. 100-148. 100th Congress, 1st Session. Washington, DC: US Government Printing Office, 1987.

Department of the Navy

Naval Support Force Antarctica. *Operation DEEP FREEZE 89/90 End of Season Report*.

Department of State

Conference on Antarctica. Washington, DC: US Government Printing Office, 1960.

Foreign Relations of the United States. A collection of State Department historical documents published regularly by the US Government Printing Office, Washington, DC.

United States Treaties and Other International Agreements. A collection of the full texts of treaties and other agreements published regularly by the US Government Printing Office.

National Science Foundation

Antarctic Journal of the United States. Published quarterly.

Facts about the United States Antarctic Program. July 1986.

The Role of the National Science Foundation in Polar Regions. 19 June 1987.

The United States Antarctic Program, 1990.

United States Antarctic Research Program Information. No. 4, 11 December 1986.

Office of Management and Budget

Budget of the United States States Government. Published each fiscal year by the US Government Printing Office, Washington D.C.

The President

The Public Papers of the President of the United States. A collection of presidential papers published annually by the US Government Printing Office, Washington, DC.

Australian Government Sources

"Antarctica Under Threat?" *Australian Foreign Affairs Record,* Vol. 56, No. 9, September 1985.

"Australia's Participation in SIBEX-1 Cancelled." *Australian Foreign Affairs Record,* Vol. 55, No. 2, February 1984.

Department of Foreign Affairs and Trade, Fact Sheet on Australia, "Australia and the Antarctic Environment," April 1990.

Hayden, Bill, "Keeping Tension Out of the Last Continent." *Australian Foreign Affairs Record,* Vol. 56, No. 1, January 1985.

Hawke, Bob, "Antarctica's Future," *Australian Foreign Affairs Record,* Vol. 60, No. 11, November 1989.

"The Value of the Antarctic Treaty System." *Australian Foreign Affairs Record,* Vol. 55, No. 9, September 1984.

Other Official Writings

Behrendt, John C., ed. *Petroleum and Mineral Resources of Antarctica.* Geological Survey Circular 909. Washington, DC: US Government Printing Office, 1983.

Bush, W.M., ed. *Antarctica and International Law: A Collection of Interstate and National Documents.* London: Oceana Publications, Inc., 1982.

Heap, John, ed. *Handbook of the Antarctic Treaty System.* 6th ed. Cambridge, England: Polar Publications, April 1989.

Negroponte, John D. "The Success of the Antarctic Treaty." *Department of State Bulletin,* Vol. 87, No. 2123, June 1987.

Wright, N.A. and P.L. Williams, eds. *Mineral Resources of Antarctica.* Geological Survey Circular 705. Washington, DC: US Government Printing Office, 1974.

Periodical Articles

Abbee, James. "Operation DEEP FREEZE." *The Air Reservist.* Vol. 37, No. 2, Spring 1985.

"L'Antarctique: Le Retour du Grand Sud." *Le Vif/L'Express* (Brussels). 19 May 1989.

Beck, Peter J. "Antarctica at the United Nations, 1985: The End of Consensus?" *Polar Record.* Vol. 23, No. 143, 1986.

_____. "Britian's Antarctic Dimension." *International Affairs.* Vol. 59, No. 3, Summer 1983.

_____. "British Antarctic Policy in the Early 20th Century." *Polar Record.* Vol. 21, No. 134, 1983.

_____. "A New Polar Factor in International Relations." *World Today.* Vol. 45, No. 4, April 1989.

_____. "Preparatory Meetings for the Antarctic Treaty, 1958-59." *Polar Record.* Vol. 22, No. 141, September 1985.

Bergin, Anthony. "Recent Developments in Australia's Antarctic Policy." *Marine Policy.* Vol. 9, No. 3, July 1985.

Brigham, Lawson W. "The Soviet Antarctic Program." *Oceanus.* Vol. 31, No. 2, Summer 1988.

"First Committee Reviews Question of Antarctica for Third Time." *UN Chronicle.* Vol. 23, No. 2, February 1986.

Henderson, Mark. "Assignment Antarctica." *Translog.* Vol. 15, No. 4, April 1984.

Joyner, Christopher C. "Security Issues and the Law of the Sea: The Southern Ocean." *Ocean Development and International Law.* Vol. 15, No. 2, 1985.

Luard, Evan. "Who Owns the Antarctic?" *Foreign Affairs.* Vol. 62, No. 5, Summer 1984.

Mitchell, Barbara. "Undermining Antarctica." *Technology Review.* Vol. 91, No. 2, February/March 1988.

"Norway in the Antarctic." *News of Norway.* Vol. 41, No. 7, 18 May 1984.

Parfit, Michael. "The Last Continent." *Smithsonian.* Vol. 15, No. 8, November 1984.

Peterson, M.J. "Antarctic Implications of the New Law of the Sea." *Ocean Development and International Law.* Vol. 16, No. 2, 1986.

Scully, R. Tucker and Lee A. Kimball. "Antarctica: Is There Life After Minerals?" *Marine Policy.* Vol. 13, No. 2, April 1989.

Shell, Ellen Ruppel. "Solo Flights into the Ozone Hole Reveal Its Causes." *Smithsonian.* Vol. 18, No. 11, February 1988.

Simoes, Jefferson. "Brazilian Antarctic Research Programme." *Polar Record.* Vol. 22, September 1984.

Triggs, Gillian. "The Antarctic Treaty Regime: A Workable Compromise or a 'Purgatory of Ambiguity'?" *Case Western*

Reserve Journal of International Law. Vol. 17, No. 2, Spring 1985.

Weller, Gunter, et al. "Laboratory Antarctica: Research Contributions to Global Problems." *Science*. Vol. 238, 4 December 1987.

Zorn, Stephan A. "Antarctic Minerals: A Common Heritage Approach." *Resources Policy*. Vol. 10, No. 1, March 1984.

Zumberge, James H. "Mineral Resources and Geopolitics in Antarctica." *American Scientist*. Vol. 67, No. 1, January/February 1979.

Reports

Kimball, Lee. A. *Antarctic Minerals Convention*. Washington, DC: International Institute for Environment and Development-North America, July 1988.

——————. *Report on Antarctica*. Washington, DC: International Institute for Environment and Development, December 1987.

——————. *Report on Antarctica*. New York: World Resources Institute, November 1989.

Polar Research Board, National Research Council. *Antarctic Treaty System: An Assessment*. Washington, DC: National Academy Press, 1986.

——————. *U.S. Research in Antarctica in 2000 AD and Beyond: A Preliminary Assessment*. Washington, DC: National Academy Press, 1986.

Newspapers

The International Herald Tribune, Paris
The New York Times
The Times, London
The Washington Post

Abbreviations

AIL	*Antarctica and International Law*
APG	Antarctic Policy Group
ATCM	Antarctic Treaty Consultative Meeting (used with Roman Numerals to designate specific meetings)
ATS Handbook	*Handbook of the Antarctic Treaty System*
BIOMASS	Biological Investigations of Marine Antarctic Systems and Stocks
CCAMLR	Convention on the Conservation of Antarctic Marine Living Resources
CRAMRA	Convention on the Regulation of Antarctic Mineral Resource Activities
CSAGI	*Comité Spécial de l'Année Géophysique Internationale*
FRUS	*Foreign Relations of the United States*
ICSU	International Council of Scientific Unions
IGY	International Geophysical Year
MMC	Marine Mammal Commission
NASA	National Aeronautics and Space Administration
NIEO	New International Economic Order
NOAA	National Oceanic and Atmospheric Administration

NSB	National Science Board
NSC	National Security Council
NSF	National Science Foundation
NSFA	Naval Support Force, Antarctica
OES	State Department's Bureau for Oceans and International Environmental and Scientific Affairs
OMB	Office of Management and Budget
OPEC	Organization of Petroleum Exporting Countries
OTA	Office of Technology Assessment, US Congress
PPP	*Public Papers of the President*
PRB	Polar Research Board of the National Research Council
SCAR	Scientific Committee on Antarctic Research
UN	United Nations
UNCLOS	United Nations Conference on the Law of the Sea
US	United States
USSR	Union of Soviet Socialist Republics
VXE-6	US Navy's Antarctic Development Squadron 6

Index

The Author

Colonel Frank G. Klotz, US Air Force, currently assigned to the US Mission to the North Atlantic Treaty Organization, Brussels, wrote this book while he was a Research Fellow at the National Defense University.

Colonel Klotz has served in the Pentagon on the Air Staff and in the Office of the Assistant Secretary of Defense for Manpower, Reserve Affairs, and Logistics. He also taught Political Science at the US Air Force Academy, where he specialized in defense policy and American government, was a White House Fellow and Special Assistant to the Deputy Secretary of State, and commanded a Minuteman III missile squadron at Grand Forks Air Force Base, North Dakota.

He is a distinguished graduate of the US Air Force Academy with a Bachelor of Science degree in International Affairs and Political Science. He attended Oxford University on a Rhodes Scholarship and earned a Master of Philosophy degree in International Relations and a Doctor of Philosophy degree in Politics. In 1983, the US Jaycees named him one of the Ten Outstanding Young Men of America for that year.

NSF Photo by Ann Hawthorne

Scientists pose with Opus the Penguin at the South Pole.